Bulgarian Frescoes

Feast of the Root

Bulgarian Frescoes

Feast of the Root

Tsvetanka Elenkova

Photographs and English translation by Jonathan Dunne

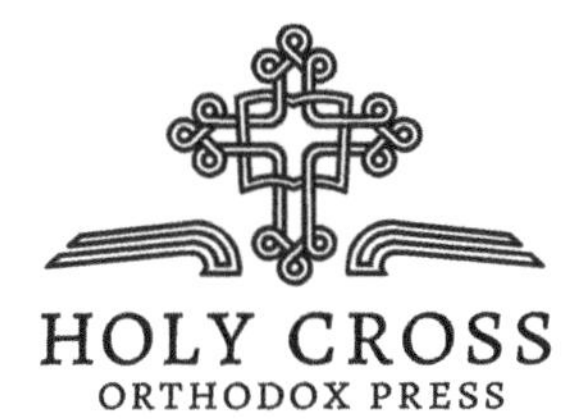

Brookline, Massachusetts

Published by

Holy Cross Orthodox Press
Hellenic College, Inc.
50 Goddard Avenue
Brookline, Massachusetts 02445

ISBN: 978-1-960613-12-7

These essays first appeared in Bulgarian in the book Български фрески: празник на корена (*Bulgarian Frescoes: Feast of the Root*) published by Omophor (Sofia) in 2013 with the blessing of His Eminence Metropolitan Dometian of Vidin and theological editing of the Right Reverend Bishop Sioniy of Velika.

Cover Image: Descent into Hell from Seslavsti Monastery

Publisher's Cataloging in Publication

(Provided by Cassidy Cataloging Services, Inc.)

Title: Bulgarian frescoes : feast of the root / Tsvetanka Elenkova ; photographs and English translation by Jonathan Dunne.

Description: Brookline, Massachusetts : Holy Cross Orthodox Press, [2025] | Translation of: Bulgarski freski: praznik na korena (Sofia : Pokrov Bogorodichen, 2013).

Identifiers: ISBN: 978-1-960613-12-7

Subjects: LCSH: Mural painting and decoration--Bulgaria. | Icons, Bulgarian. | Christian art and symbolism--Bulgaria. | Fasts and feasts--Orthodox Eastern Church, | Orthodox Eastern Church--Doctrines.

Classification: LCC: ND2800 .E4413 2025 | DDC: 755.2/094977--dc23

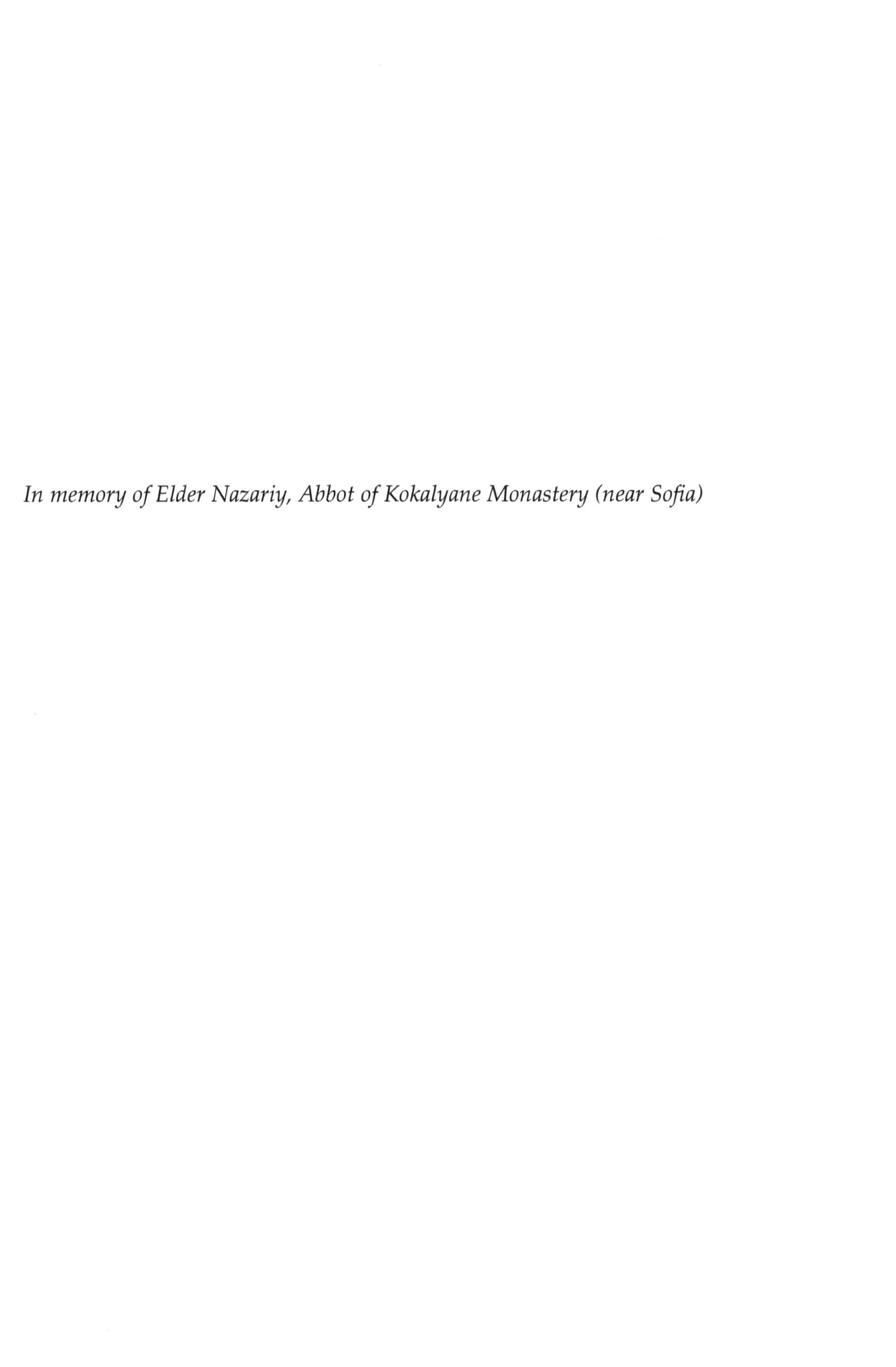

In memory of Elder Nazariy, Abbot of Kokalyane Monastery (near Sofia)

CONTENTS

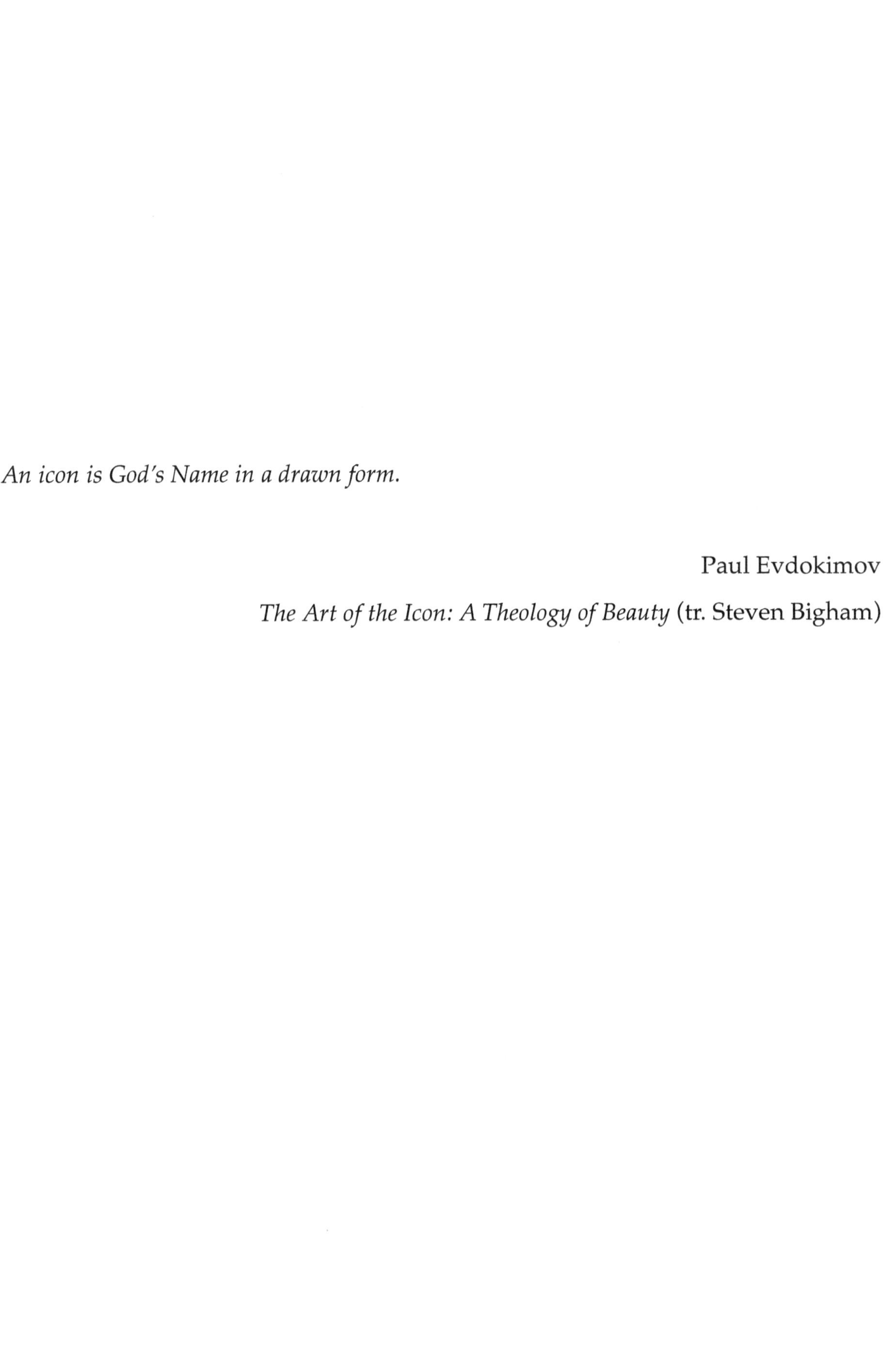

An icon is God's Name in a drawn form.

Paul Evdokimov

The Art of the Icon: A Theology of Beauty (tr. Steven Bigham)

Preface to the Bulgarian Edition

(2013)

'In spiritual things you have to be a "thief" and exploit if possible every moment,' says Elder Ieronymos of Aegina,[1] and it seems these words of his fit the context of the present Christian essays most closely. The book is the result of a pilgrimage to 140 Bulgarian monasteries, which I visited with my family in the period 2006-2012, the highlights of which I consider to be our meeting and friendship with Archimandrite Nazariy – *Dyado* Nazariy, as he is known by everybody, former abbot of Kokalyane Monastery – and our introduction to the unique frescoes of Seslavtsi Monastery. Which we fell in love with forever. At the same time, I read mainly Orthodox literature, quotations from which are included in the essays: *Theology of the Icon* by Leonid Ouspensky, *The Journals of Father Alexander Schmemann 1973-1983*, *The Philokalia*, *The Ladder of Divine Ascent* by St John Climacus, *Beginning to Pray* by Metropolitan Anthony of Sourozh, *Instructive Words* by Archimandrite Seraphim

1 Peter Botsis, *The Elder Ieronymos of Aegina*, tr. Holy Transfiguration Monastery (Brookline, MA: Holy Transfiguration Monastery, 2007), p. 204.

Aleksiev, *Saint Silouan the Athonite* by St Sophrony of Essex, *The Elder Ieronymos of Aegina* by Peter Botsis, *The Garden of the Holy Spirit: Saint Iakovos of Evia* by Stylianos Papadopoulos, *From Portrait to Icon* by Stamatis Skliris, *The Church at Prayer: The Mystical Liturgy of the Heart* by Archimandrite Aimilianos of Simonopetra, and of course the book I consider to be the highest achievement with regard to icon painting – *The Art of the Icon: A Theology of Beauty* by Paul Evdokimov. All of them, people and books, have taught me something along the way. From Elder Nazariy, I received a barely visible sign of the cross as a shield to turn to before any undertaking. From the Cursing of the Fig Tree, the only fresco of its kind on Sofia's Holy Mountain, I learnt that Absolute Virtue and Good, Jesus Christ, even when he curses, in fact blesses. From his hands, instead of ammunition, comes light. From Evdokimov, I understood that frescoes are a kind of hieroglyph. And the frescoes themselves taught me something that Dostoevsky wrote in a letter to Natalia Fonvizina after his release from prison camp in Siberia in January 1854: 'There is nothing finer, profounder, more attractive, more reasonable, more courageous and more perfect than Christ, and not only is there not, but I tell myself with jealous love that there cannot be. Even if someone were to prove to me that the truth lay outside Christ, I should choose to remain with Christ rather than with the truth.'[2]

Bulgarian frescoes are imbued precisely with this love for Jesus Christ. And although the book has in its title 'Feast of the Root,' which refers theologically to the Virgin Mary and in particular to the Feast of the Annunciation, in this instance it has acquired a wider meaning – that of the Savior, of Orthodoxy as the root of the Bulgarian people, which has enabled them to survive for centuries, of their Tree of Life.

I wish in particular to thank my husband, Jonathan Dunne, who was responsible for the photographs, an important historical legacy of abandoned holy places, outstanding because of their documentary value. Also, our son, Gabriel, who had already visited a hundred

2 Malcolm Jones, *Dostoevsky and the Dynamics of Religious Experience* (London: Anthem Press, 2005), p. 7.

monasteries by the time he was two. And, of course, Iliana Alexandrova and Plamen Sivov, the publishers of the first, Bulgarian edition (2013). I offer my heartfelt thanks to the Right Reverend Bishop Sioniy of Velika for his initial reading and indispensable help as regards the Orthodox canon. I hope this work may contribute to the lifting of the Bulgarian people's subdued spirit and the realization of true values.

— Tsvetanka Elenkova

Preface to the American Edition

(2025)

Twelve years after the first, Bulgarian-language edition of this work, which is already out of print, we return to the beloved holy places (this time in an English translation) gifted to us by this pilgrimage, a pilgrimage that happened just in time (we would barely have the strength to carry it out today), like most things by God's will. It opened our spiritual eyes so that we could gaze on the unfolded Bible of Bulgarian frescoes, whose Word like 'living water' flows to and from our hearts to reveal to us the unending beauty of Orthodoxy, the only 'spring of water gushing up to eternal life' (Jn 4:14).

— *Tsvetanka Elenkova*

Christ Pantocrator

The Translator of Man

Who is Christ? Not only the one we know about from the Bible and Sacred Tradition, but also the one we communicate with on a personal level along the way by means of the Holy Spirit, who was pleased to descend on the Apostles and all those who have faith in the Son. For even if Christ says, 'Unless you see signs and wonders you will not believe' (Jn 4:48), those who have experienced him accept what was said by Einstein as a personal confession: 'There are two ways to live your life. One is as though nothing is a miracle. The other is as though everything is a miracle.' Christ is an experience precisely, and herein lies the greatest miracle. We experience him every day – some through their daily bread, others through trials along the way, still others by experiencing him the way the elder Iakovos Tsalikis experienced David of Euboea: 'Because I experience Saint David within.'[3] And, 'No one comes to the Father except through me' (Jn 14:6).

And there is the Pantocrator from Eleshnitsa (fig. 1-1) – the bitterness in his look, which flows down to his chin as he forcibly takes a sip, the image that is closest to that of St Catherine's Monastery at Sinai.

Or the Pantocrator from Seslavtsi (fig. 1-2) – the skepticism in slightly narrowed eyes mixed with a knowledge of betrayal, even by those nearest to him. 'Because if Christ was betrayed by his closest friends, in whom should we hope in this world if not in him?' says the Bulgarian elder Nazariy.

The Pantocrator from Alino (fig. 1-3) has a wrinkle between the eyebrows like a candle (this area is one of the most important in iconography, where various symbols can be detected – a chalice, a flower, a flame, wings, a fishbone, and even eyes), like a torch burning inside a seed (the oval of his face), which cracks the seed so it can send out shoots above the black soil. Wings for a new life. Since what else is the candle's flickering flame if not the constant flapping of wings that enclose the primeval darkness. There where the Lord made his hiding place, as it says in the Psalter, the uncreated light. Also, this is the only Pantocrator with slightly parted lips. God the Word. The young man who in the fresco Christ Angel (fig. 1-4) is permeated with clarity of mind, his forehead an open book. Who in the fresco Christ Emmanuel has a stone lodged between his eyebrows – the cornerstone. Because this is the way of Christ from his first sermon in the temple as a child – from the cornerstone on which the temple is built – to the Almighty, the candle.

3 Stylianos Papadopoulos, *The Garden of the Spirit: Saint Iakovos of Evia*, tr. Dimitri Kagaris (Clearwater, FL: Orthodox Witness, 2018), p. 178.

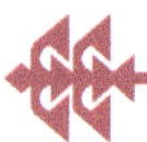

The way from the stone to fire. The way of holiness, enlightenment. Not burning. This is why the face in Christ Emmanuel has the color of stone, but the Pantocrator has the soft tones of flame.

The Pantocrator from Iliyantsi (fig. 1-5) already bears the expression of someone to whom everything is clear. He has a spanner between his eyebrows. The spanner that is so plain to see in the fresco Christ in the Tomb (Nedelishte, fig. 1-6). There, where his torso from his belly to his shoulders resembles a waistcoat, ready to be taken off. Under which can be seen the true body of the one who will resurrect, of the triangle-Trinity formed by the three dots of his nipples and navel. The draining blood seems to be going in the other direction, flowing into his body, driving home like arrows that pierce him, since 'the kingdom of heaven has suffered violence, and the violent take it by force' (Mt 11:12).

The Pantocrator from Strupets (fig. 1-7) is strict, tormented, time has erased an eye. The outline from his eyebrows to his chin forms a heart. But the Savior is also bread, like his stomach – a round loaf with the sign of the cross in the fresco Christ in the Tomb (Strupets, fig. 1-8), into which the water flows from his throat. Bread mingled with tears, as in the folktale 'The Three Brothers and the Golden Apple,' since this world is the world of the snake. He is also a flatfish that has been caught in the fresco Christ in the Tomb (Malo Malovo and Radibosh, figs. 1-9,10). Hands resting on the heart of his stomach (Alino, fig. 1-11).

There are also Eastern elements in some of the images of Christ Pantocrator (from a later iconographic period, the eighteenth-nineteenth centuries): almond-shaped eyes (Kurilovo), the letter omega, resembling an Egyptian symbol (Iskrets), emphatically folkloric details (Dolni Pasarel, fig. 1-12).

His awe-inspiring beauty (a combination of delicate features and distance) is noticeable in frescoes from the Church of the Nativity in Arbanasi (figs. 1-13,14) and St Stephen's Church in Nesebar (fig. 1-15). The latter has the mosaic feel of the icon of St Theodore Stratelates in Patleina Monastery. A vivid awareness of his own presence and identity. The same with which he refuses to answer the question, 'Are you the Messiah, the Son of God?' (Mt 26:63).

In the Pantocrator from Rakovitsa (fig. 1-16) only the outline and colors are left. The details have faded over time. But still clear is the figure of a dove that ascends from the waist to the halo. This dove is perhaps a layer of the Book of the Gospels which Christ usually holds in his left hand. But here his hand, like the other, is

raised aloft in blessing. With the gesture of a martyr who has nothing in common with his tormentors, the unquestioning gesture of pain and its transition to non-pain, of victory over pain.

The Christ in the Tomb by Theophanes the Cretan in St Nicholas' Monastery at Meteora, perhaps the best expression of the way of the Savior, the Savior as way, which portrays his body as a ladder that climbs from the apple of the groin (temptation) through the heart of the stomach (because we feed with the heart) and the steps of the ribcage to the light of the mind (eternal life), through the arduous passage of the clavicle (the eye of the needle), receives its simplification and stylization in the Pantocrator from Rakovitsa. For there is an inseparable connection between the frescoes Christ in the Tomb and Christ Pantocrator. One is impossible without the other, and vice versa. Not by chance are they to be found in the most sacred parts of the church – the altar and the central dome – symbolizing Christ's heavenly and earthly kingdom.

Christ in the Tomb is contained within the Pantocrator – the outstretched Word that flies towards the Light. Just as Noah's dove found land. Just as the dove of the Holy Spirit strains towards the Virgin Mary's womb, towards Christ as he is baptized in the Jordan River.

God, as well as being Maker of all things visible and invisible, is also a Translator, our Guide, who carries us through the narrow passage. Who translates heavenly things for our weak human eyes, so they don't go blind like those of Saul on the road to Damascus.

'Action precedes divine vision,' says the elder Ieronymos of Aegina. 'God first created the body and afterwards breathed in the soul.'[4]

So, creating man from the dust in a direct, literal way and then breathing into his nostrils the breath of life, God gave a spiritual dimension to his translation, affording it the only true meaning – that of the Holy Spirit.

4 Peter Botsis, *The Elder Ieronymos of Aegina*, p. 223.

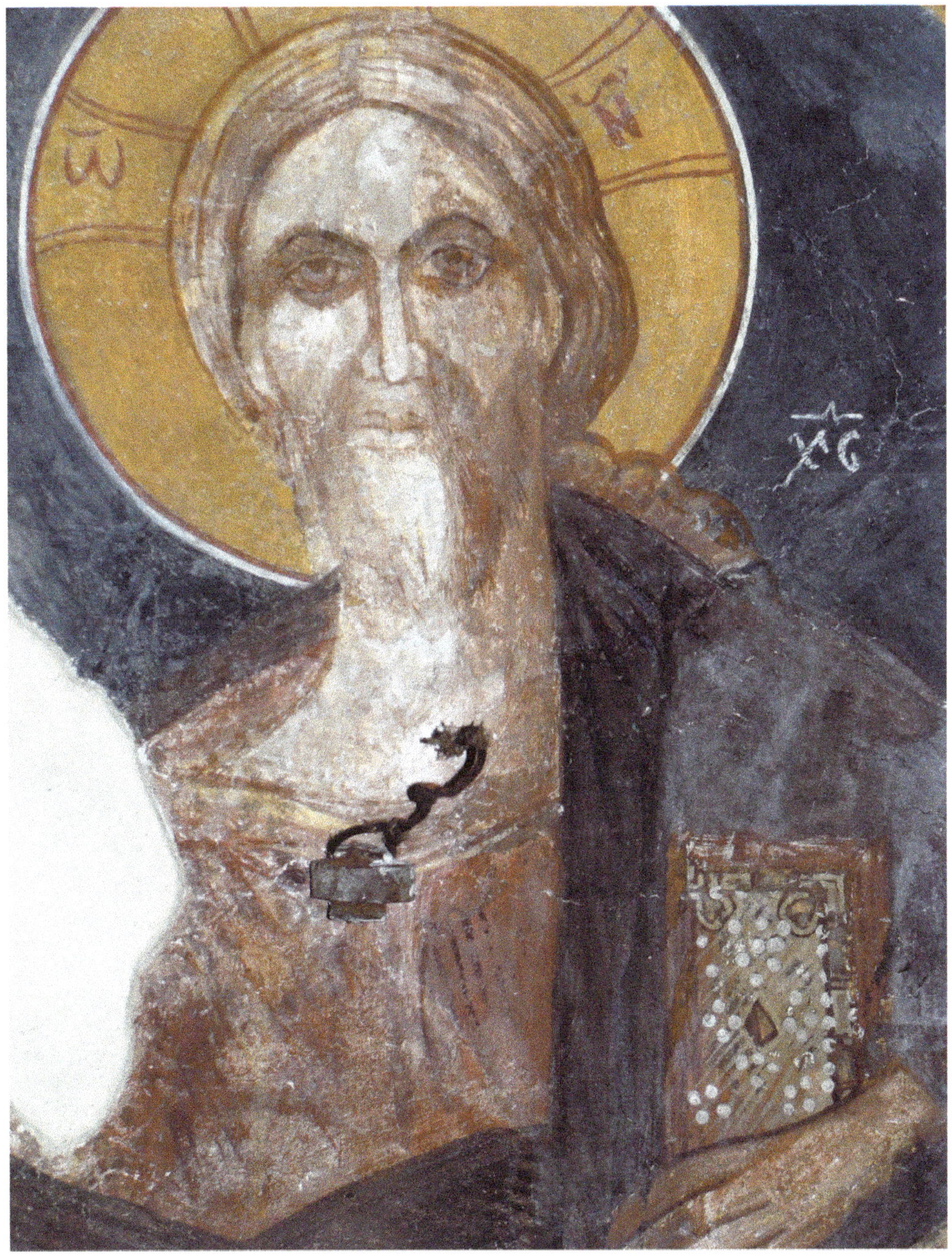

Fig. 1-1

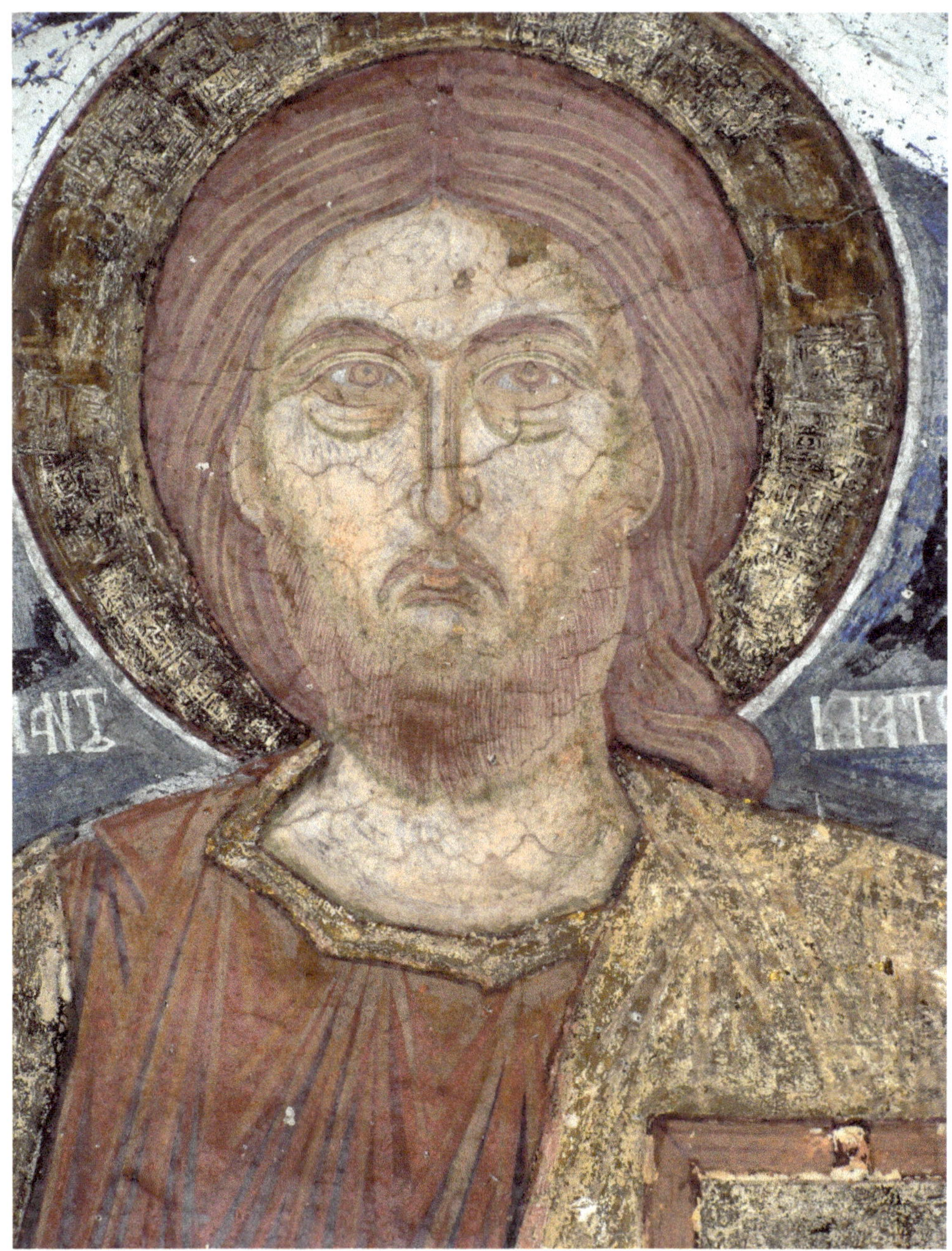

Fig. 1-2

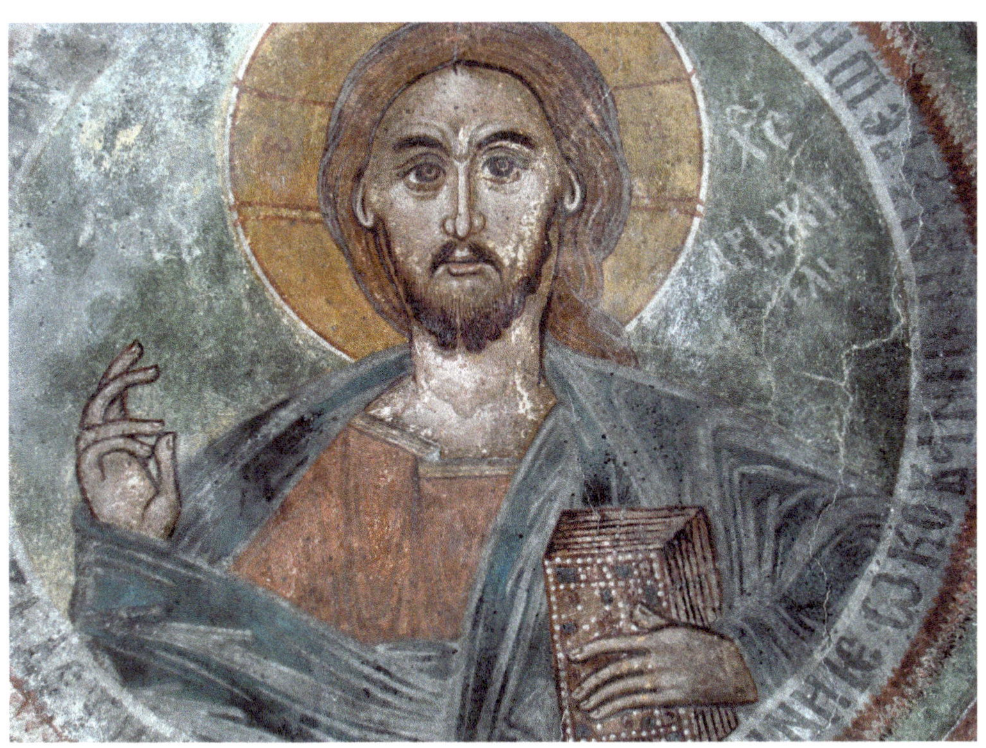

Fig. 1-3

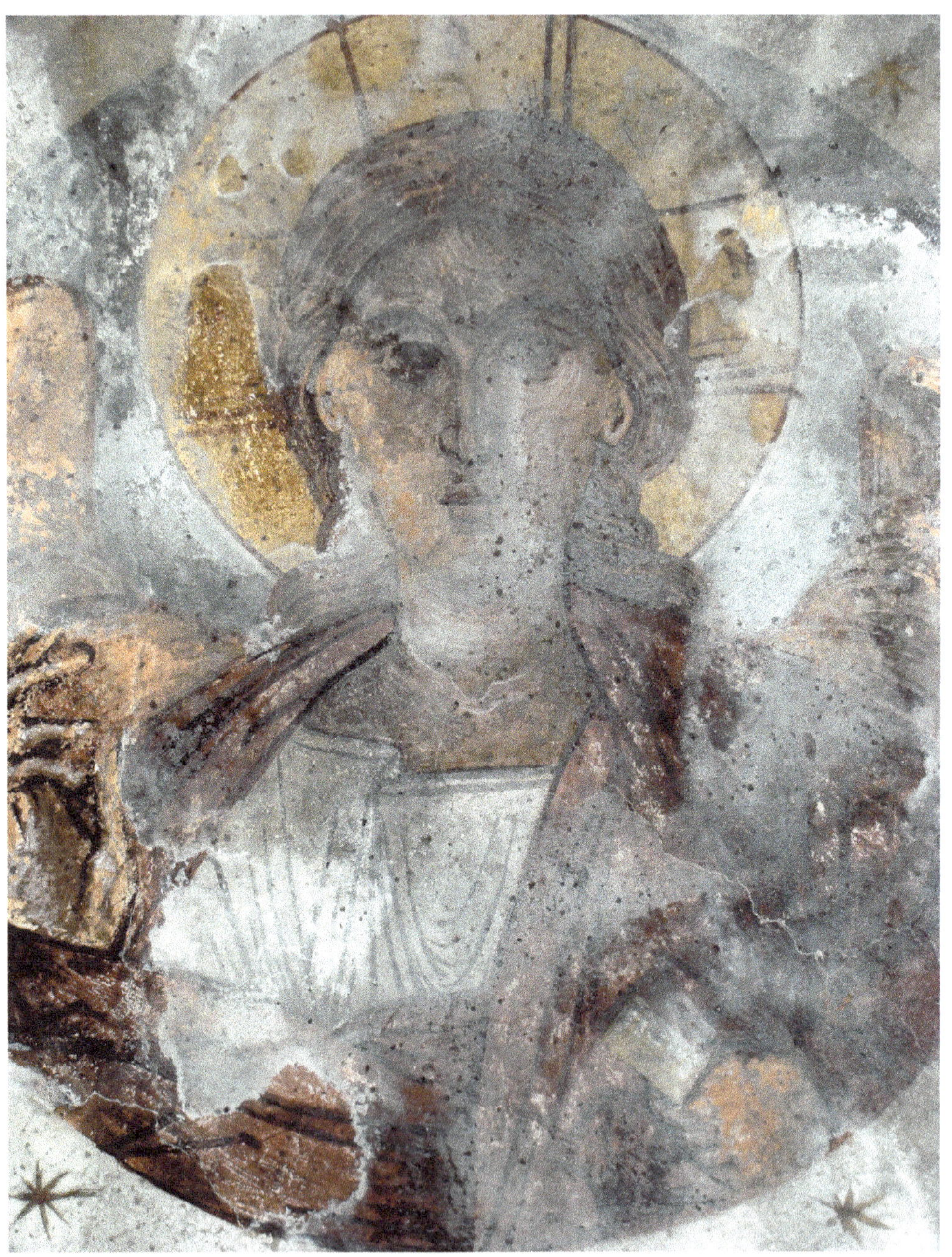

Fig. 1-4

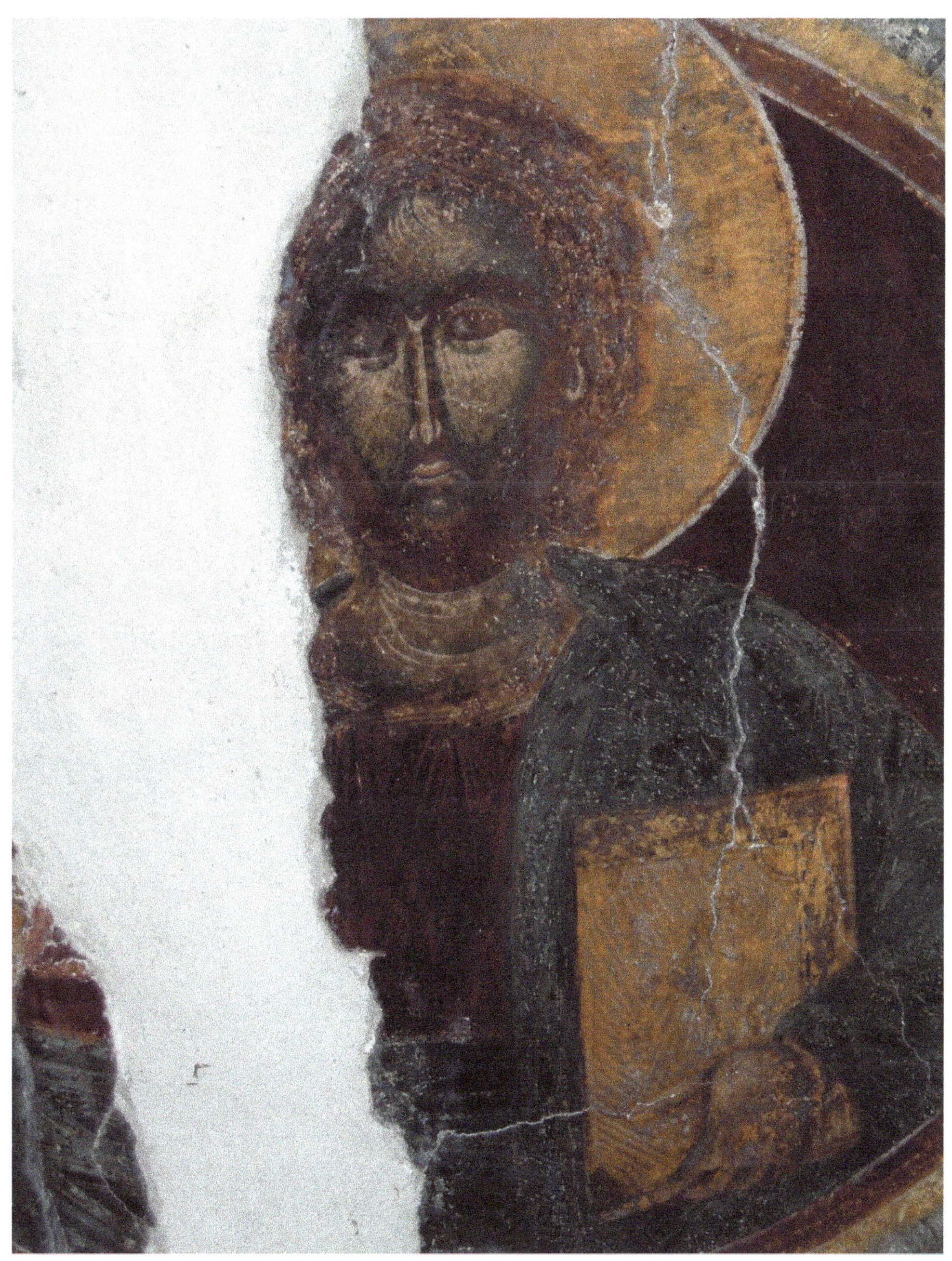

Fig. 1-5

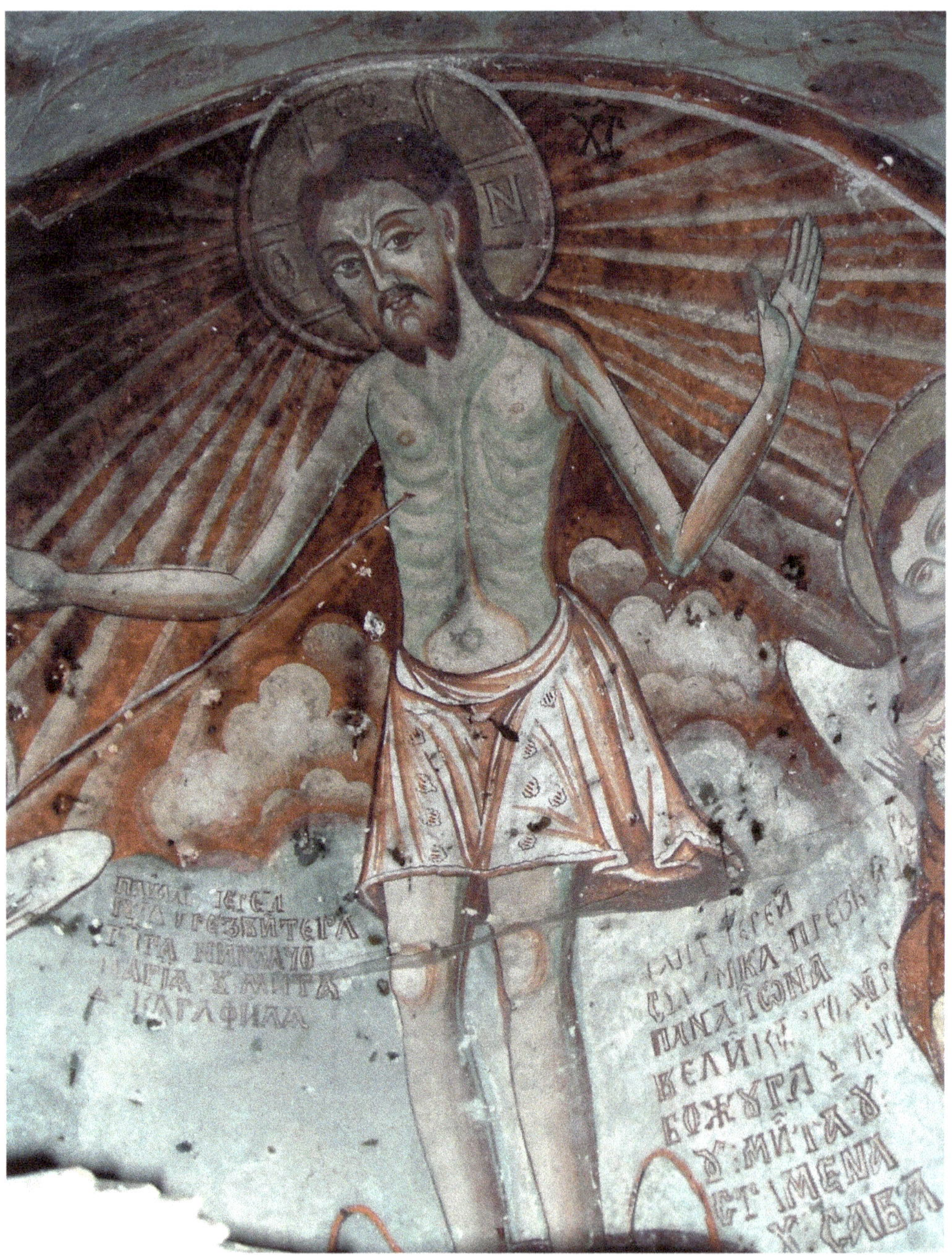

Fig. 1-6

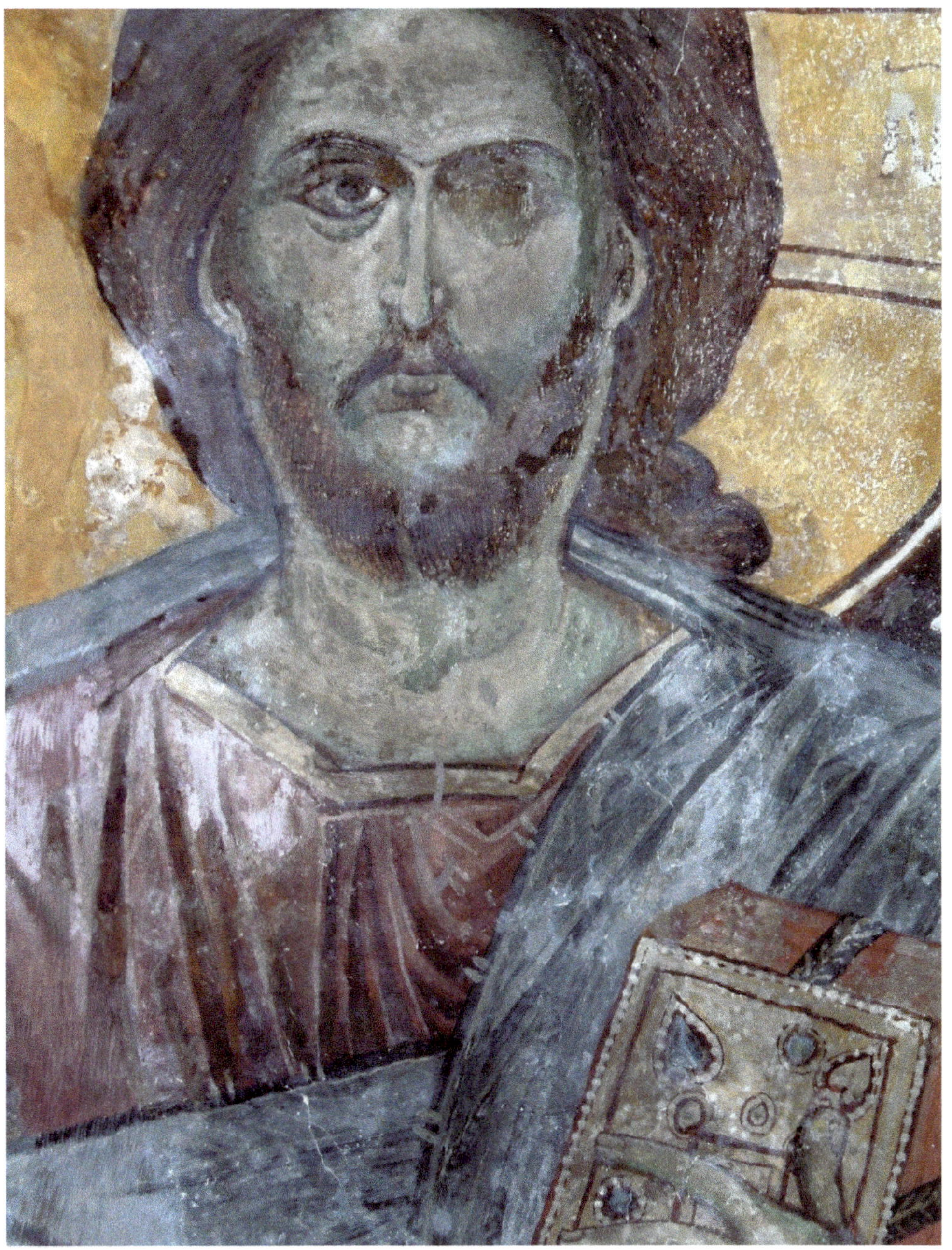

Fig. 1-7

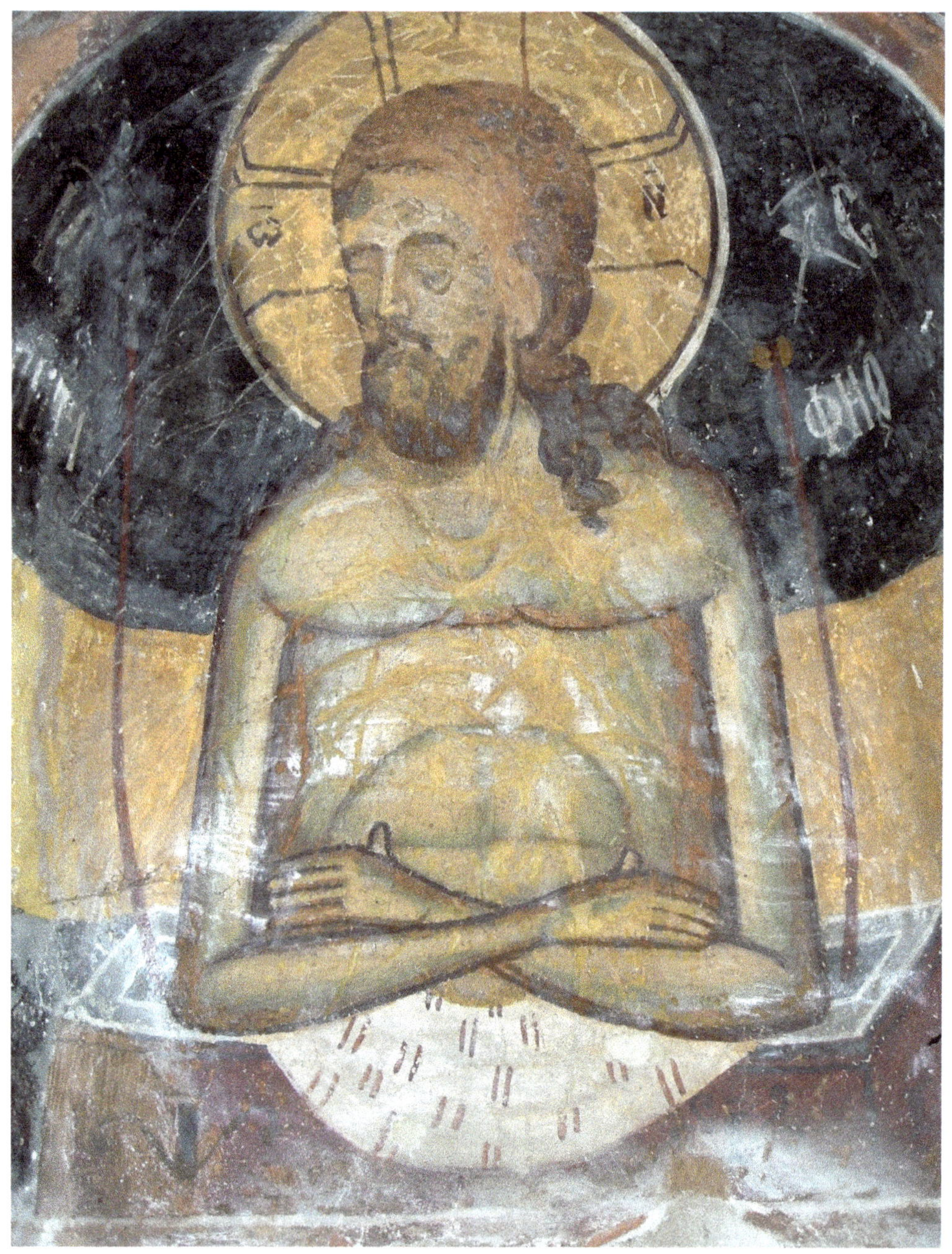

Fig. 1-8

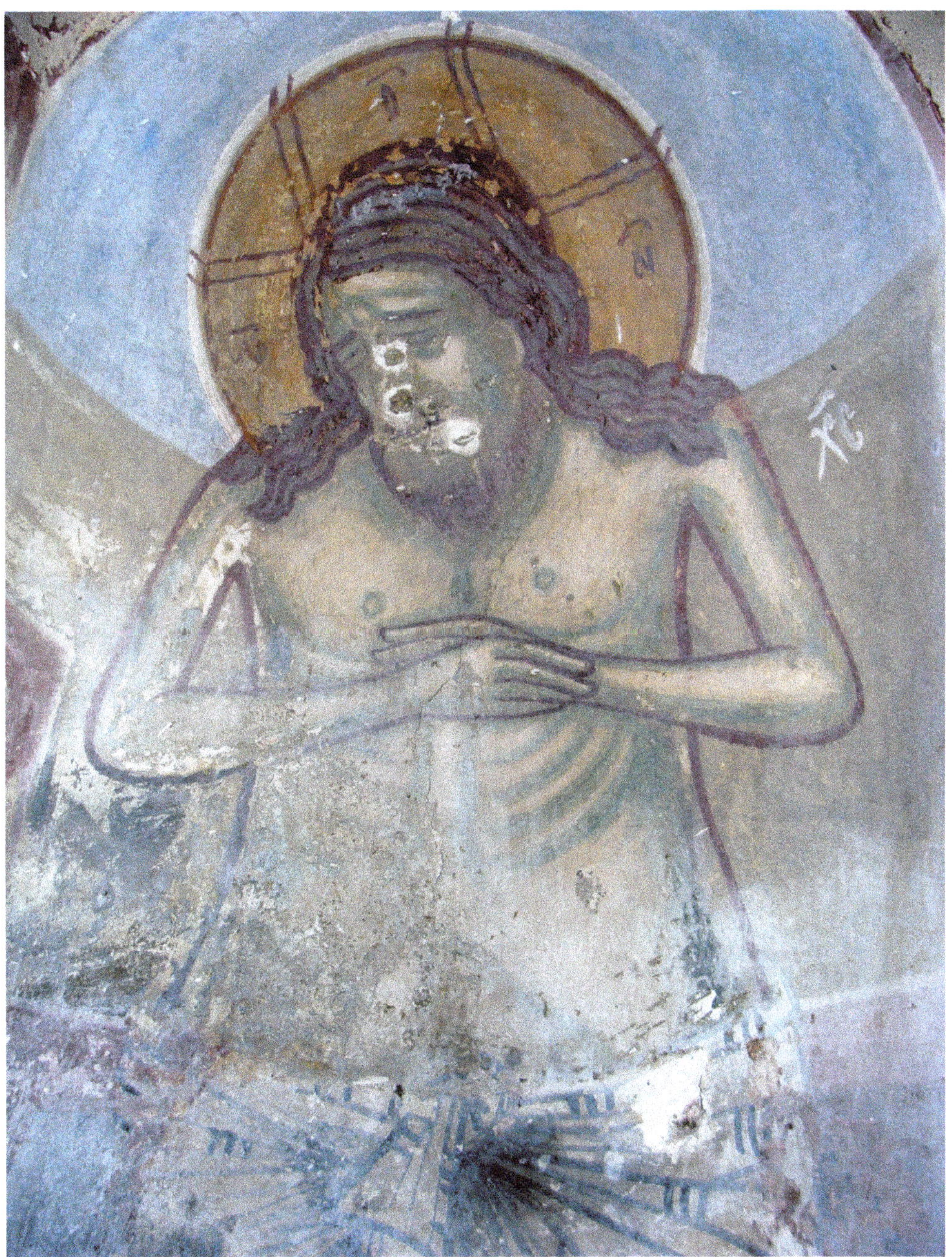

Fig. 1-9

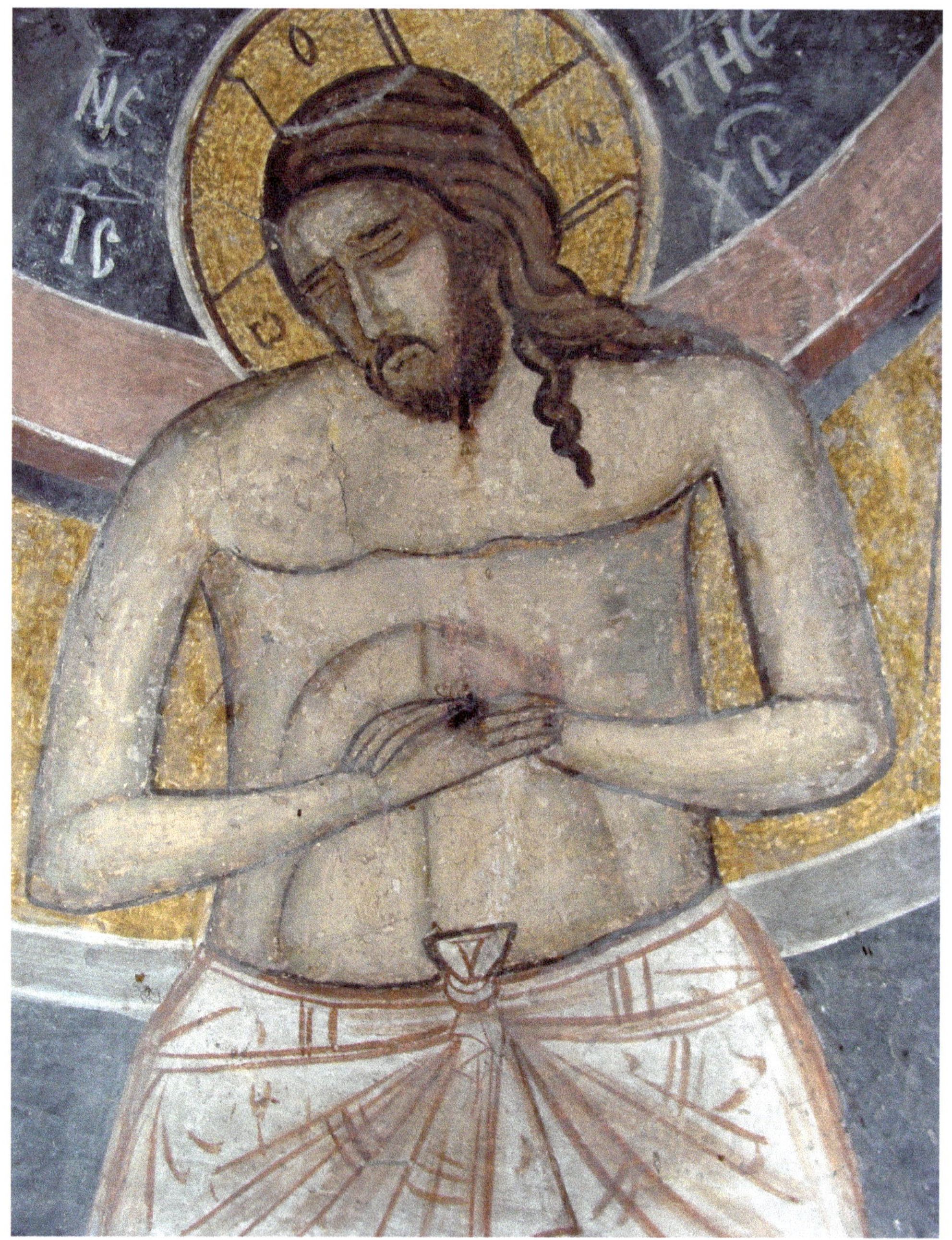

Fig. 1-10

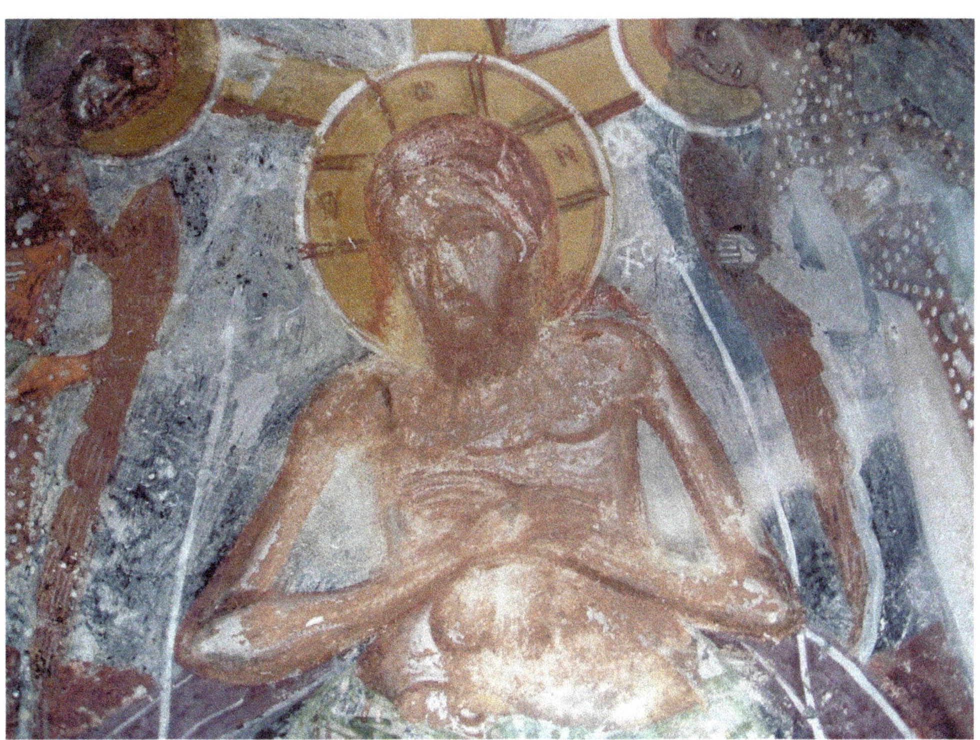

Fig. 1-11

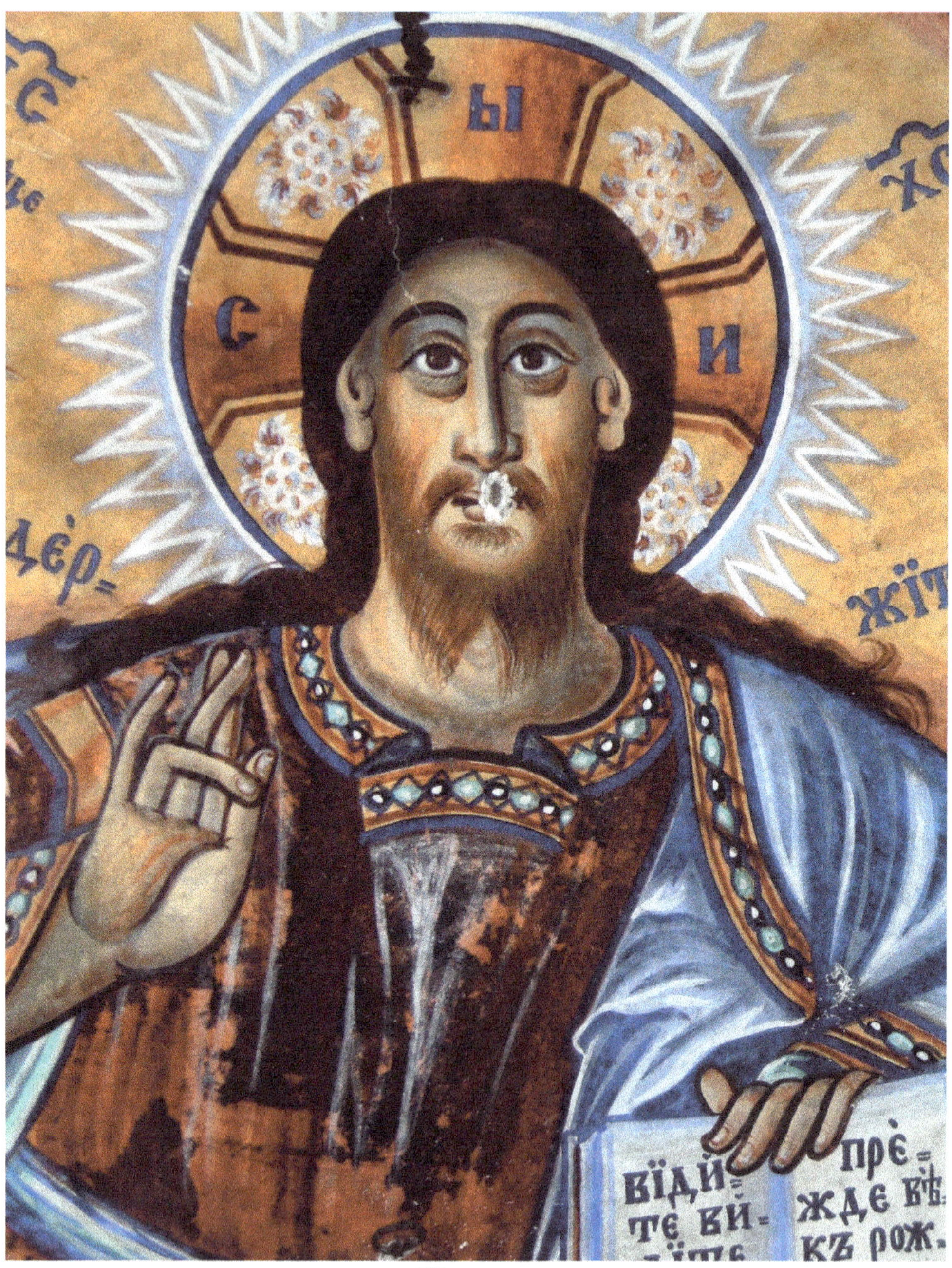

Fig. 1-12

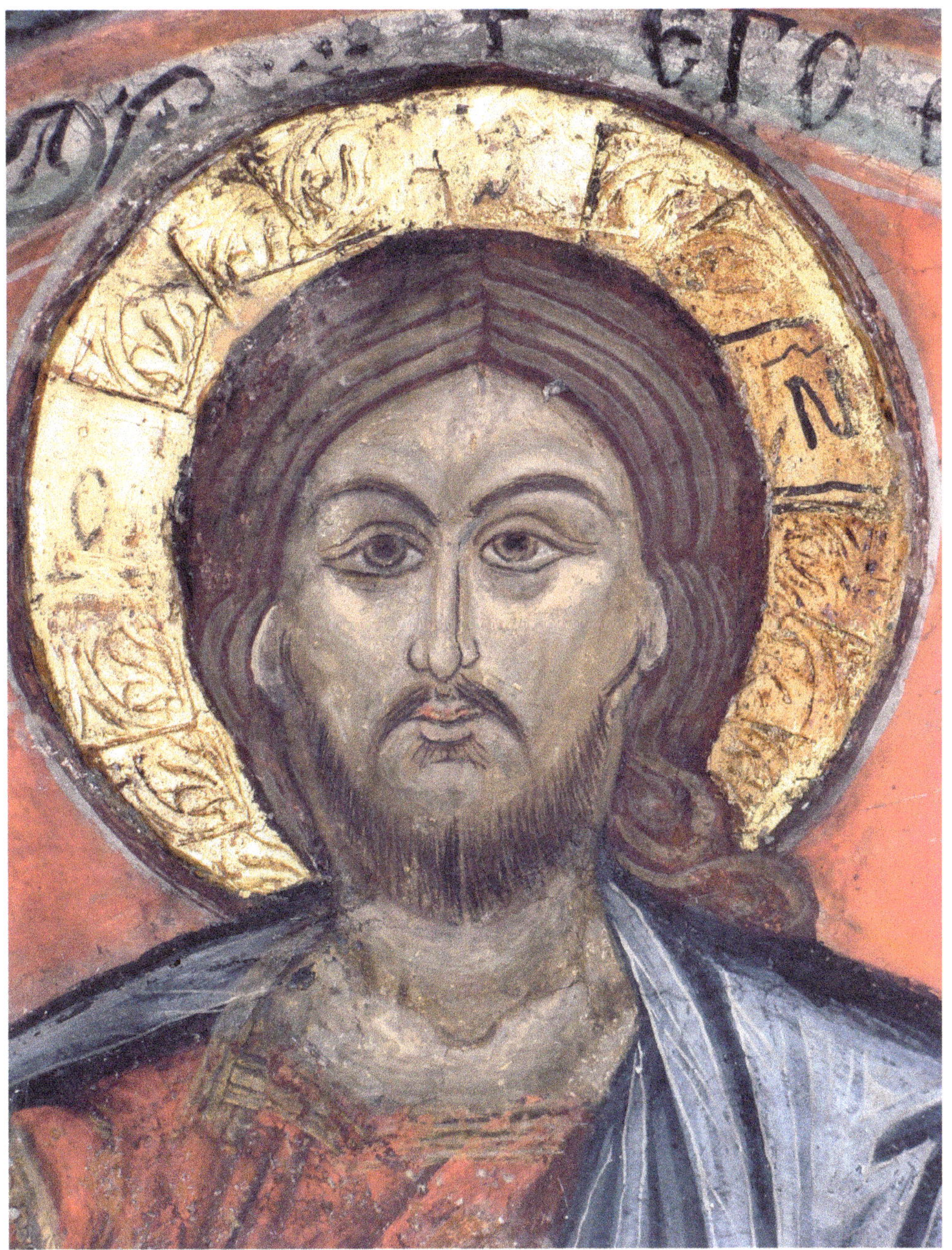

Fig. 1-13

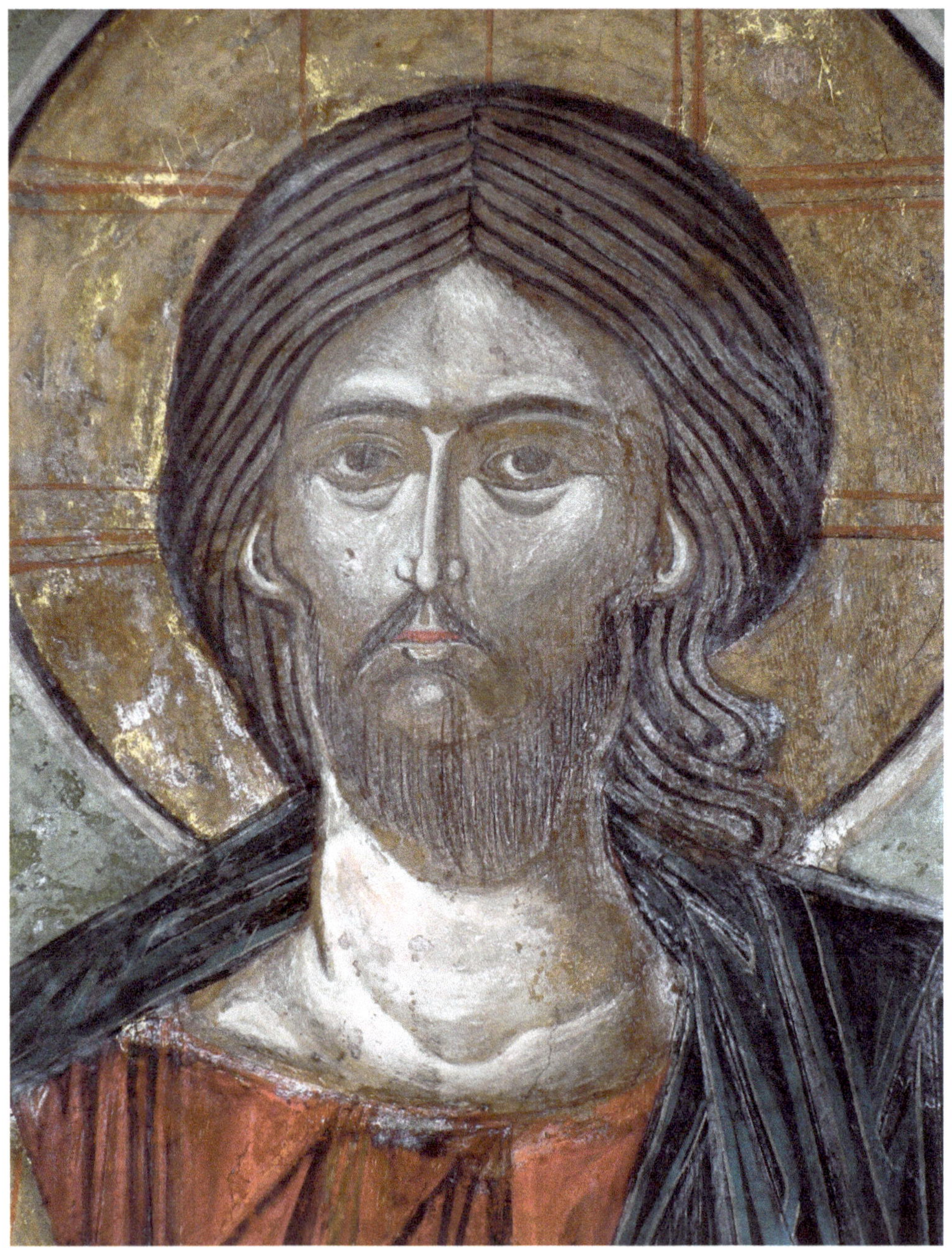

Fig. 1-14

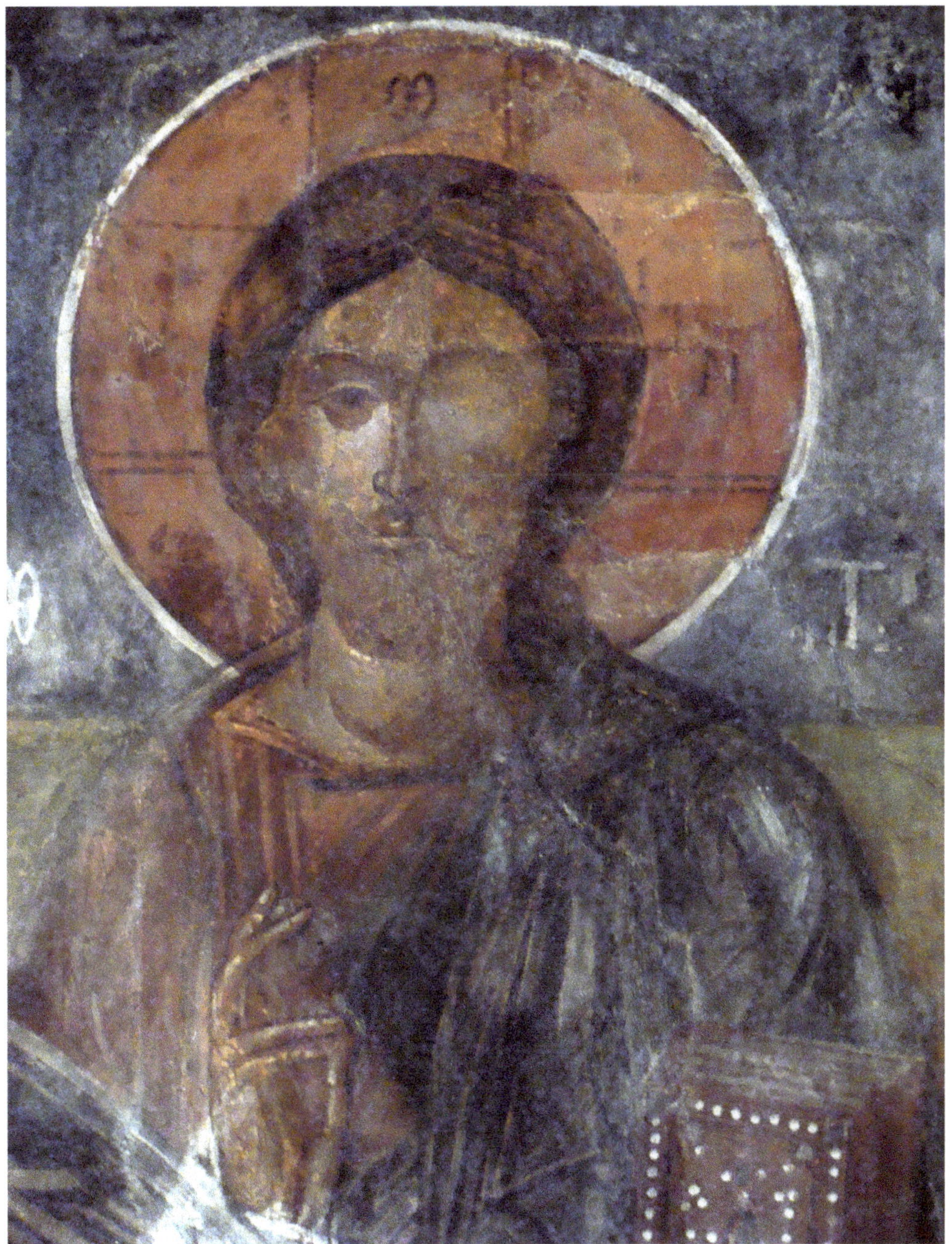

Fig. 1-15

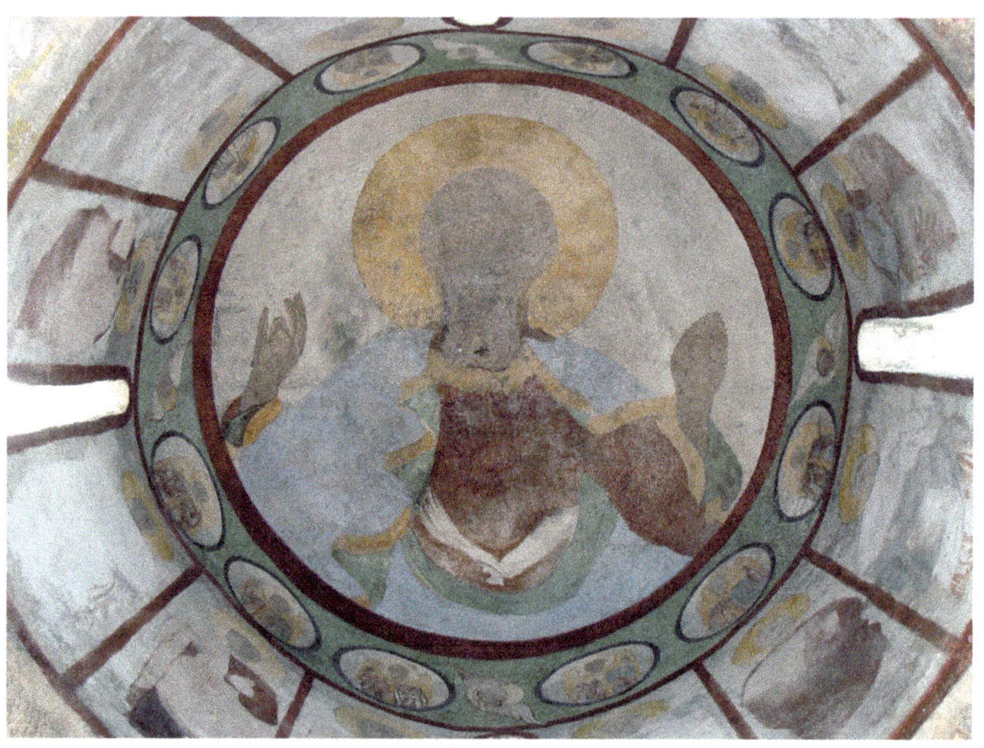

Fig. 1-16

Nativity

The Eye of a Needle

The light is a star, the Infant a spool. The Virgin Mary no longer holds a distaff and spindle. She is the Mother of God – what she had to spin, she has spun. It is up to him now to knit the shirt of the world in silence and word, in parables.

The principal relationship, as in the Annunciation, is between her and the Light. Between her and the Infant. The Light-Word. The incarnate Light. But in an interaction like that of the Deesis, where the Son is the bridegroom and the Mother the bride. Because the main message of the Nativity, apart from the fact that 'the light of knowledge dawned upon the earth' (Troparion of the Nativity), is precisely the intimate, deeply saving link between mother and son, the realization of the plan of the Incarnation through the Virgin Mary and of the first deification, the saving road of Adam through Christ. Not by chance do artists paint the Infant in the manger wrapped like a cocoon, about to spread his wings, filling them with blood, becoming the only bird that has nowhere to lay its head, but with a body like a soul. Like Lazarus' body, symbol of human resurrection, like his own body, devoid of its shroud, which the Angel of the Lord points towards. And that of the Nativity, reminiscent of a fish that monks, hunters of men, catch with their own bare hands.

So the Infant contains within himself not only his own soul, but also his Mother's (which is also sometimes depicted like a cocoon – Rakovitsa, fig. 2-1), Lazarus', deified humanity's once it has shed its old garment. He is not only his own Resurrection, he is the Resurrection of the world. He is the way to the manger. And from the manger on upwards. To where the Christmas Star points.

The letter L determines the position of the Mother's body in relation to her Son. She is drawn perpendicularly to the manger, her head turned towards or away from him. The second of these gestures expresses tiredness, exhaustion. Waiting in agony for what is to come. In the Nativity from Eleshnitsa (fig. 2-2), this is shown by the oversized hand under her chin, which borders on forgetfulness and hardship. When because of the long wait, painful time, time is so prolonged you almost lose track of it, falling into timelessness, into eternity. Like the monk Ero from Armenteira Monastery in Galicia, who kept on begging the Virgin Mary to reveal eternity to him. And standing under a tree in the courtyard, listening to the nightingale's trills, he drifted off in such a way that when he came to, he couldn't recognize a single face. Three hundred years had gone by.

Only in Eleshnitsa is the Mother's position parallel to that of the Son. This balances the double gesture of the averted head and hand. The image of the young mother gives character to the whole composition: she has masculine radiance (Boboshevo),

her bed resembles a mandorla, but one that is made of matter (Alino, fig. 2-3), she lies on a geometrical plane with a fragile body (Strupets), her halo is inscribed in the larger, material mandorla like a pupil in an eye (Karlukovo), in the white of an eye (St Stephen's, Nesebar; Church of Sts Peter and Paul, Veliko Tarnovo, fig. 2-4). The eye of God.

Albeit not directly, in the fresco of the Nativity, God the Father is invariably present. The fresco of the Holy Trinity is seemingly embedded in that of the Nativity. As are the frescoes of the Baptism and the Resurrection.

The cave of the Nativity is another characteristic detail. Not only as a place, but also as a symbol of the womb, of life in anticipation of the Resurrection, of Hell. There where the Infant already steps, so he can go on to what he has to accomplish.

In some frescoes, the Mother climbs into the cave on her knees, holding out her hands to the Infant, like those thousands of pilgrims flocking from the harbor to her church on the Greek island of Tinos. She climbs in an inner Golgotha, a Golgotha-womb, concave, the opposite of Christ's, though in fact they are one and the same (Seslavtsi, fig. 2-5). In other frescoes, the cave is painted so skillfully and knowledgeably from a geological point of view that the chosen color (including the Mother's clothes) is the same as the rock that makes up the mantle: peridot (Iliyantsi, fig. 2-6). In another fresco, the cave is tied at both ends like a scarf (Ivanovo). Because 'whatever you bind on earth will be bound in heaven' (Mt 16:19).

Although all in swaddling clothes, the Infant is always with his head raised. He greets the Mother, blesses her. Even with restricted hands, he blesses with the gesture of his head.

In a kind of sequence, the star's movement and the Mother's inner ascent establish the two main forms that are to be found in the most spectacular frescoes of the Nativity – from Dolni Pasarel and the Church of Sts Michael and Gabriel in Arbanasi. From a compositional point of view, the frescoes are built around one form (the hourglass) and inscribed in the other (the eye).

In iconography, the detail contains the whole, and the whole fits inside the detail, just as all frescoes are superimposed on top of each other, and one is an expression of all, and vice versa. Like the reflection of a hill on a body of water, or a serviette folded in four, which we cut and, when it opens, the shapes are multiplied.

The archetypal form found in most frescoes of the Nativity is that of the Way. The narrow way like the eye of a needle, which the Savior talks about in parables. And

nothing expresses the Nativity as deeply as two symbols: the hourglass and the eye, which underpin the images from Dolni Pasarel and Arbanasi. The eye is in fact an hourglass, only the two arcs face inwards.

At its narrowest point, the hourglass from Dolni Pasarel (fig. 2-7) borders on cumulus clouds in the heavenly world and hills in this world. Among the hills, right in the middle, are depicted the Mother and Child, and the only link between the two worlds is the Christmas Star, which hangs over the manger after guiding the Magi a long way to the chosen place, thus forming the letter L between heaven and earth. Because the eye of a needle is not straight vertically or horizontally. It is an angular shape. And the difficulty of passing through it is not just because the entrance is narrow, but because it is folded. There is no entrance as narrow as one that is folded. However strong the jet may be, if the hose is bent, the supply of water will be cut off.

So the way the Magi travel, each from his own place, following the star, coming together in front of the Infant's cave, is nothing other than the route each of us must take to the Savior. Where the earthly way finishes or takes another direction. And the real direction is neither forwards, nor back, nor down, but only up towards the light, on the bundle of rays of the Christmas Star, which has stopped over the manger. Passing through the only possible place, which the star illuminates: the Christ Child. Because 'I am the way, and the truth, and the life. No one comes to the Father except through me' (Jn 14:6).

Through the hourglass, horses, sheep and other animals continue to flow like grains of sand. The painter from Dolni Pasarel has wisely introduced a shepherd who has grabbed the reins of three horses and wants to lead them over the hill, but they pull back. Because he isn't the real shepherd. While the reins of the bull and donkey lowering their heads over the manger descend like streams to the proper place for food and water. Bowing their heads.

In the largest fresco of the Nativity in Bulgaria, the one in the Church of Sts Michael and Gabriel, Arbanasi (fig. 2-8), the hourglass is closed inside a huge eye, in the centre of which, the very pupil, are the Mother and Child. The pupil is half black, half white, like the heavenly bodies depicted in images of the Crucifixion and Creation. The eye's lower edge is red because of the soil, the red clay of Creation, the fatigue, weeping and pain of this world, while the white beneath the upper edge is the heavenly kingdom with its angels and cherubim.

Seen from above, the hourglass represents an eye with a pupil at its narrowest point. The two together provide the scheme for a cross with seven rays: four horizontal

rays going in the four directions of the world, one stuck in the earth, another in the sky like Jacob's ladder, and the seventh where the horizontal and vertical meet: the passage, the pupil, the cornerstone with its enormous weight, after whose victory over death nobody has to die alone since they die together with Christ.

The fresco of the Nativity contains all the basic eschatological truths – about birth, death and resurrection, about God's economy. And perhaps it conceals an answer to the most important human question of all: the meaning of life, the way. Which begins by seeing the star, ends with worship of the Infant beneath the star's light and continues through the eye of the needle, through the cornerstone, upwards, all along the bundle of rays.

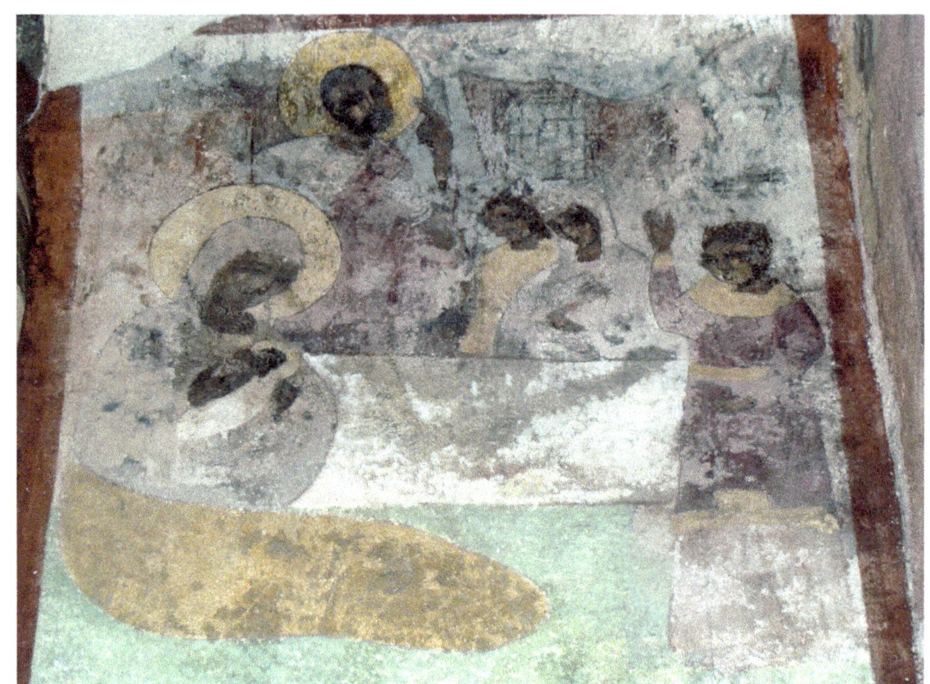

Fig. 2-1

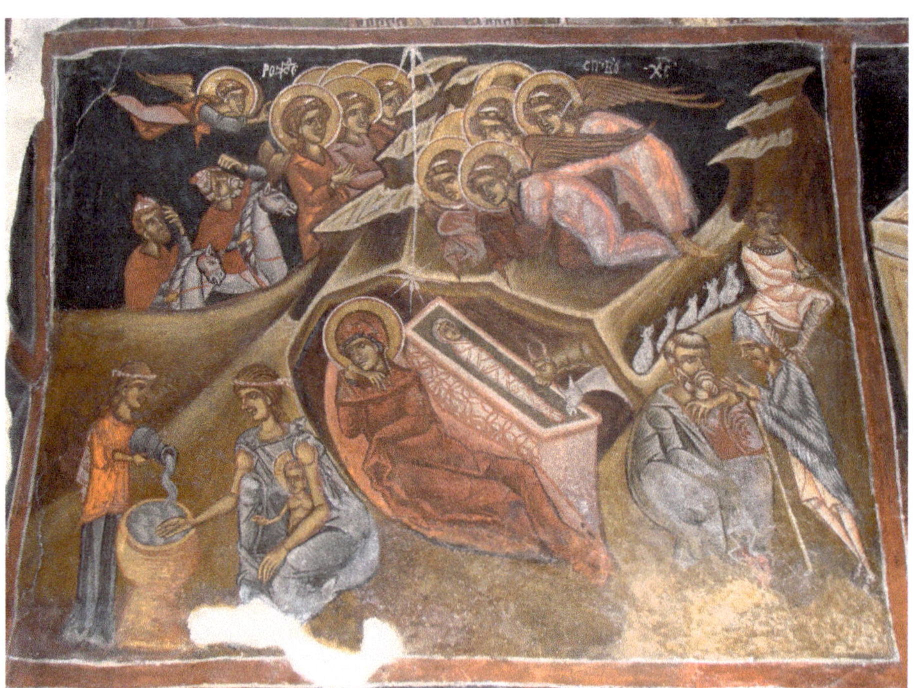

Fig. 2-2

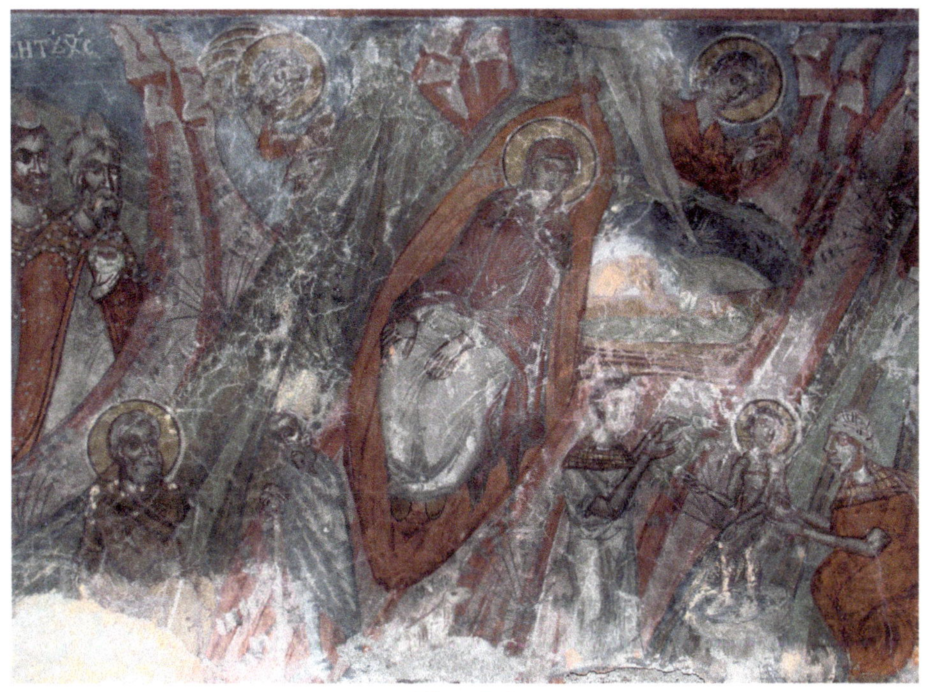

Fig. 2-3

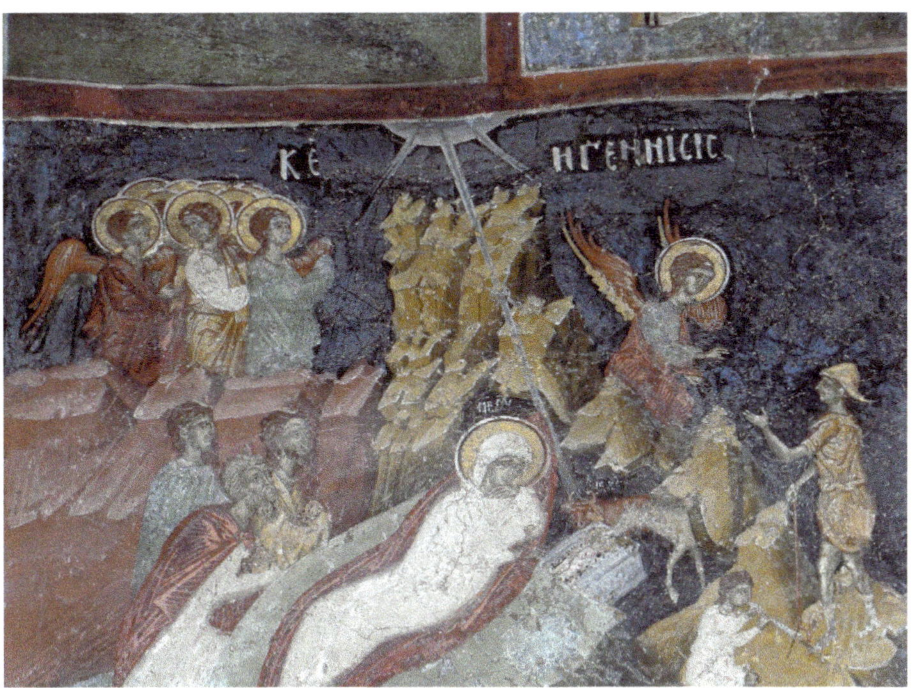

Fig. 2-4

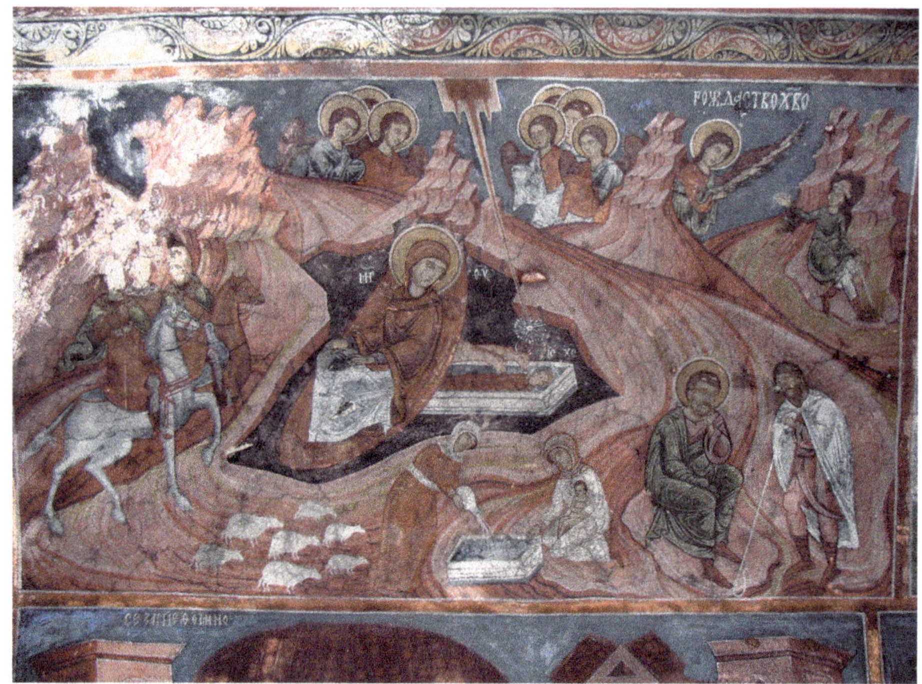

Fig. 2-5

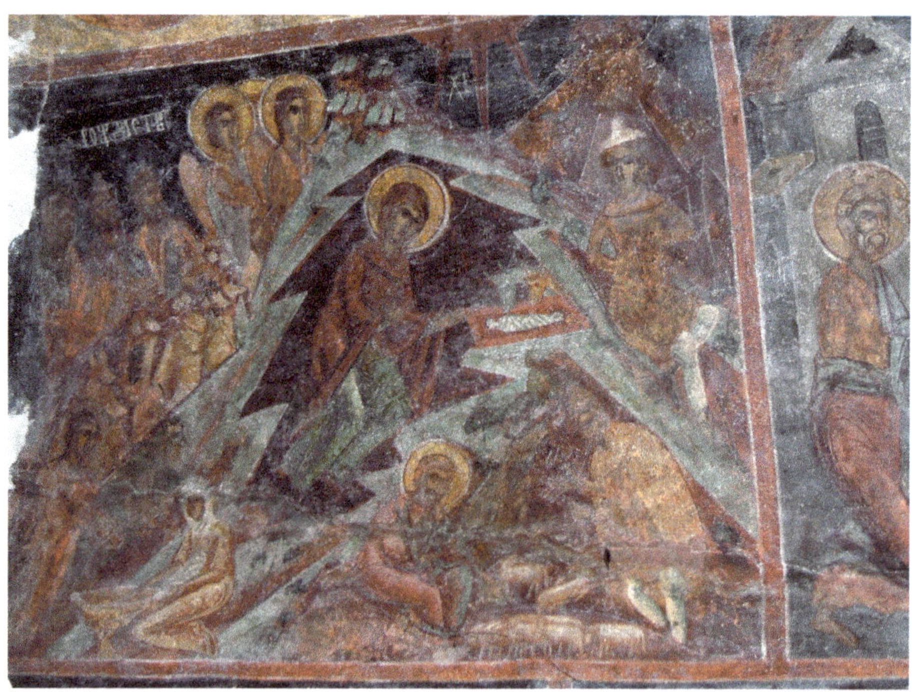

Fig. 2-6

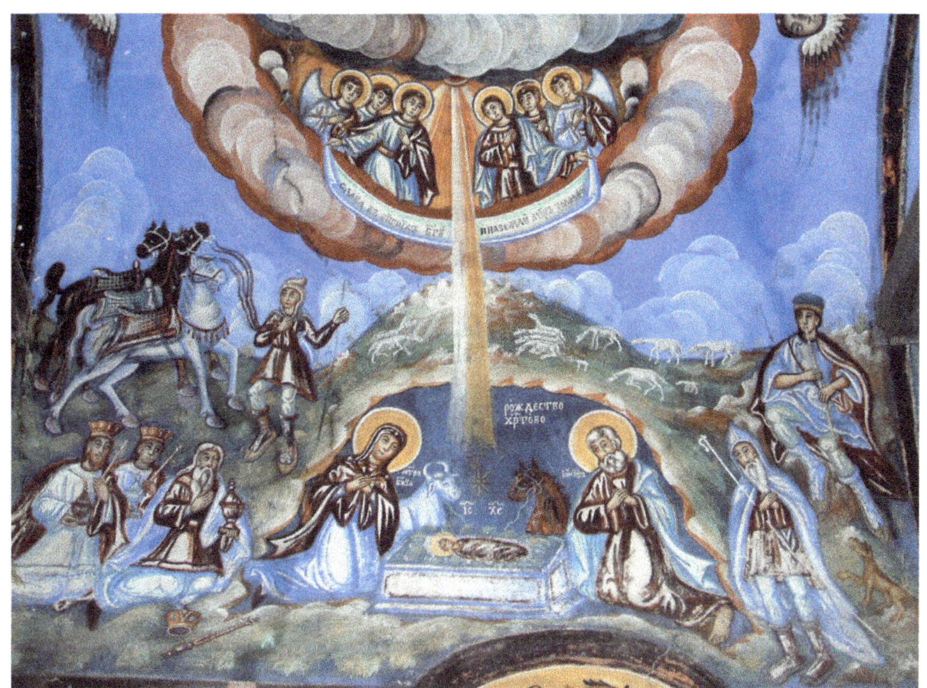

Fig. 2-7

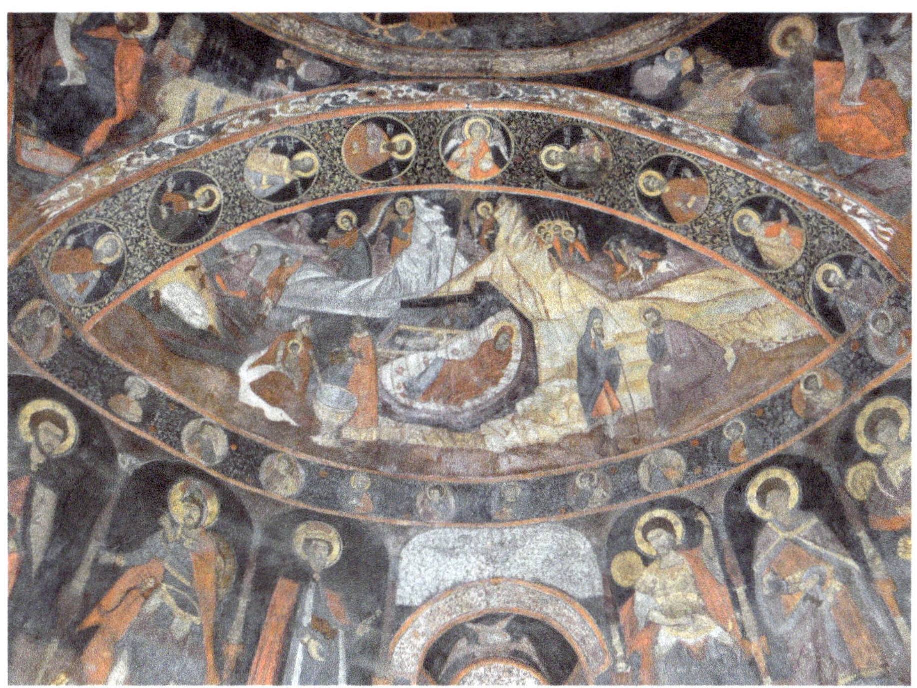

Fig. 2-8

Theophany

The Fulfillment of the World[5]

5 This essay discusses three events in the life of Christ: Candlemas or the Presentation of Jesus in the Temple when he was a baby (2 February), Christ among the Teachers or the Finding in the Temple when he was aged twelve, and Theophany or the Baptism of the Lord when he was thirty (6 January).

Evil, which has no original essence but is merely the resistance of the free creature to Him that is before all ages – to God – cannot be absolute. Therefore evil in the literal sense does not, and cannot, exist. All evil effected by free beings must live like a parasite on the body of the good.

— St Sophrony of Essex, *Saint Silouan the Athonite*[6]

We all know what delousing is. You take off your clothes and pass through a disinfecting environment. Techniques that are familiar to us mostly from war films or the like. For us, baptism is a kind of delousing. Jesus Christ himself passes through it, his original purity is testified to by the Holy Spirit, the keeper of the entrance. That is why evil has no place in him, it cannot be injected like a wasp's foreign egg in the cocoon's insides, which it liquefies in order to appear not as a butterfly, but as a parasite. The Savior himself bears witness: 'I will no longer talk much with you, for the ruler of this world is coming. He has no power over me' (Jn 14:30).

And yet he passes through the Jordan River. And yet he is baptized by the Baptist, who proclaims that he is not worthy to 'untie the thong of his sandals' (Mk 1:7). He doesn't do this as a justification or proof – even in front of Pilate he doesn't defend himself. Justification pertains to those who are captive to sin. Rather, he does this to become one of us, lowering his divine nature to that of a human, in an act of condescension. Taking up his cross. Setting out on a mission that is not to change the law, the world, but to fulfill it. The strength of evil in the world resides precisely in its mimicry, its inability to be distinguished from good, because of 'imperfection in human good, and the inevitable presence of some pretence of good in evil.'[7]

'Do not think that I have come to abolish the law or the prophets; I have come not to abolish but to fulfill' (Mt 5:17), says the Savior, and this is what defines his saving mission: the knowledge of who he is, and following the path according to which 'even the hairs of your head are counted' (Mt 10:30). Change in the world consists in its fulfillment.

From an early age, Christ fixes the coordinates of this fulfillment. What child has not let go of his mother's or father's hand in a throng of people and got lost at least once, even if only for a minute, but in order to be found in the Temple of the Lord?

6 St Sophrony of Essex, *Saint Silouan the Athonite*, tr. Rosemary Edmonds (Crestwood, NY: St Vladimir's Seminary Press, 1991), p. 117.
7 St Sophrony of Essex, *Saint Silouan the Athonite*, p. 117.

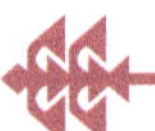

What child has not sat at table, raised on a cushion as on a throne, but in order to preach in the temple with the characteristic dome like an egg shell over his head, with the characteristic shape of his hair, whose curls seem to delineate the labyrinths of his thought (Christ among the Teachers, Seslavtsi, fig. 3-1), with the characteristic garment that looks as if letters have been scrawled all over it (Christ Emmanuel, Alino)? What child has not been taken from his mother for the first time, like Christ being placed in the arms of Simeon the Righteous? Reaching out his hand as far as it will go towards his Mother (Presentation of Jesus in the Temple, Strupets, fig. 3-2) – hers is unusually big (Eleshnitsa, fig. 3-3) – and yet blessing the witness, because the Son is not his Mother's property. Regardless of the obvious spatial link between them, which is indicated by the zigzagging ornamentation (Bilintsi, fig. 3-4). It is precisely these scenes from Candlemas that mark this first separation: from the arms of Simeon the Righteous through his foray to the temple to his best friend, John the Baptist. Like us, through childhood and puberty to the adult age of thirty, Christ gradually moves away from his family, in order to utter the now famous remark, 'My mother and my brothers are those who hear the word of God and do it' (Lk 8:21). He outgrows his family. He walks alone into the wilderness. Despite his Mother's sad look.

And there is the Savior, standing in the middle of the river. Very important are the gestures and positioning of his feet, his hands, the shrunken stomach. This is perhaps the only fresco, together with the Crucifixion, where we see Christ in his human nakedness. More than that, perhaps the only fresco where he is depicted completely naked, without even a girdle around his loins, emphasizing not the gender, but the shape of the stomach (Boboshevo). The whole of Christ's priesthood from his baptism to his crucifixion is his placement in the context of a sinful world, outside the gates of heaven, and in fulfillment of God's Word, which is his fight against sin, unlike our ancestors, who opposed God's Word. Fulfillment, which is humility and the attainment of true freedom, unlike the freedom in evil which flowed from the Tree of Knowledge through the mouth of the serpent, in the opposite way to how freedom flowed from the Holy Spirit on the Apostles at Pentecost or on Christ's head at the Theophany (Zemen, fig. 3-5). It is precisely this filling from one outpouring to another, from not good freedom to freedom in God, that Christ came to achieve. In this consists the only real great change of the world, then and always.

Christ in the Jordan, unlike Adam and Eve in Eden, out of which flow four rivers, has stepped on the snake and the mythological creatures, as in the Resurrection he has stepped on Adam's skull, on the first rung of the earthly ladder (Iliyantsi).

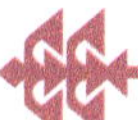

The earth beneath his feet is cracked, he stands in the middle between two shores – the ruler of this world and the kingdom of heaven (Strupets). He has stepped on a piece of land like Noah's Ark in the watery element, sanctifying it with his hands (Alino, fig. 3-6), his feet are gathered together in a triangle for better support (Seslavtsi, fig. 3-7), his posture is even that of one who dances over the sin of the world (Radibosh). His hands bless, his arms are crossed on his chest (Rakovitsa). The contours of the river proceed from his strong hair, whose prototype is that of Samson, the folds of his stomach have the outline of a church (Eleshnitsa, fig. 3-8), of a bell (Dolni Pasarel, fig. 3-9), of a portrait even (Preobrazhenie, fig. 3-10). Christ is personalized in the river, he is the face, one of the Holy Trinity, to whom God the Father testifies out loud for the first time. His posture is that of one who surrenders himself completely to the Father and the Holy Spirit, with outstretched arms and legs beneath the dove, which hangs like a fruit different from the apple (Preobrazhenie). Christ has yet to walk on the water, the water is still milk, as if it came into being with his footsteps (St Stephen's, Nesebar, fig. 3-11). He is armed in the first place with his will and awareness of the Father's will for him. The greatness of God's love, of God's gesture towards us, resides precisely in his humility, the lack of imposition. In the one who is 'standing at the door, knocking' (Rev 3:20), but only comes in when he is invited.

In God's delicacy towards people, sending Christ as an example, lies also the future of the world, in the words of Patriarch Kirill of Moscow: 'Man's choice always has an eschatological perspective, because on this, whether he will go along the path of life or the path of death, depends the course of human history and its final outcome.'[8]

8 Translated from an article by Patriarch Kirill published in Bulgarian as 'Божият замисъл за човека и свободната воля: Есхатологическа перспектива' in the magazine Християнство и култура (vol. 1/58, 2011).

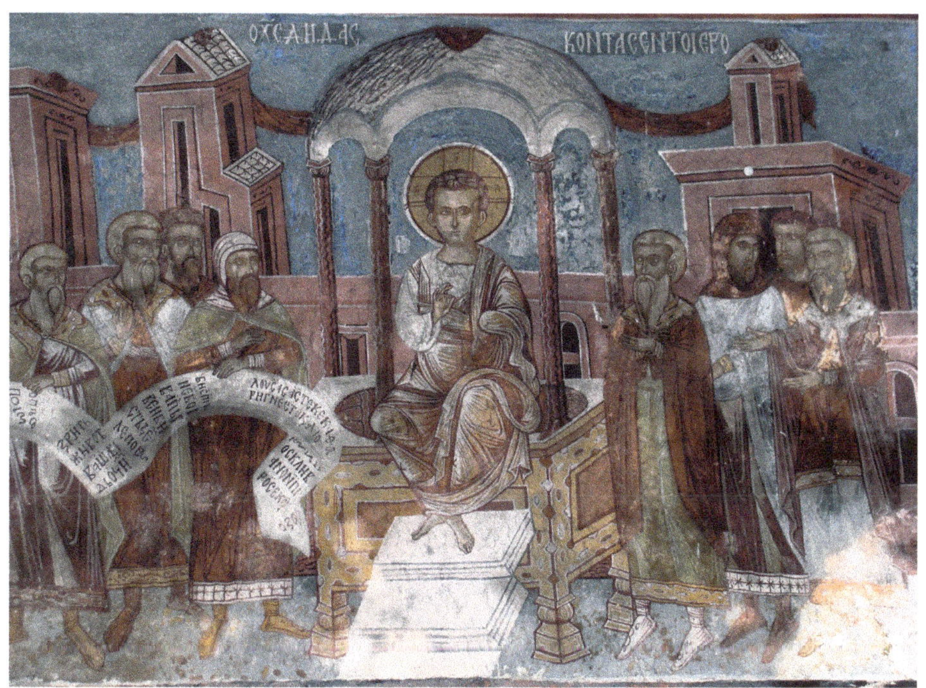

Fig. 3-1

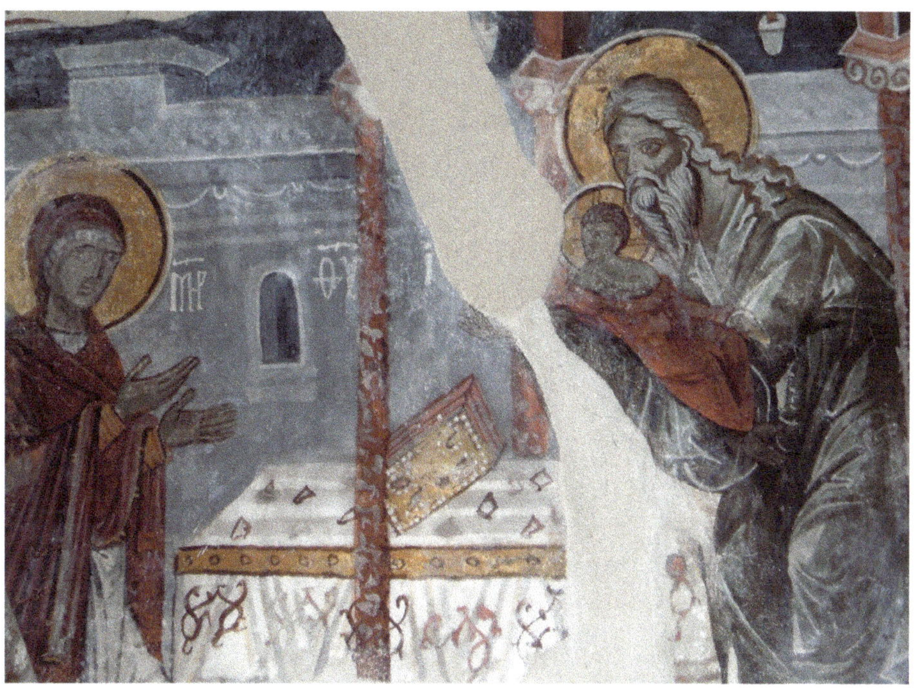

Fig. 3-2

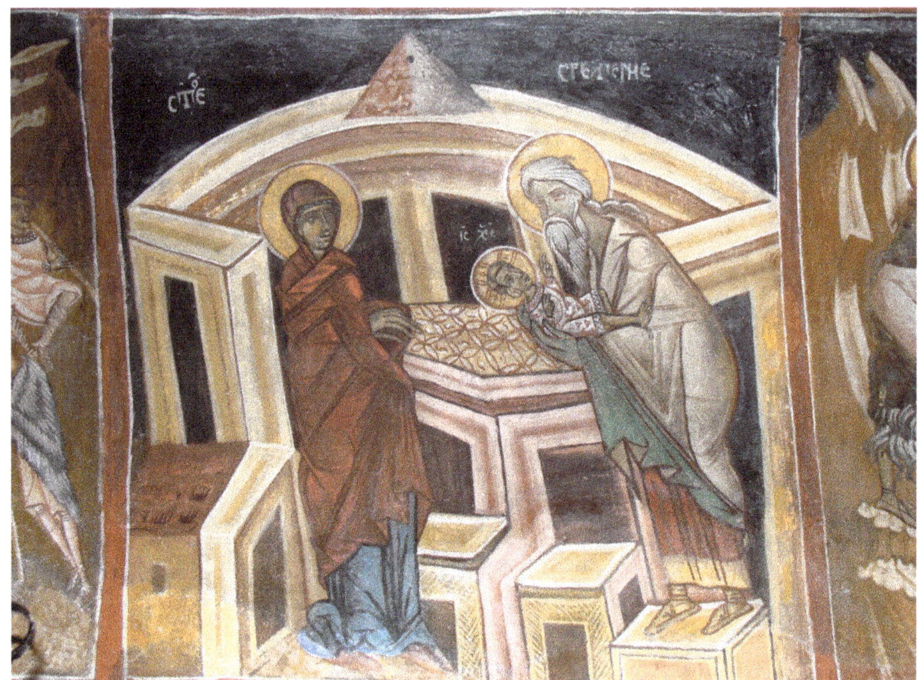

Fig. 3-3

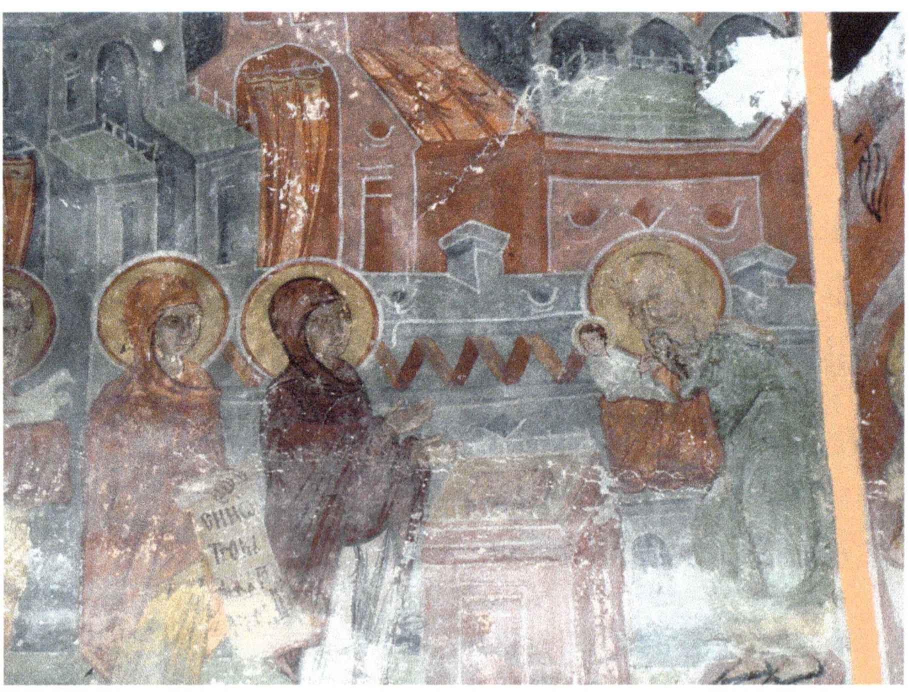

Fig. 3-4

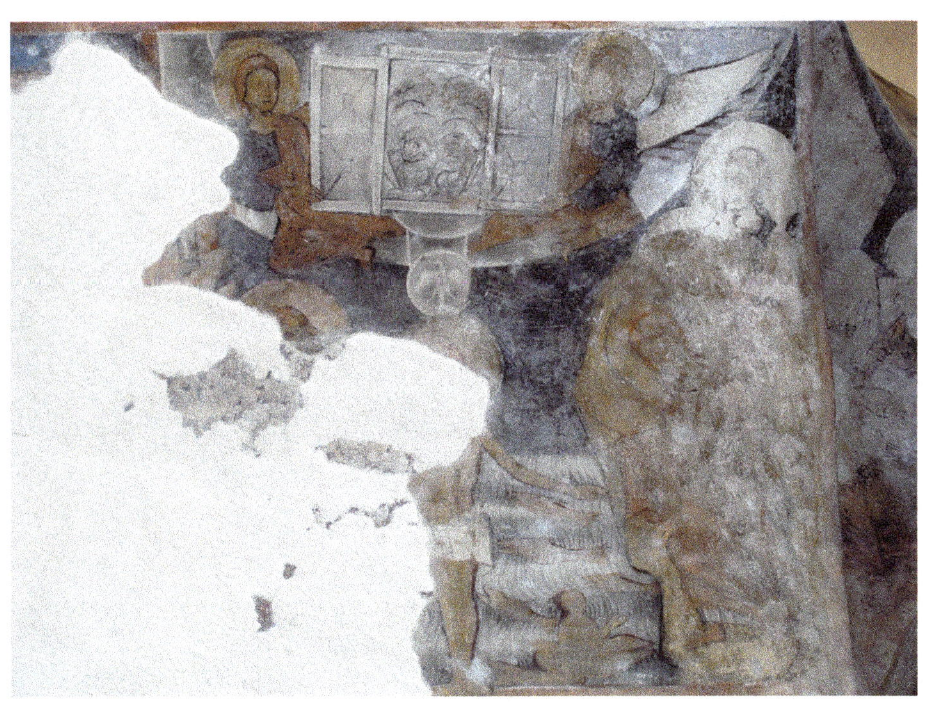

Fig. 3-5

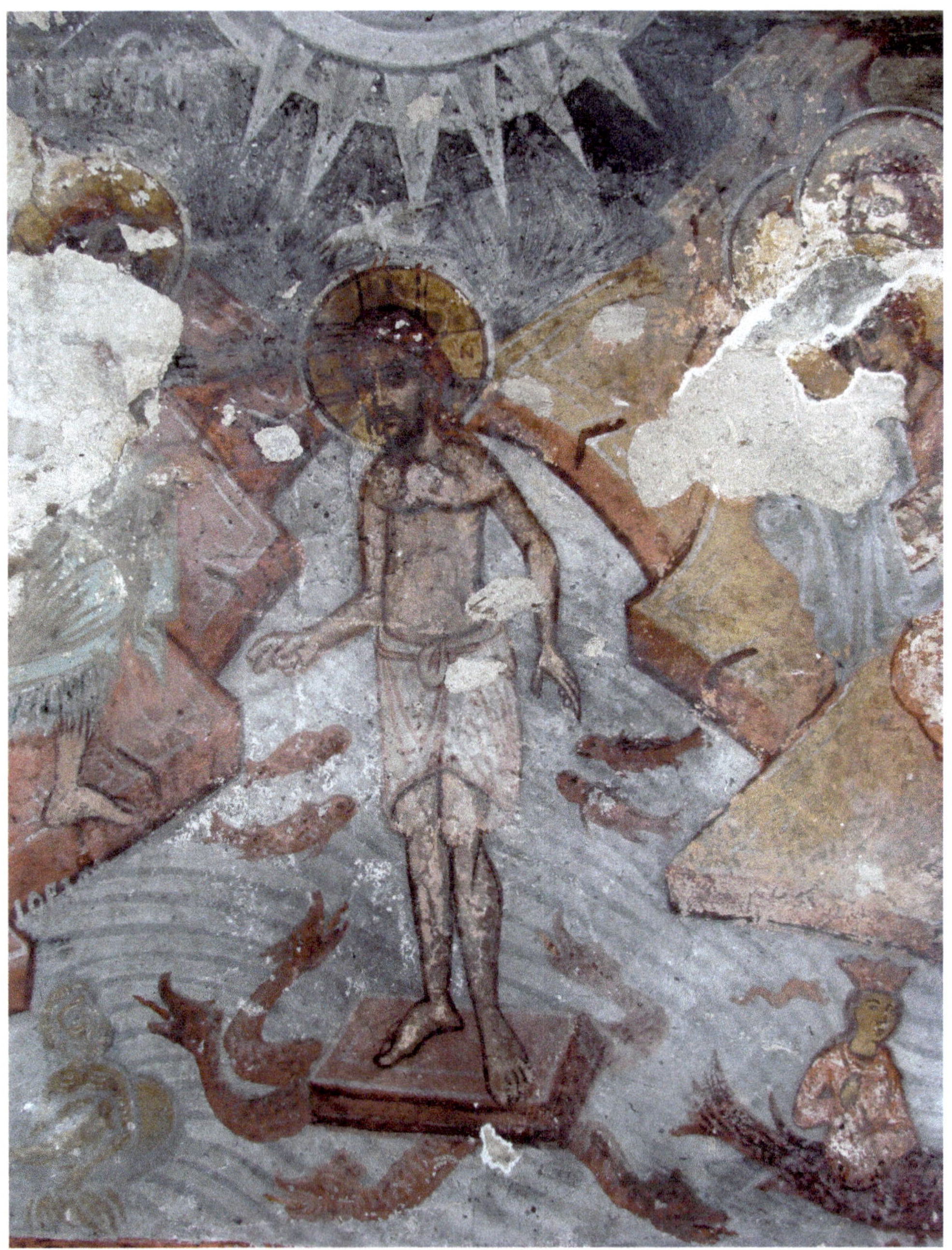

Fig. 3-6

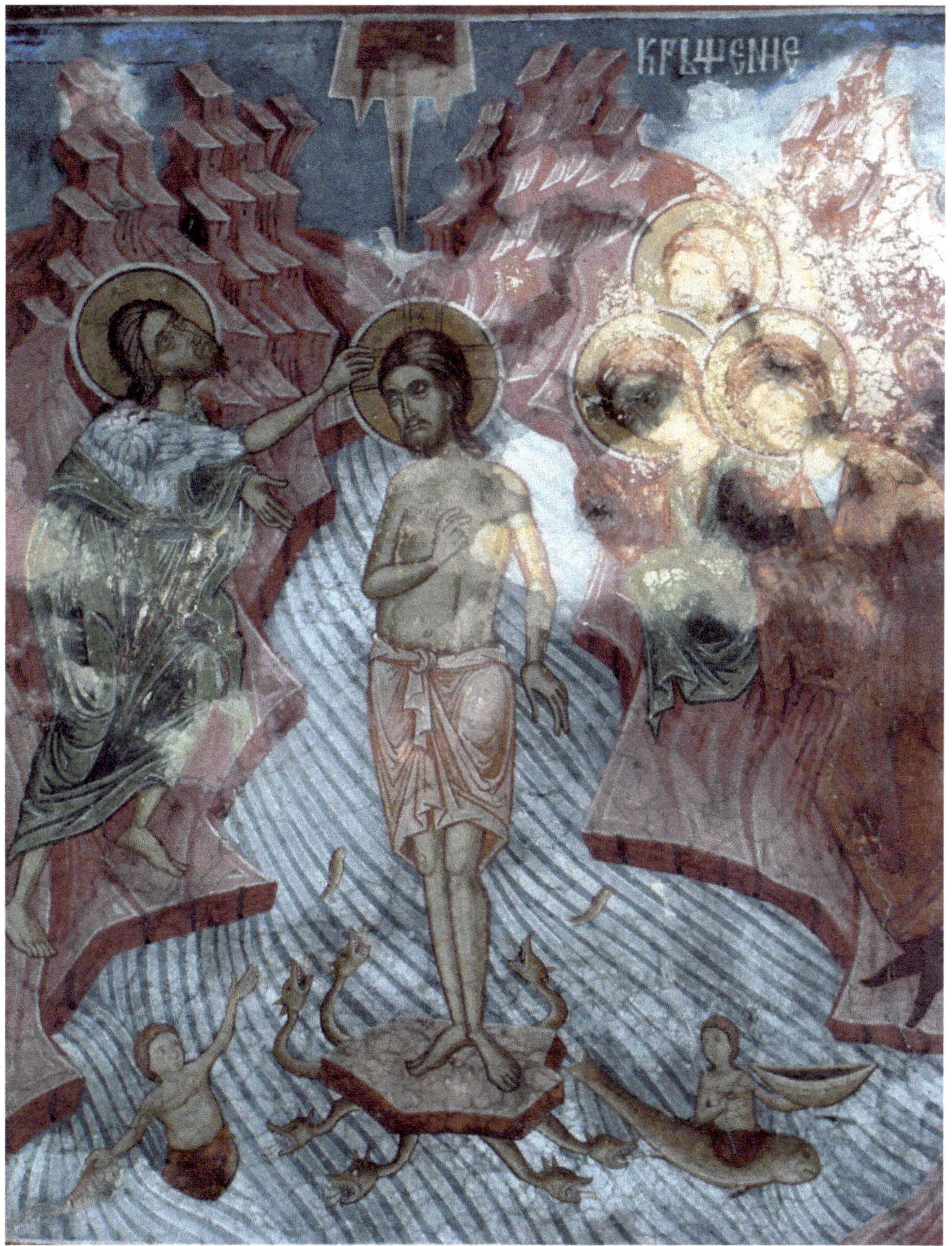

Fig. 3-7

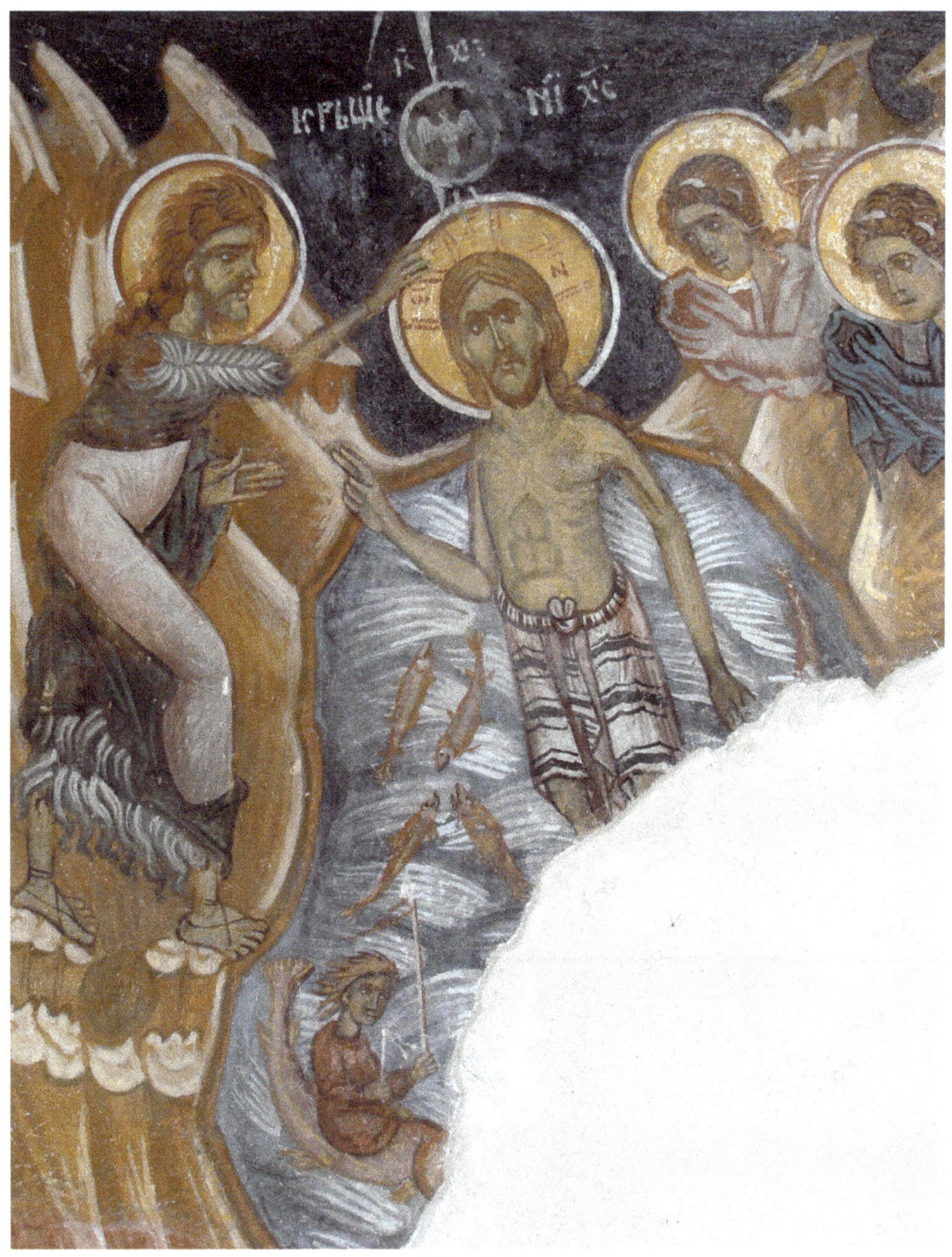

Fig. 3-8

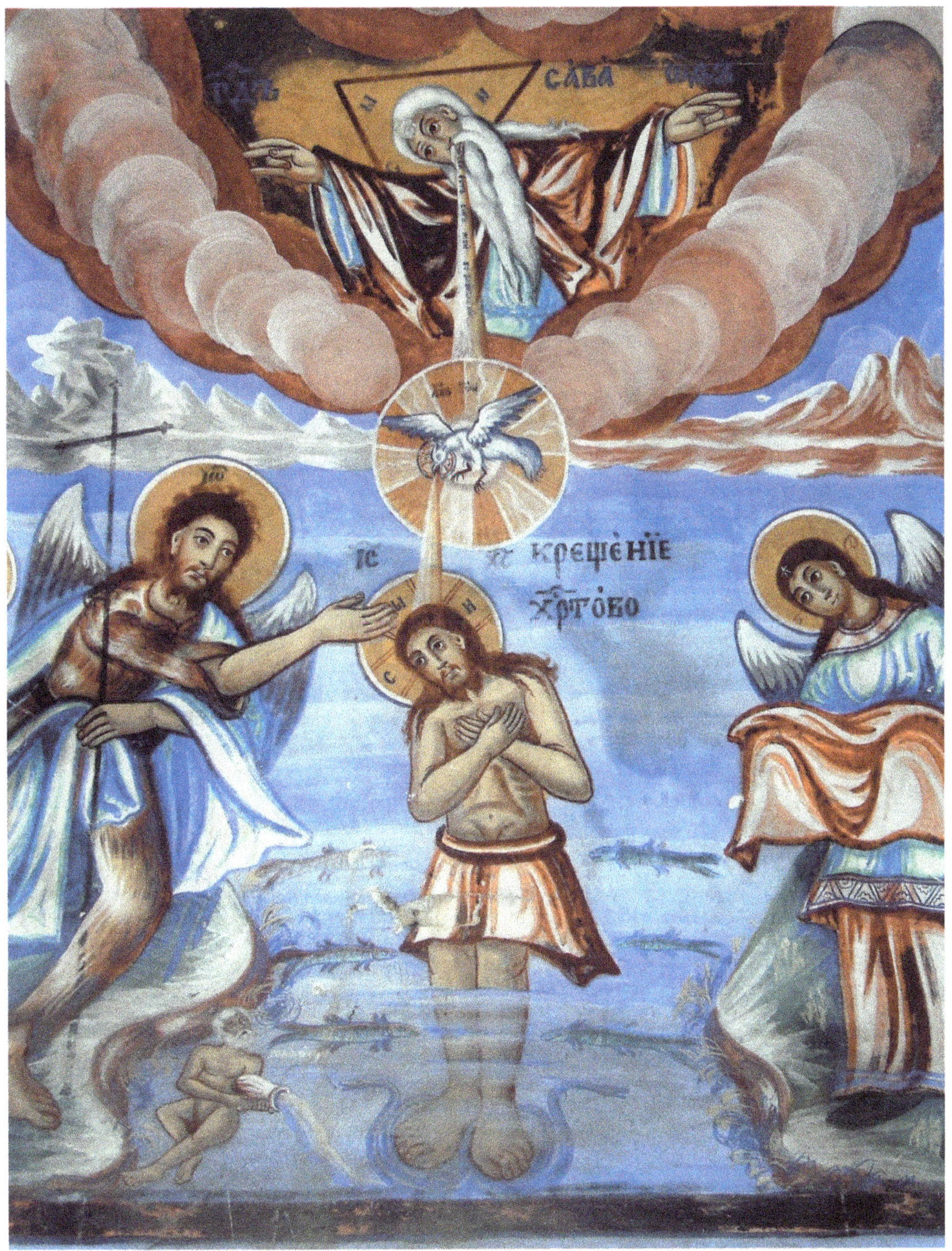

Fig. 3-9

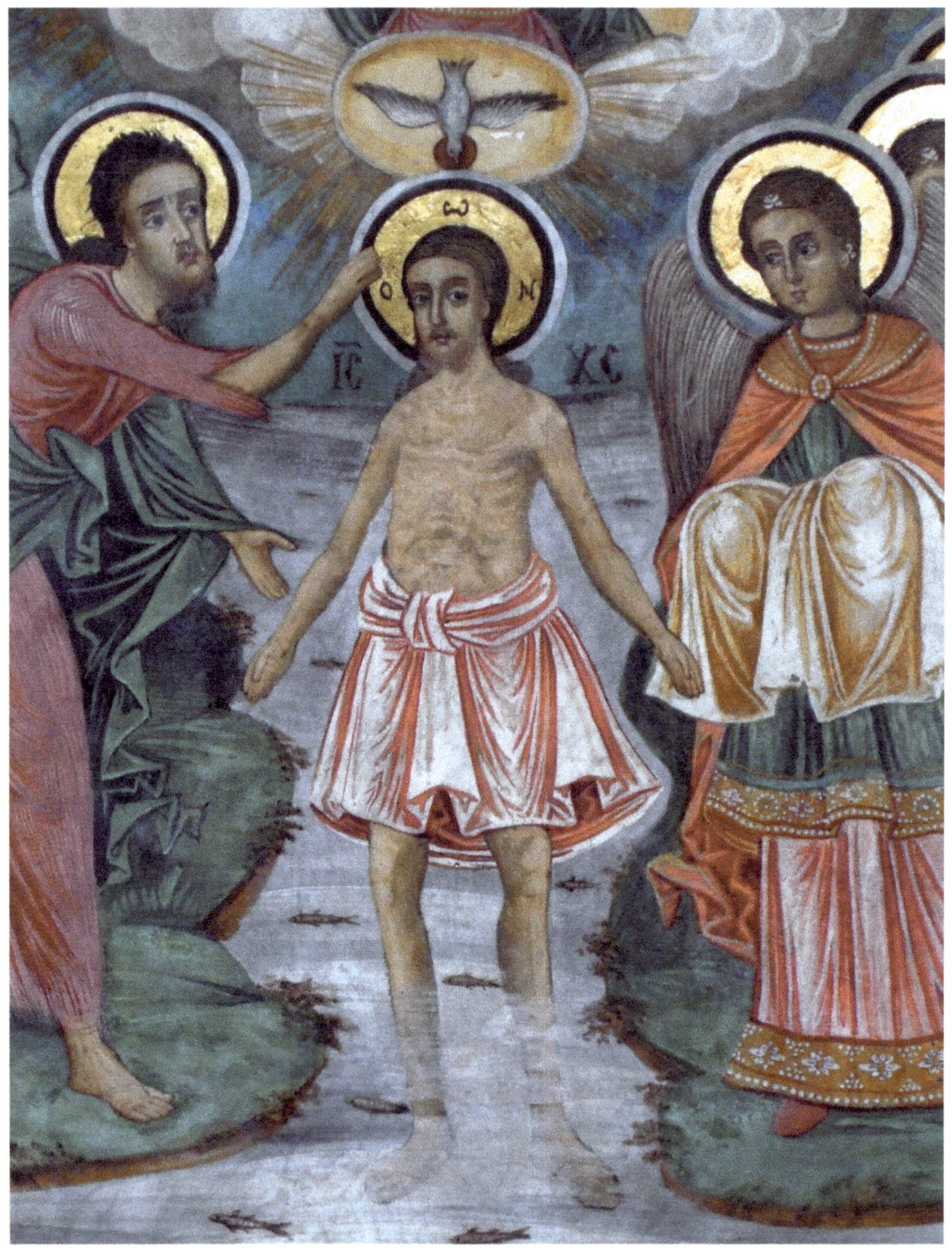

Fig. 3-10

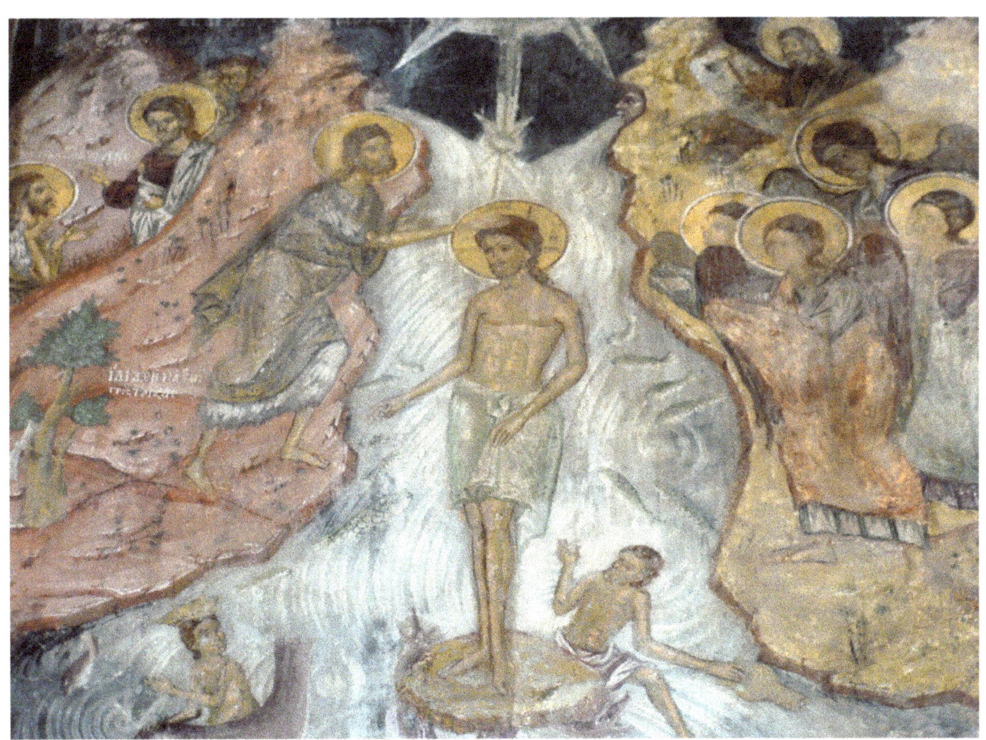

Fig. 3-11

Annunciation

The DNA of Life

The Annunciation is the only fresco painted not only on the walls of churches, but also on the icon screen, on the holy doors at its centre, the approach to the Holy of Holies. Because of the grandiose message it brings – of Christ's condescension, gathering the world in a single gesture from the Creation to the Resurrection.

For what else is that ray (line) of light directed towards the halo (circle) around the Virgin Mary's head if not the combination of linear human and cyclical cosmic time, in order to bring about eternity (the cross)?

Just as, according to the latest research by NASA, more than four billion years ago a meteorite crashed into a still empty earth, carrying the building blocks of DNA for life on the planet. Or as, biologically, life is sown in the womb by a single spermatozoid breaching the egg's outer shell and membrane all the way to the nucleus, where it releases its DNA, giving birth to a new heart. The first human organ to start working, when the embryo is barely three weeks old, the organ where, according to St Macarius of Egypt,[9] the soul is to be found.

Based on this same identity between the sacred and its material support, in his painting *The Annunciation*, Ivan Mrkvička depicted the Virgin's conception as a beam of light falling directly on her womb, carrying the divine seed-dove, which will be sown any moment. A cloud, like a hand, obscures the moon because of the sanctity of the sacrament, which is the only creation from eternity to the present, before the angels, a sacrament for them as well. The Virgin has been prostrated by the light's power, like the Apostles at the Transfiguration. In his work, Mrkvička, who also painted Alexander Nevsky Cathedral in Sofia, seems to summarize all the icons of the Annunciation: the spirit is seed, the Virgin's head her womb.

Or as St Nicholas Cabasilas writes, the plan of the Incarnation would have been impossible without the Virgin's will and faith.[10] Faith, which according to St Sophrony of Essex isn't just a psychological category, but 'an active manifestation of God's power in us.'[11]

---

9 St Macarius of Egypt, *Fifty Spiritual Homilies of Saint Macarius the Egyptian*, tr. A. J. Mason (London: Aeterna Press, 2014), homily 41.

10 Nicholas Cabasilas, 'Homily on the Annunciation', <https://www.johnsanidopoulos.com/2013/03/homily-on-annunciation-by-st-nicholas.html>, section 4.

11 St Sophrony of Essex, Духовни беседи (*Spiritual Talks*, Sofia: Omophor, 2006), a translation from a Russian edition by M. Meilakh (1997), p. 23.

The main scene of the Annunciation is in fact the communion between the Holy Spirit and the Virgin Mary, between the symbols of divine holiness and of human holiness by grace. Archangel Gabriel is the displaced centre, the witness of the new Creation. The spiritual world with its angelic ranks was created before man. For this reason, he bears witness. Just as the fallen angel, Satan, taking the form of a serpent, bears false witness at the Tree of Knowledge, leading Adam and Eve to sin, Archangel Gabriel, his exact opposite, bears witness with a true word at the Annunciation, holding a blossoming flower. The icon of the Annunciation is an intermediate station between the Fall and the Resurrection.

This is how it has been seen by the painters of four Bulgarian monasteries – Alino, Seslavtsi, Boboshevo and Eleshnitsa – and a church in the village of Berende, northwest of Sofia (close to the Serbian border).

In Alino (fig. 4-1), the light rushes towards the Virgin's head, as the flower turns its petals in the direction of the sun. One of the sun's rays, which looks like a flower, separates from the others and touches her halo. Light of light, which here, like Jacob's ladder, is shown going in both directions – not only from God to man, but also from the Virgin Mary, the first deified human and symbol of human perfection, to God. God's benevolence towards the Mother of God is so great the Holy Spirit turns towards her like a second sun.

In Seslavtsi (figs. 4-2,3), the scene is conveyed even more intimately. The light descends from around the corner of the façade – in other frescoes, we see it passing between black clouds (the iconostasis at Chepino, figs. 4-4,5) or even perched on a window (the altar at Dolna Beshovitsa) – in the form of three rays (symbol of the Holy Trinity) and of the letter 'M,' the first of Mary's name, and reaches her halo above the purple veil, which is like the wall of a womb. The two circles (the halo and the veil) overlap in a figure of eight, the symbol of the eighth day, the Resurrection, ready at any moment to open before the aspiring dove-seed, right where the Virgin Mary has timidly raised her hand with the ring finger projecting slightly forwards. Like Sleeping Beauty, she will prick her finger on a spindle – God's word of love and pain (curse or crucifixion), which will also save her. The hand is that fragile symbol of the door, which opens before God's might and then immediately closes, allowing nothing and no one else. It should be noted here that the Virgin's hand is pressed tightly against her body, as if in plaster, and this rigidity in the movement once again emphasizes her complete surrender to God's will.

The symbols of the spindle and the figure of eight, of virginity and eternity, can be found in other examples of icon painting, like those in the complex of Our Lady of Tinos (Panagia Megalochari) and St Sophia Cathedral in Kyiv (an eleventh-century mosaic), but depicted in a more traditional way – the Virgin with a crown or else spinning.

The church in Berende (fig. 4-6) brings out the dogma of active faith. Only in this fresco does the light pierce the Virgin's halo and directly touch her bowed head. Her mantle, eyebrows, eyes, lips, posture, all point to a downward motion like that of falling marbles. The Virgin, who descends like descending light. The ecstasy of humility, so close to the ecstasy of the Crucifixion, when the light has already penetrated her soul – a rational beginning, becoming part of her will. This categorical outpouring of grace is transmitted precisely through the ray in the form of a flask, from which the dove, the Holy Spirit, will pour out at any moment.

In the Virgin's face, we read humility and sorrow, so identical, that humility from the first of the three preparatory weeks before Lent, which is the first virtue, as opposed to the original sin of pride, the first weapon we use to fight against the spirits of malice under heaven during the forty-day fast.

The only cheerful Virgin is the one in Boboshevo (figs. 4-7,8), whom the dove rushes towards in a mandorla and with a halo like a fly embedded in amber, in a precious stone.

While the humility in Alino is shown by the Virgin's spinning action with her disproportionately large, alien hand, and in Seslavtsi by the pricking of her finger on a spindle, in Berende, Boboshevo and also Eleshnitsa (figs. 4-9,10) the distaff is in the form of a spanner, while in Eleshnitsa the spindle hangs over a detail of the column that resembles the cup from the Last Supper. The spanner is her key to the heart of God, to the kingdom of heaven, to people, to her own strong-willed heart. Where it all begins.

It is worth mentioning here that in no other fresco than the Annunciation from Alino is the depiction of Archangel Gabriel so close to, and yet so far from, that of Archangel Michael. His wings, spread in ecstasy, like a pair of scales – the same scales Archangel Michael holds in his right hand, the scales on the cross, a measure of righteousness (in Boboshevo, his scepter forms a cross with the end of his epitrachelion) – are ready to fly off at any moment, in a love dance or a fight to the death. Like the Virgin Mary, he also reflects love and pain, Annunciation

and Crucifixion. In his hand, he holds a scepter, but it is a blossoming lily. His posture is like the flight of the Holy Spirit – that descending or falling dove hit by a stone or in a mating ritual, which almost touches the ground before dizzily rising again to the heights. The dying, lovesick dove with legs and wings asymmetrically scattered about its body; the love that invariably contains pain, which is depicted in a more direct manner in the wall paintings of Boyana Church and Preobrazhenie Monastery. In the former, Archangel Gabriel's wings are a living willow hedge with heart-shaped leaves, while in the latter they look like baleen. With that function of filtering which is again characteristic of Archangel Michael.

Sacred images in Bulgarian lands, which Paul Evdokimov says are influenced by Semitism and the tragedy of those in Syrian monasteries,[12] also possess a unique figurative symbolism much closer to intimacy, much more liberated in dogma.

12 Paul Evdokimov, *The Art of the Icon: A Theology of Beauty*, tr. Steven Bigham (Pasadena, CA: Oakwood Publications, 2011), location 2721: 'In Bulgaria, we feel the more tragic influence of Syria along with the Semitic dimension of Orthodoxy.'

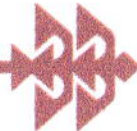

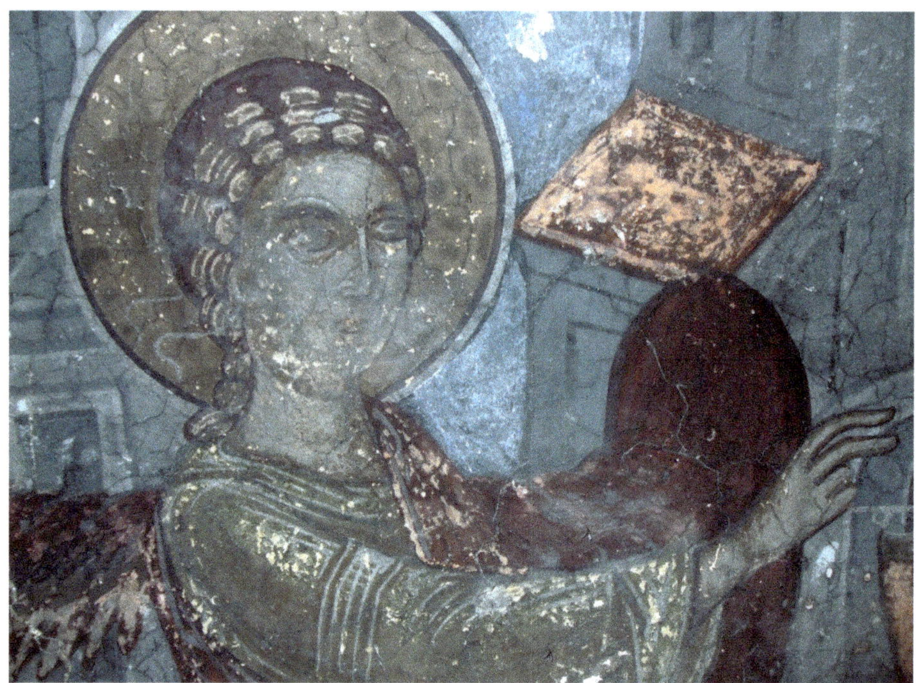

Fig. 4-2

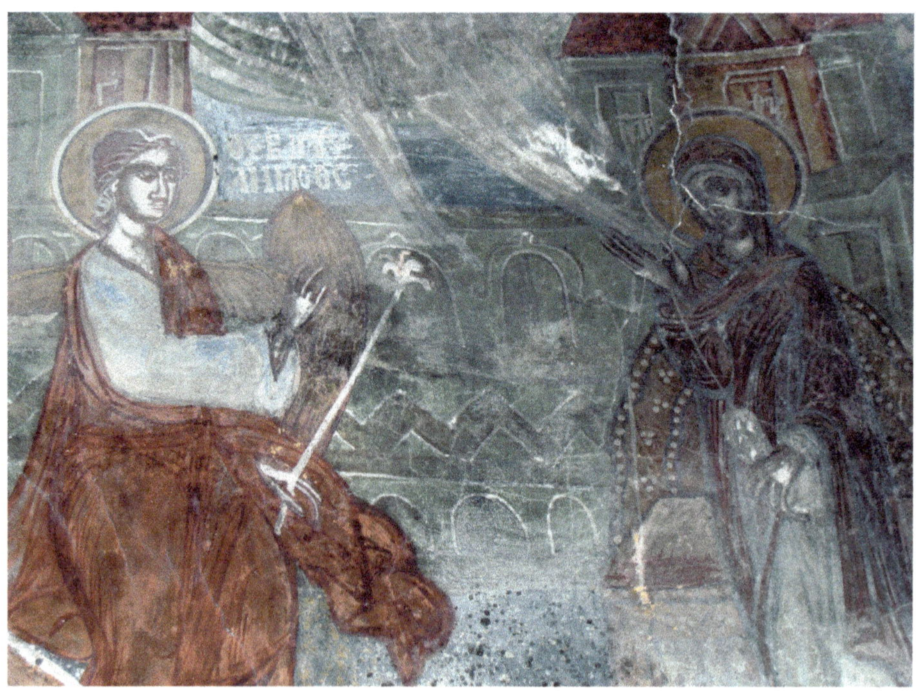

Fig. 4-1

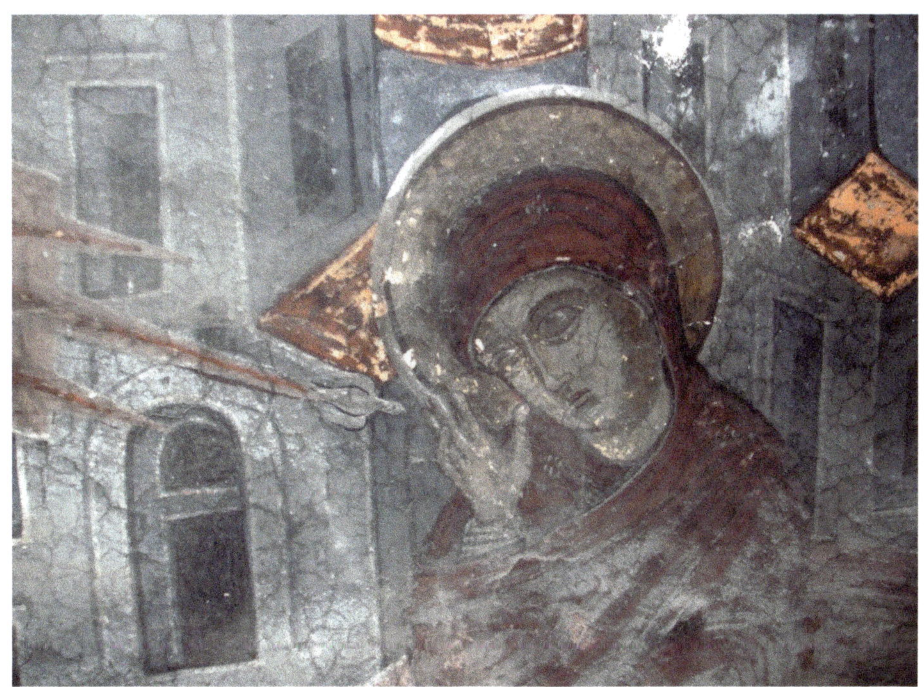

Fig. 4-3

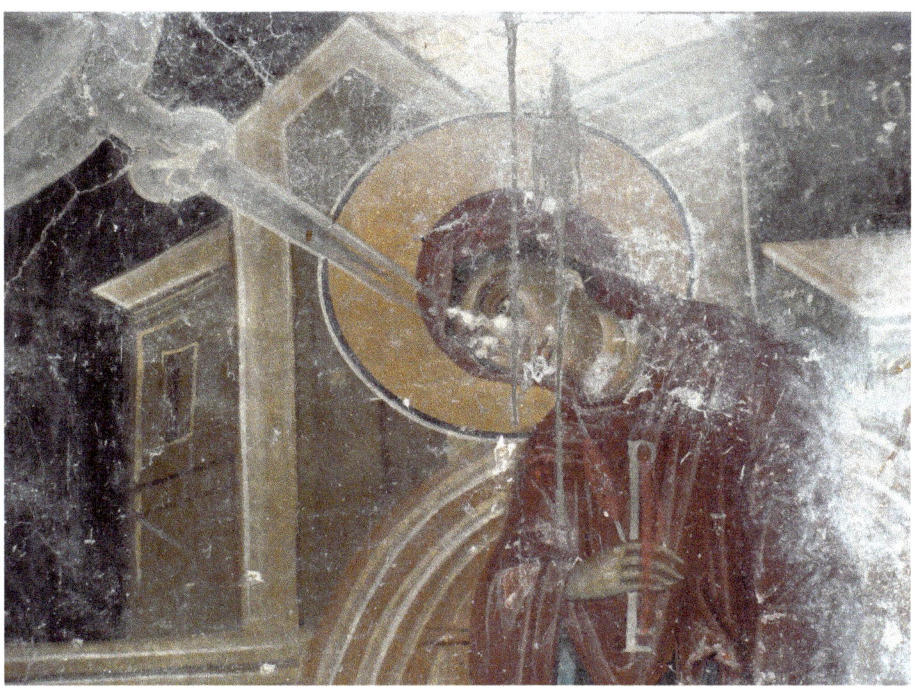

Fig. 4-6

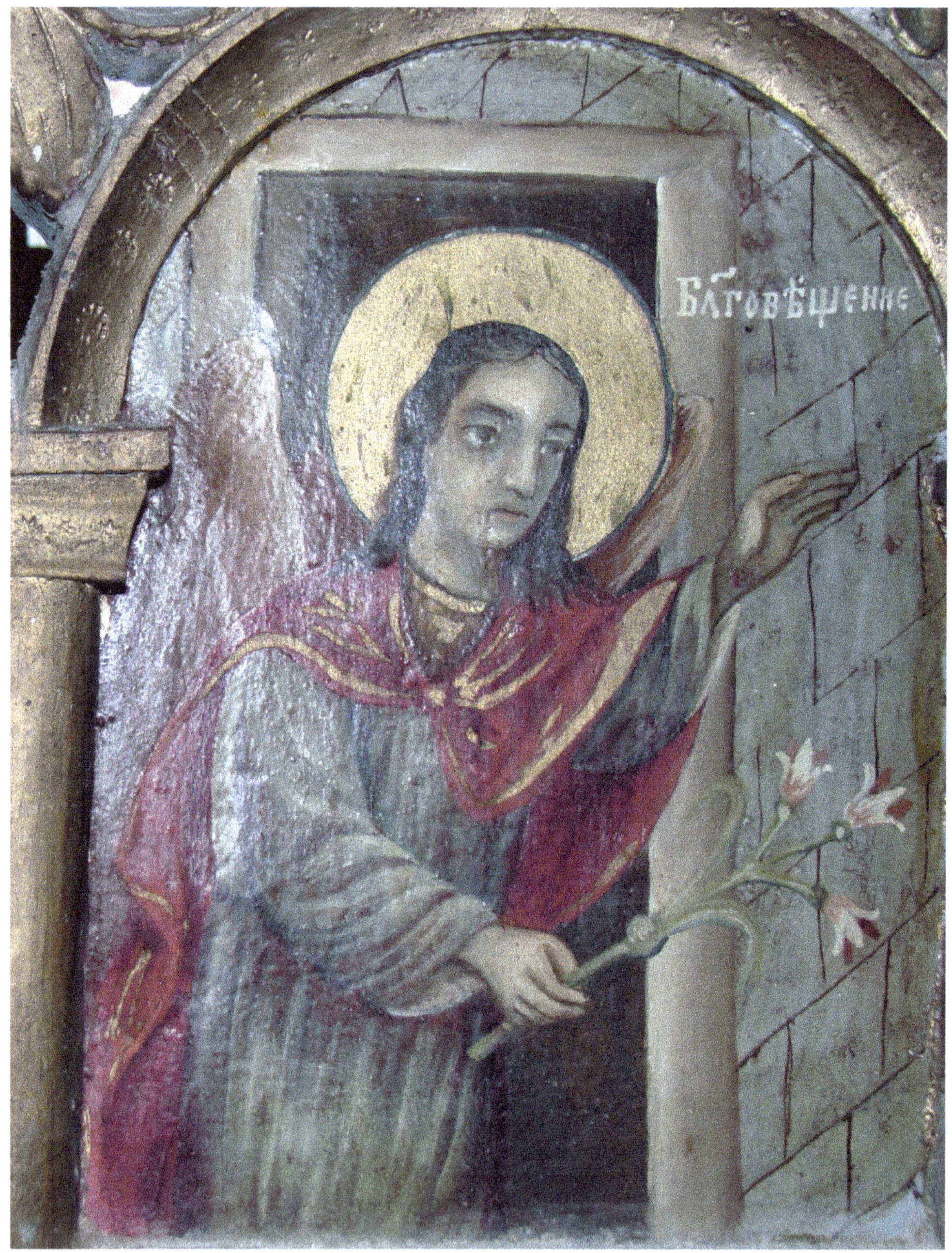

Fig. 4-4

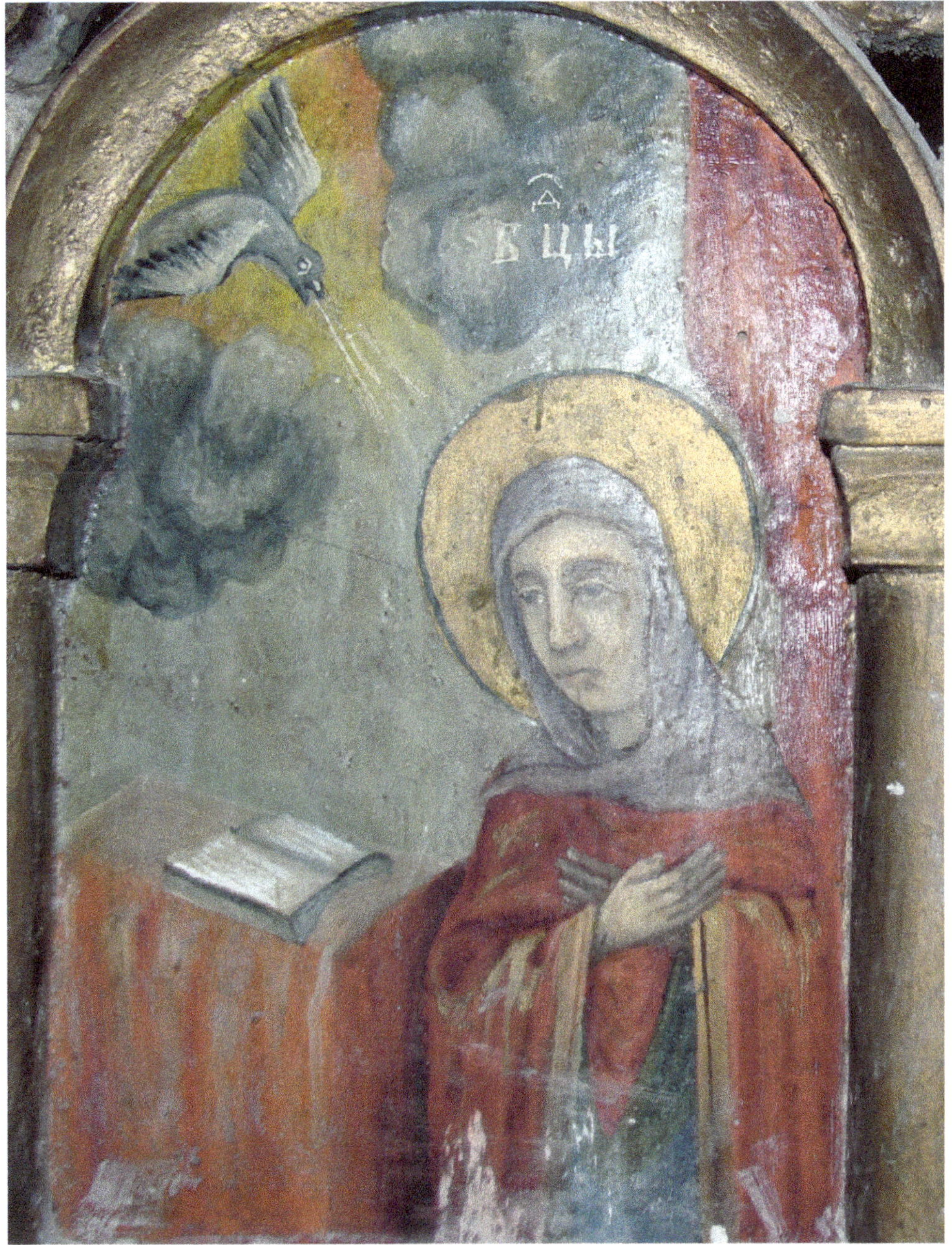

Fig. 4-5

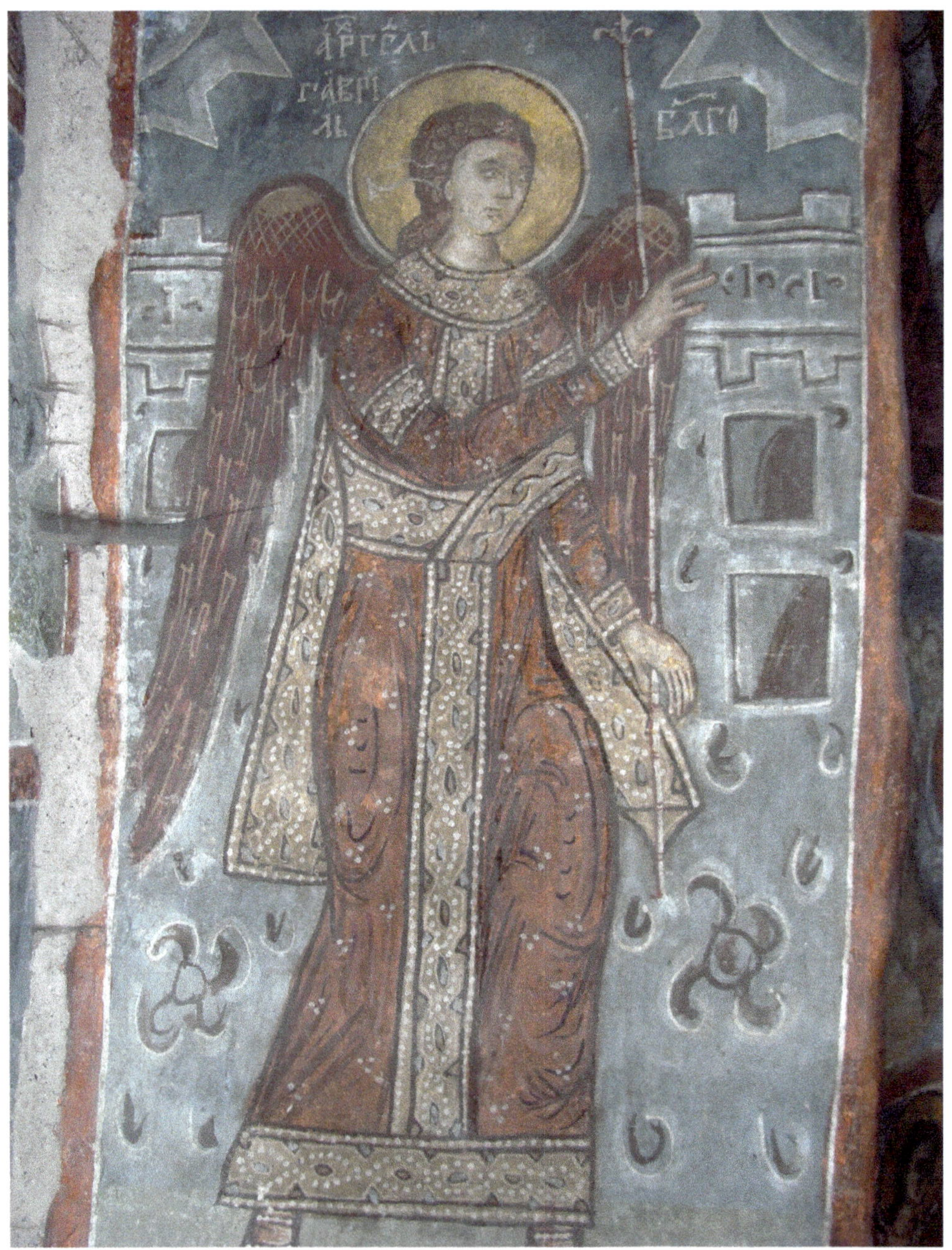

Fig. 4-7

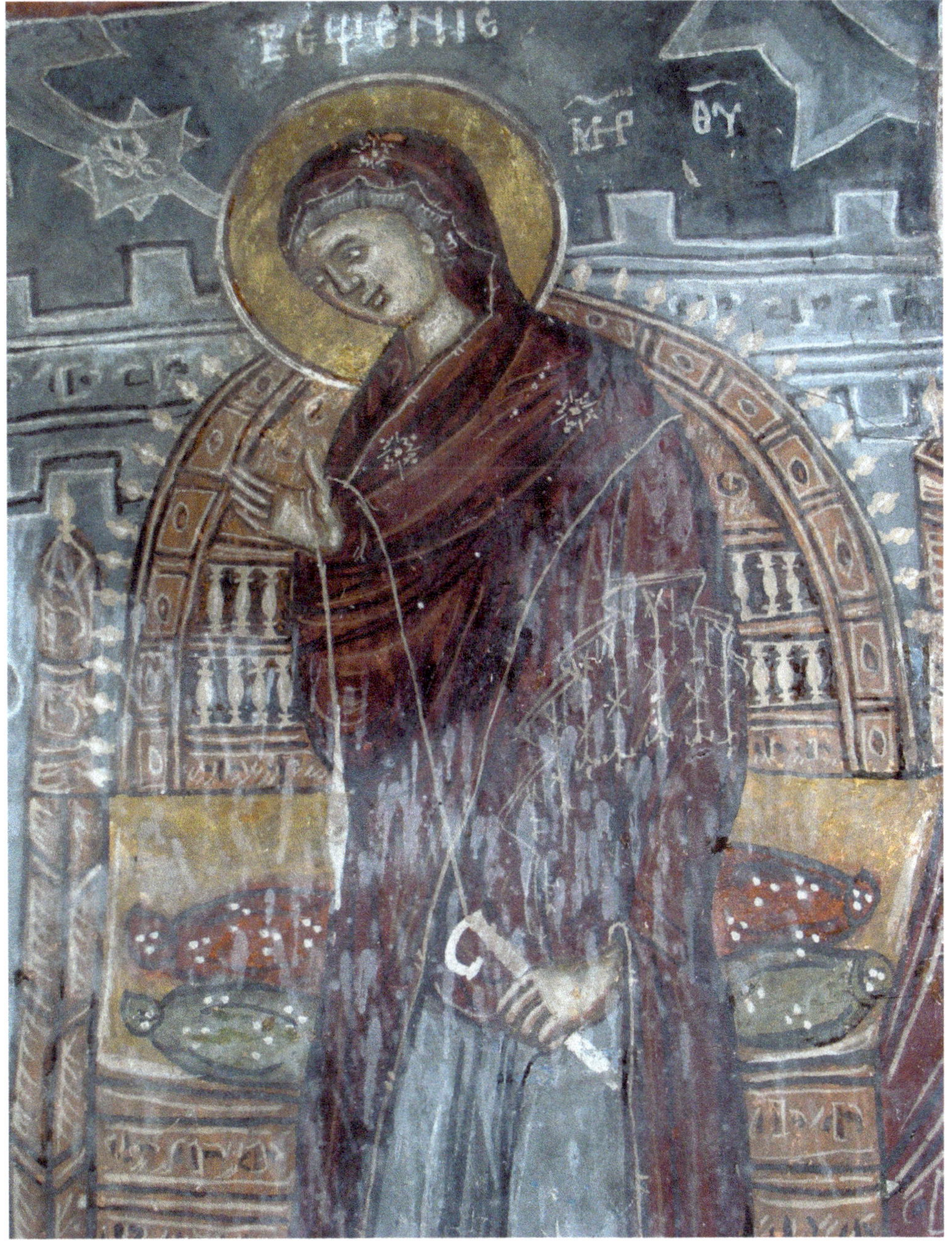

Fig. 4-8

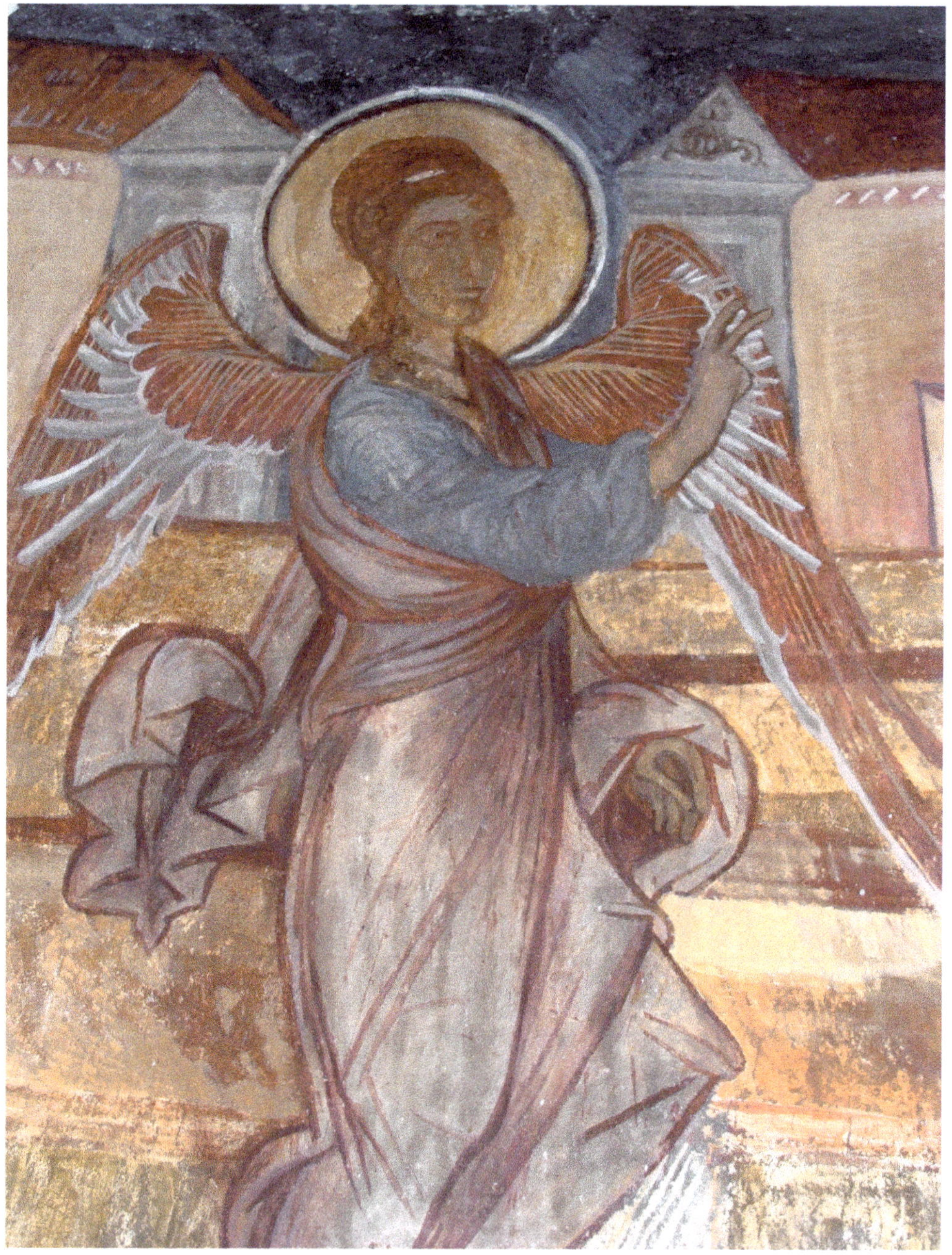

Fig. 4-9

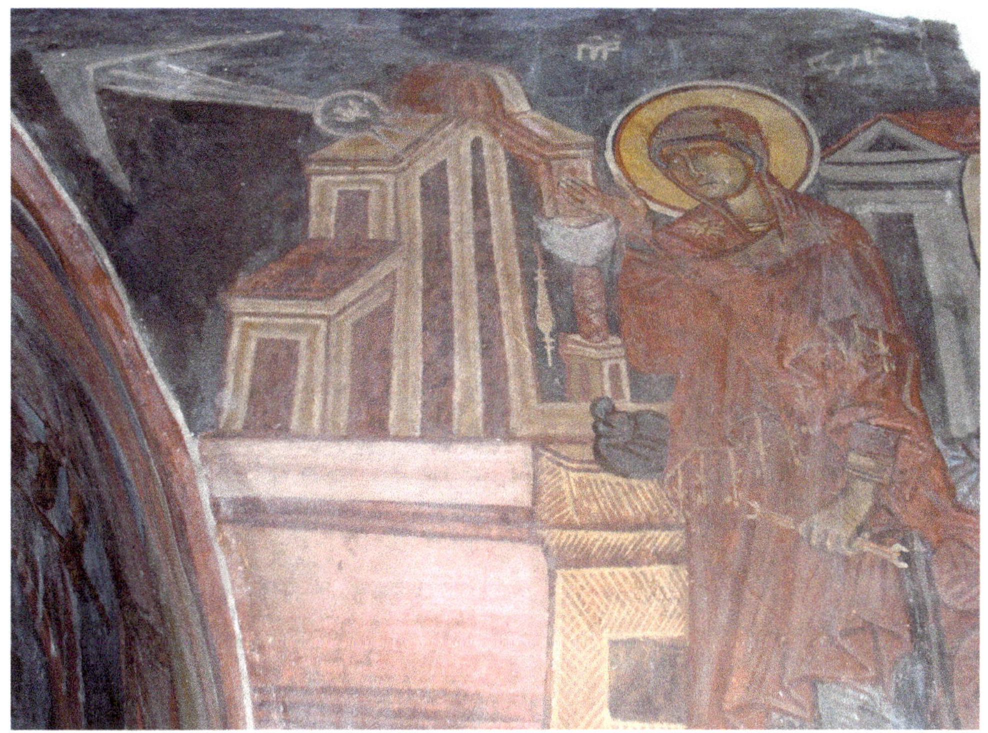

Fig. 4-10

The Miracles of Christ

The Womb of Salvation

In his book *The Sophiology of Death*, the Russian theologian Sergius Bulgakov writes, 'Every person dies with Christ, and Christ co-dies with each person in his disease, in his suffering. This is the cost of redemption.'[13] There are always two sides to this cost of redemption: Christ and us. In Bulgarian frescoes, both parties are depicted by artists in a very specific way. Nothing stands between Christ and the sick. Except for his right hand, which is directed towards the sufferer (Seslavtsi, fig. 5-1). With the two fingers of the God-man, whose message comes once again to confirm the biblical dismissal of all astrologers, fortune-tellers and assorted healers. Because, if you haven't reached that high degree of deification, which is Christ the God-man's message to us, you will be unable to cure physical and spiritual ailments. Not by chance does Christ say, when casting the demon out of the epileptic, 'This kind does not come out except by prayer and fasting,' after informing his disciples, 'If you have faith the size of a mustard seed, you will say to this mountain, "Move from here to there," and it will move' (Mt 17:20-21).

The requisite condition for healing even yourself, as St Sophrony of Essex writes, is that faith – not psychological, but ontological – which is able to generate inner energy, overcoming disease.[14] That high degree of approach to God, when the two fingers, one divine in origin, the other human, unite and like a scalpel remove unnecessary growth from souls and bodies. As in your left hand you should always hold a scroll with the Word. In one hand is the scalpel of blessing; in the other, the Word of God. This is the challenge of true healing. The combination of both. Word and deed, God and man. Because 'you will know them by their fruits' (Mt 7:20), adds the Savior, and still further, 'One does not live by bread alone, but by every word that comes from the mouth of God' (Mt 4:4).

In almost all frescoes, Christ heals from a distance, without touching the sick, except in the scene with the man born blind, when he touches his forehead with his finger, or with St Peter's mother-in-law, whose hand he grasps to lift her up from bed (St Stephen's, Nesebar, figs. 5-2,3). This touching of the forehead, the mind, seems to be telling us how important it is to change our way of thinking, to knead the flesh again, to recreate what has been created, so that we can see. Or how important it is not to let go of someone's hand, embracing it in your palm, as the Savior did to Adam and Eve in the fresco Descent into Hell, so you don't give Death the one it wanted. To intercede. Christ is our recreator, our eternal intercessor.

---

13 Sergius Bulgakov, *The Sophiology of Death: Essays on Eschatology: Personal, Political, Universal*, tr. Roberto J. De La Noval (Eugene, OR: Cascade Books, 2021), p. 152.

14 St Sophrony of Essex, Духовни беседи, p. 22-3.

Christ blesses us, Christ touches our minds, Christ pulls us out of the womb to life, co-dying with our pains, with the decisive movement of his body, with the will of his step, but also with the concentrated, albeit weary, look on his face, which in the healing of the deaf mute is averted in pain, while his body is folded in on itself, like a seed or a tear (Alino, fig. 5-4). The Savior's face as he heals us is filled with bitterness and suffering, even more than when he suffers on the cross. Christ's martyrdom does not begin and end with his crucifixion, it begins with the Temptation of Christ, when Satan like some ancient Greek statue-idol tempts him, and Christ blesses him in return (St Stephen's, Nesebar, fig. 5-5), as he blesses the fig tree on the way to Jerusalem (Seslavtsi – see the essay 'Resurrection'), because God – full love – cannot contain even an ounce of evil, so his curse is also a blessing. Christ's martyrdom consists in empathizing with martyrs, like the Good Samaritan, who, living in Christ, helps the victim of robbers, binds up his wounds and takes him to the inn, paying with his own money (St Stephen's, Nesebar, fig. 5-6). His image is doubled with that of Christ, because he doesn't act of his own will, but Christ acts in him, or he of his own will allows Christ in. 'Listen! I am standing at the door, knocking; if you hear my voice and open the door, I will come in to you and eat with you, and you with me' (Rev 3:20). In fact, the sequence of events in this fresco is reminiscent of the Wheel of Life in Preobrazhenie Monastery (fig. 5-7) or the Church of the Nativity in Arbanasi. From demonic attack to shelter, from birth to rebirth in Christ, life is not just a circle, it is a circle with martyrdom, not in our own sufferings, but in the sufferings of others. Christ reveals this to us with his earthly life – he is born in the womb of a cave, he descends into the womb of the earth after his death on the cross and heals the sick, who are lowered through a roof that is like a womb, as in the healing of the paralytic at Capernaum (Seslavtsi, fig. 5-8). There are angels there as well, like the angel at Bethesda, who stirs up the water of the pool, side by side with the thirty-eight-year-old paralytic, whom the Savior commands to pick up his bed and walk. His bed, which forms a cross with the columns of the porch (Seslavtsi, fig. 5-9). This is our own particular participation in redemption – faith. Because in all the frescoes, in the gesture, movement or posture of the one who is healed, is found a cross, which the artist uses to reveal our role in salvation – see the cross in the staggering posture of the lame man, of the man with the withered hand, in the posture of the father and his epileptic son (St Stephen's, Nesebar, figs. 5-10,11,12), or in the healing of the sick man who leans on his elbow (Podgumer).

So Christ's martyrdom and our faith – the faith of all of us who have been gathered together like empty jars at the Wedding at Cana, waiting to be filled again, with new content – are what casts out demons – prehistoric cave paintings (Demons

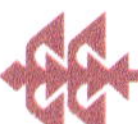

being expelled from Mary Magdalene, Seslavtsi, fig. 5-13) – no more, no less. Little black men that come out of our mouths, out of the epileptic's mouth, because 'it is not what goes into the mouth that defiles a person, but it is what comes out of the mouth that defiles' (Mt 15:11).

Christ leaves us his command as a healer: 'Take no gold, or silver, or copper in your belts, no bag for your journey, or two tunics, or sandals, or a staff; for laborers deserve their food [...] If anyone will not welcome you or listen to your words, shake off the dust from your feet as you leave that house or town' (Mt 10:9-10, 14), since 'truly I tell you, whatever you bind on earth will be bound in heaven, and whatever you loose on earth will be loosed in heaven' (Mt 18:18).

Salvation and healing begin here, not in heaven. Damnation as well. And faith – that hole like a cave in Christ's body, where Doubting Thomas is allowed to put his finger to make sure of the Savior's resurrection (Seslavtsi, fig. 5-14). With all his pain, not on the cross, but of his martyrdom, Christ exclaims, 'An evil and adulterous generation asks for a sign, but no sign will be given to it except the sign of the prophet Jonah' (Mt 12:39).

So we are born from the womb, we die in the womb, we are healed through the womb and we even believe because of it. What then is the womb, expressed in five frescoes of Christ's miracles like his five wounds (the fifth being the Parable of the Sower, Alino, fig. 5-15)? What is the cycle of life, expressed in three frescoes of Christ's martyrdom: the Wedding at Cana, the Temptation of Christ and the Good Samaritan? What is the message of the black cave paintings? The womb is a necessary precondition for salvation, where you must find a place, dig a pit, in order to bury God's seed. It has sheltered the root that turns life itself from need to help for the needy, from empty jars to jars with new content. From *fast* to *feast*, where there is no longer any room for little black men.

There is a tribe, the Meakambut, among the last remaining nomadic people today, who live deep in the jungles of Papua New Guinea and believe that life originated in a cave, where the spirit of the earth made a gap so the cave's inhabitants could emerge into the light. The door opened for a little and then closed for ever. Their handprints have been left on the walls in red and black.

The same palms that are in the frescoes of Adam and Eve admitting their guilt (Iliyantsi – see the essay 'The Ascension of Jesus') and of Apostle Peter pointing up and down (Samaritan Woman, Seslavtsi, fig. 5-16), summarizing the gesture of all those who have been healed by grace, who testify: come out of the darkness and live in the light.

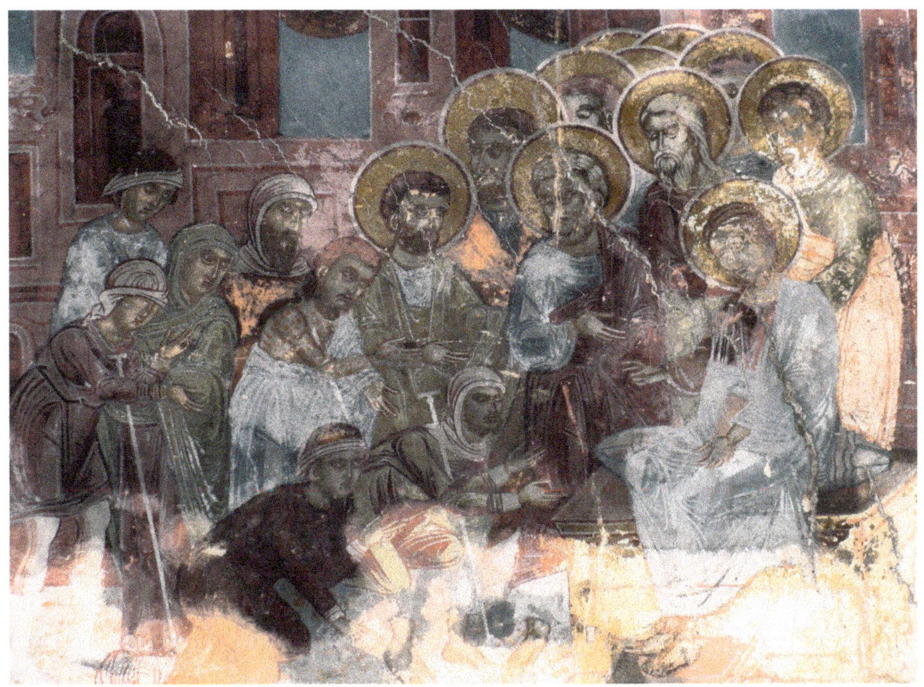

Fig. 5-1

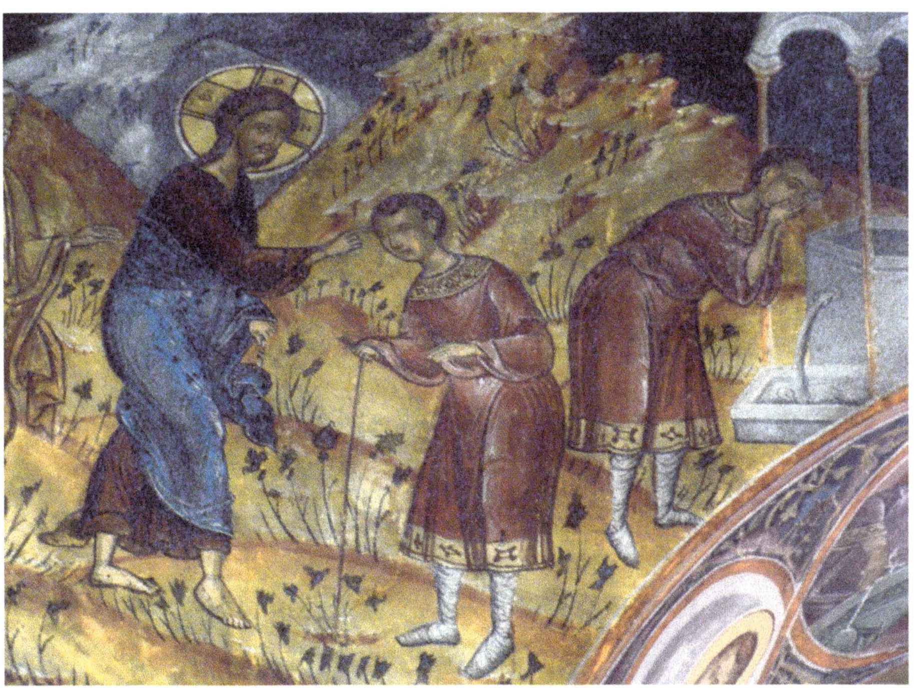

Fig. 5-2

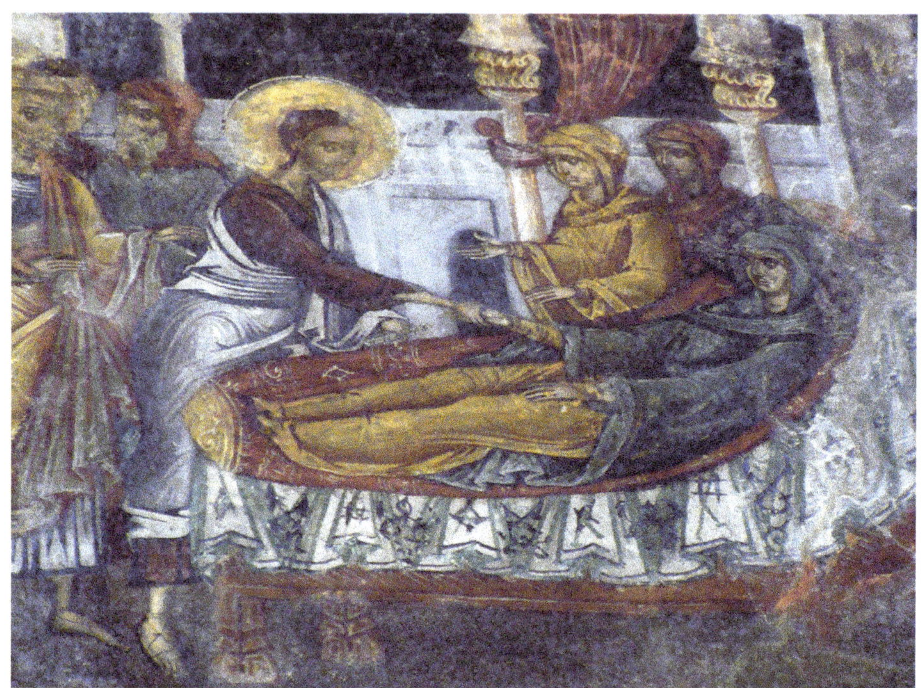

Fig. 5-3

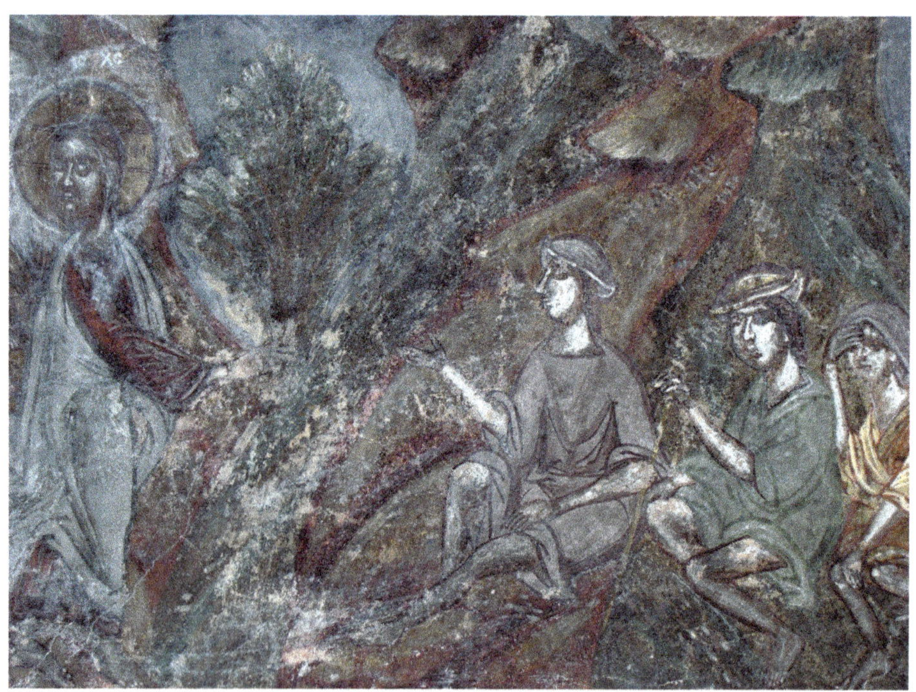

Fig. 5-4

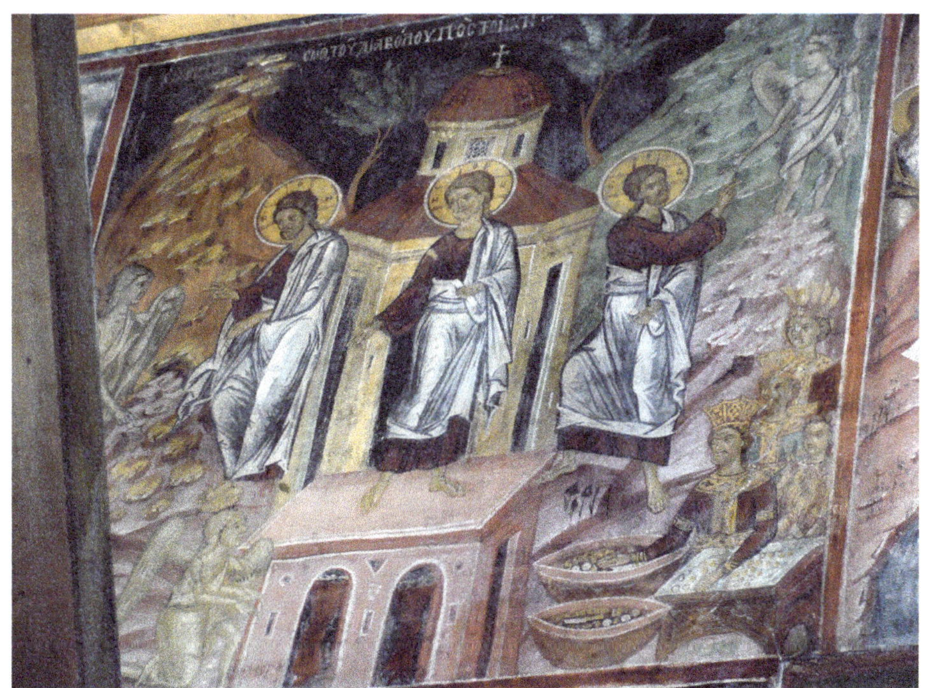

Fig. 5-5

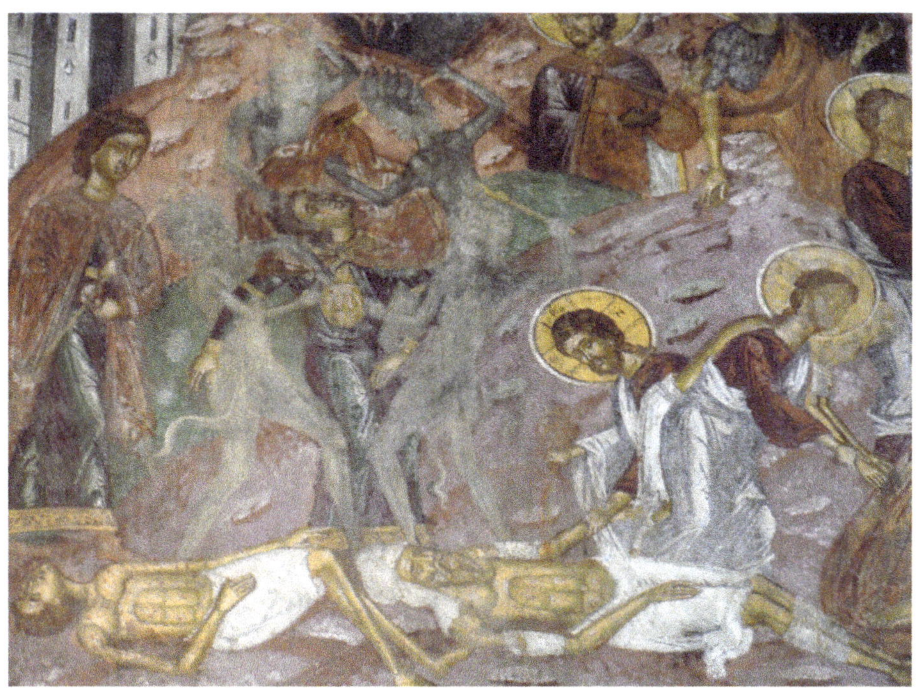

Fig. 5-6

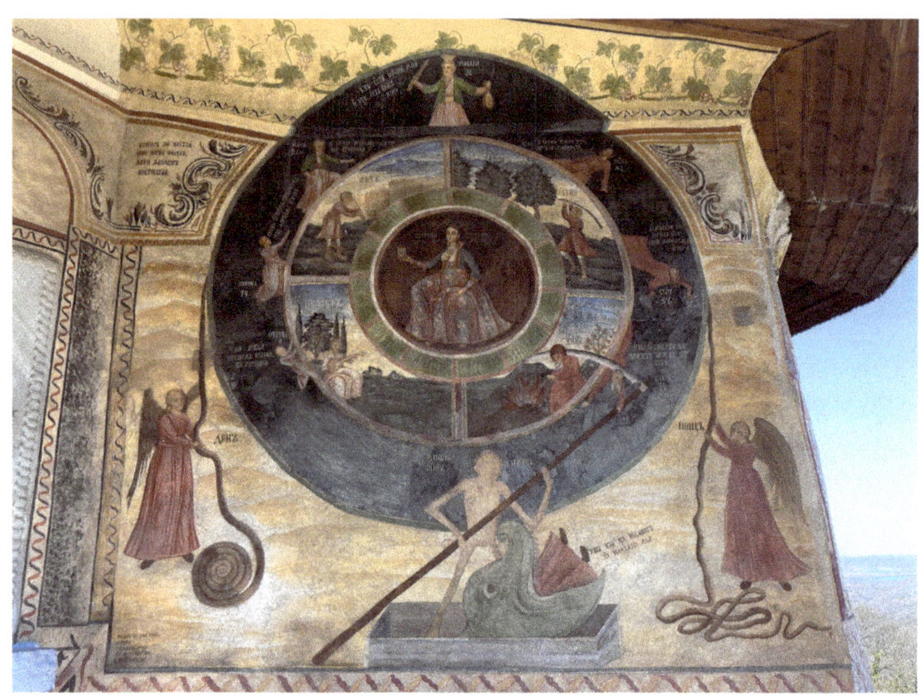

Fig. 5-7

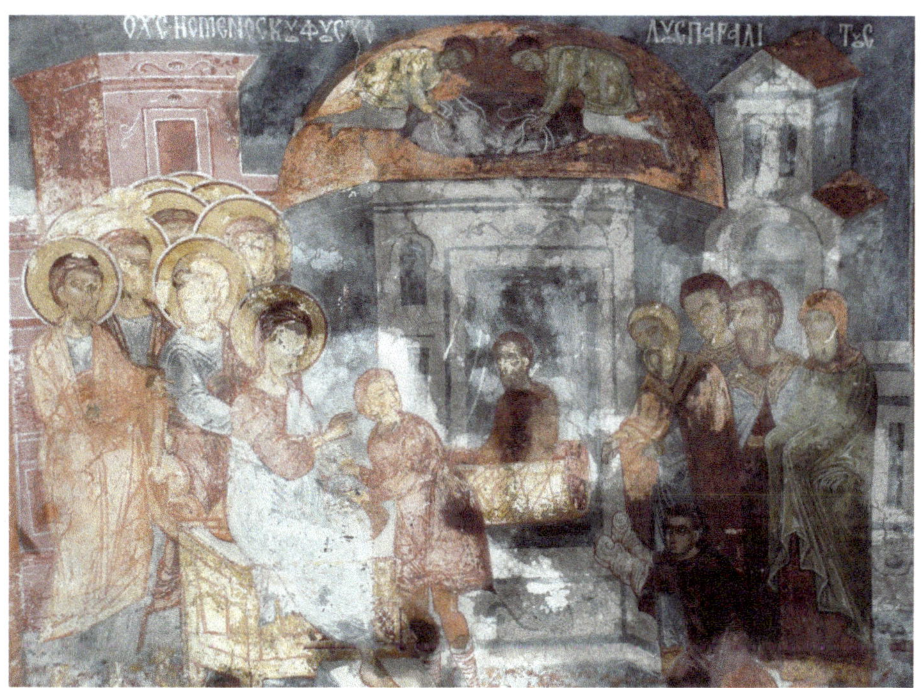

Fig. 5-8

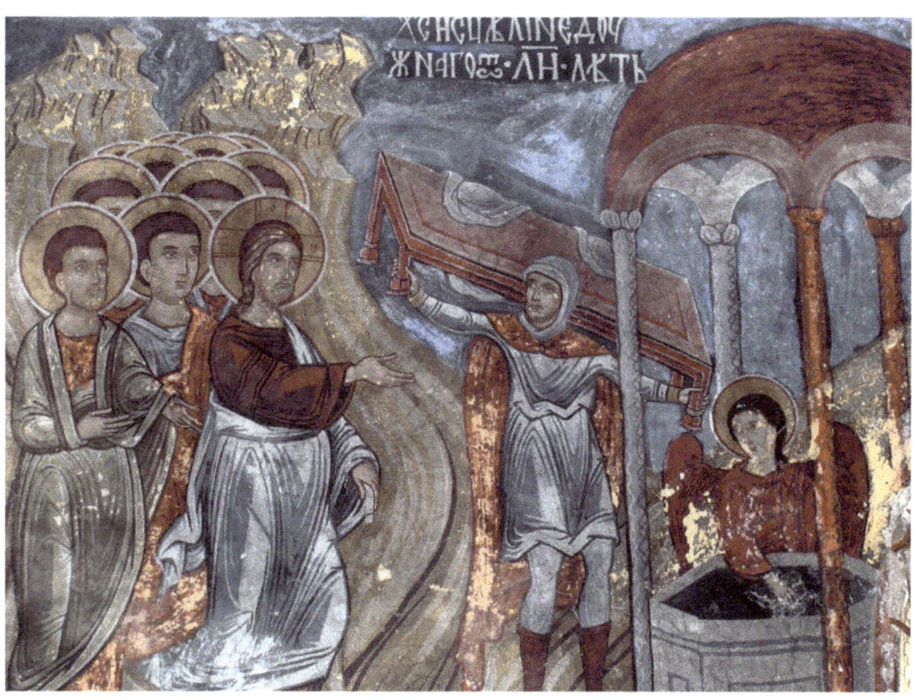

Fig. 5-9

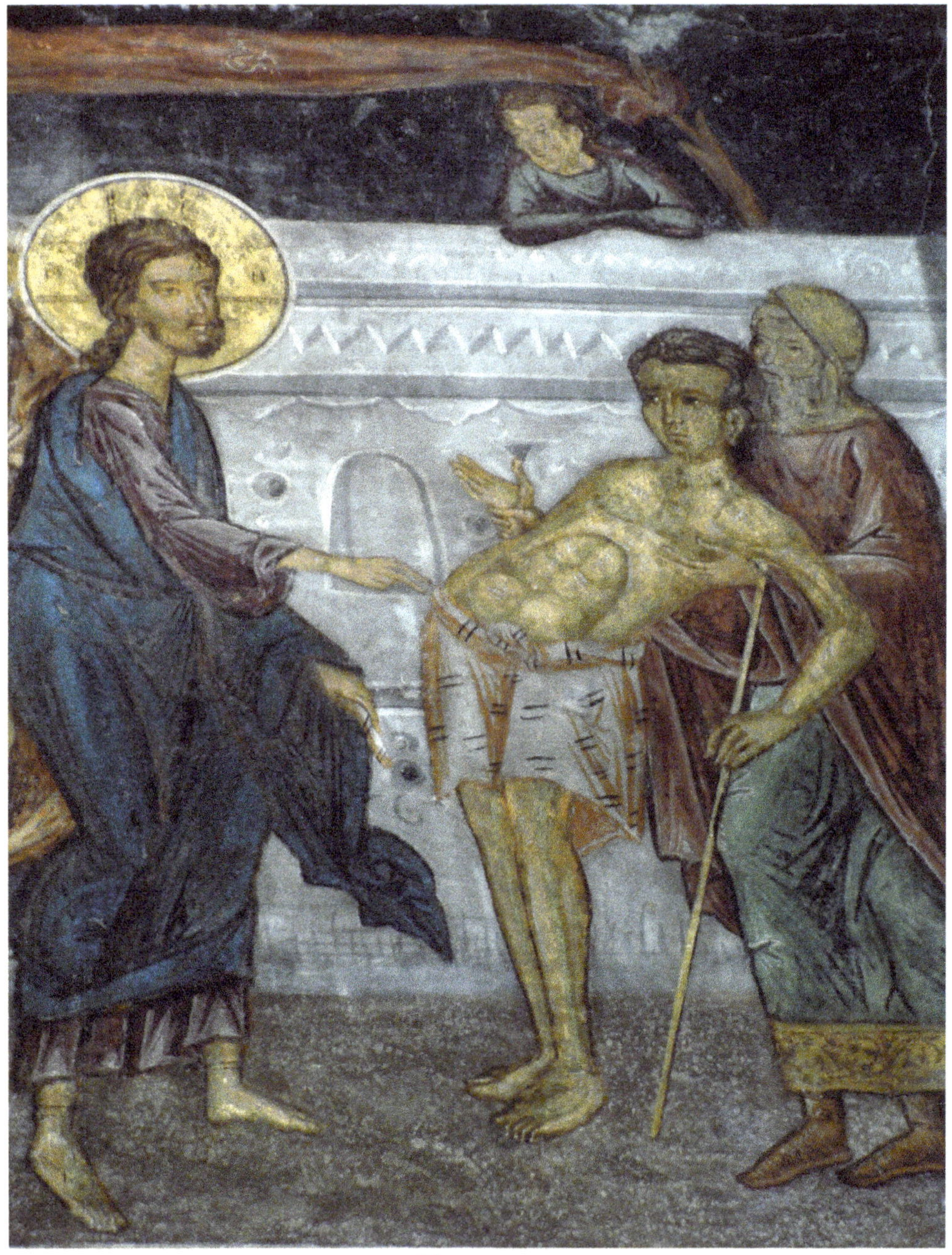

Fig. 5-10

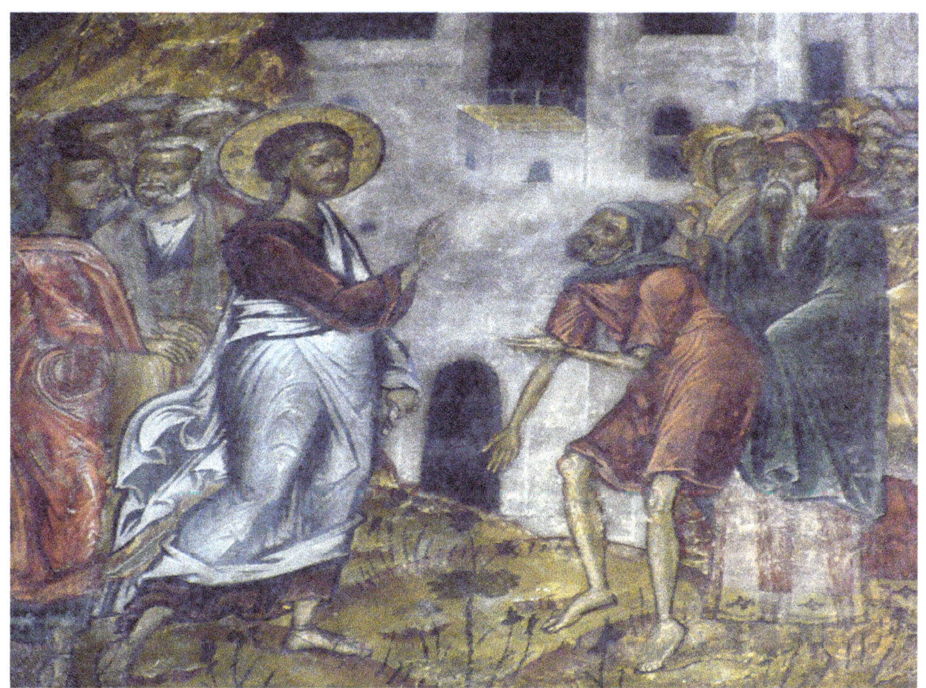

Fig. 5-11

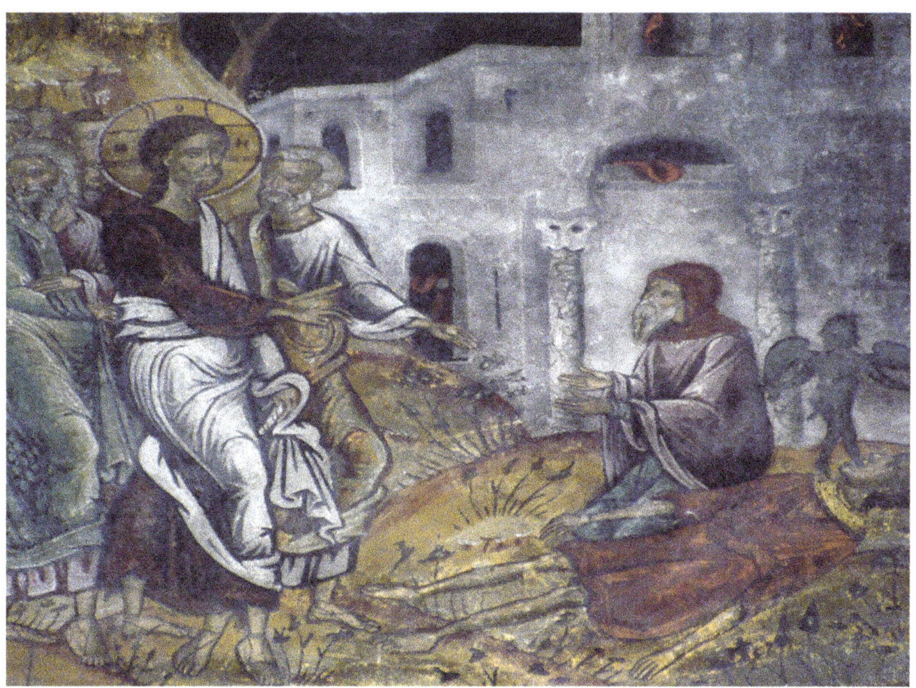

Fig. 5-12

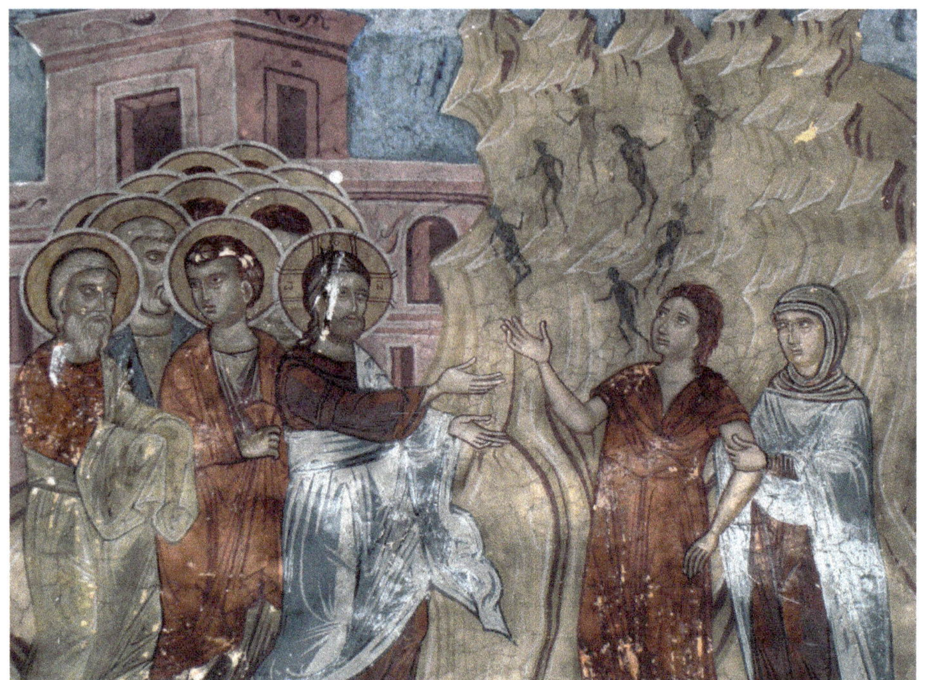

Fig. 5-13

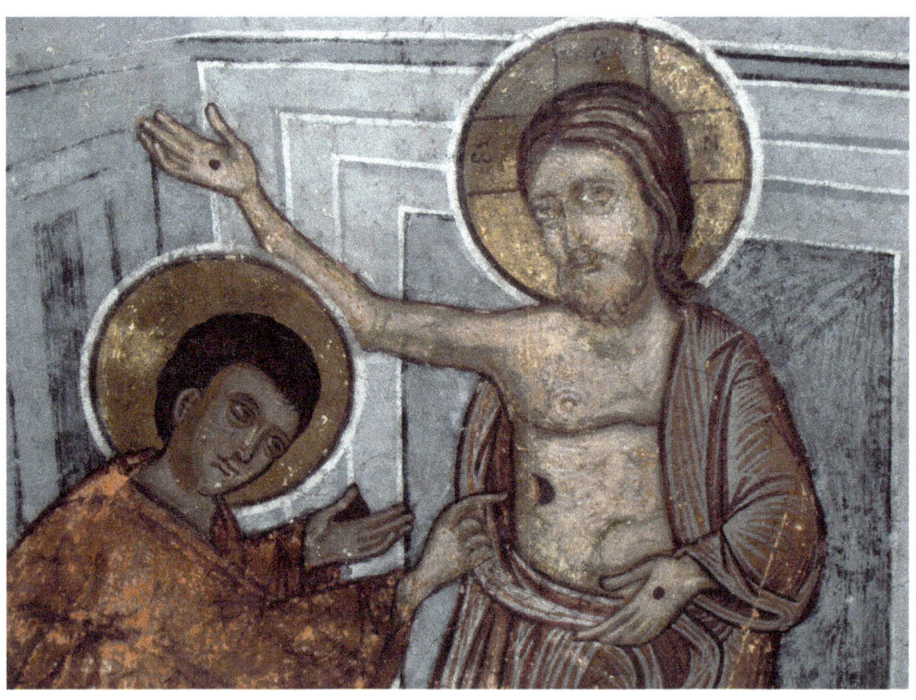

Fig. 5-14

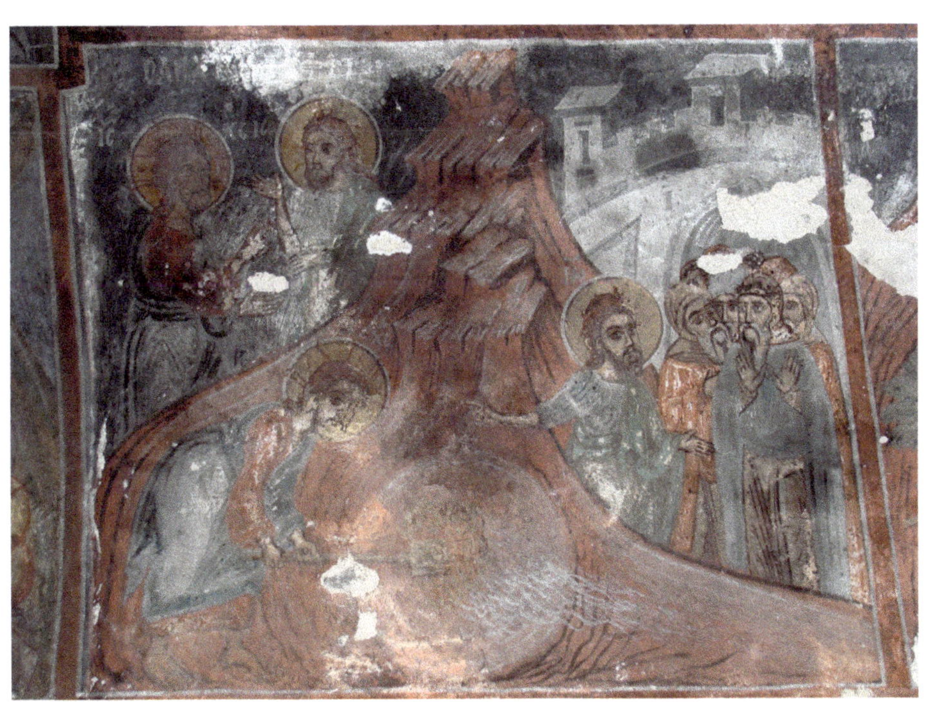

Fig. 5-15

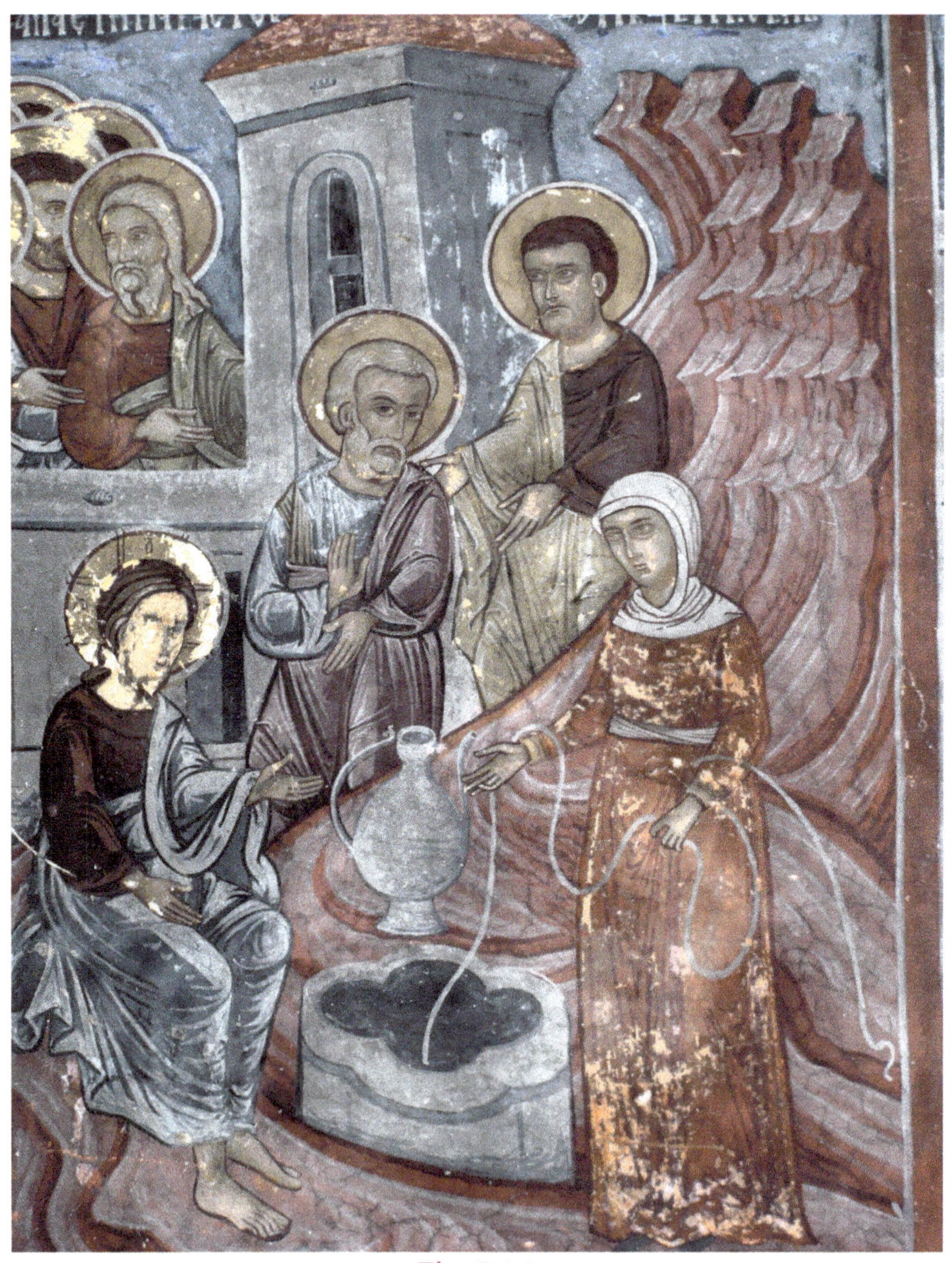

Fig. 5-16

The Last Day

The Cup of Hope[15]

15 This essay deals primarily with the events of Holy Week from the raising of Lazarus on Lazarus Saturday, through the entry into Jerusalem on Palm Sunday and the cursing of the fig tree on Holy Monday, to the Last Supper, the washing of the disciples' feet, Jesus' prayer in the Garden of Gethsemane and the betrayal and arrest of Christ on Maundy Thursday, and his being brought before Pilate on Good Friday in the morning.

In Christ, death dies: 'trampling down death by death.' From that moment on, no one dies alone; Christ dies with him in order to raise him up with him.

Paul Evdokimov, *The Art of the Icon: A Theology of Beauty*[16]

On the last day of his earthly life, Christ shows us how to accept the approach of death with dignity, turning a curse into a blessing, like his of the fig tree, and ending the day with prayer, like his in the Garden of Gethsemane, albeit the fear is diminished. Because 'no one puts new wine into old wineskins' (Lk 5:37). Because even if there is nothing in the wineskins, we have to believe he will fill them, as at the Wedding at Cana in Galilee – the first of his miracles, not by chance, and the fresco which resembles the Last Supper most closely. Above all else, Christ is this 'cup-bearer,' this high priest, who gives us the cup of life – full. The same cup he asked to be taken away from him. And who gives us kneaded bread. Not the old bread that is soaked in water to make it edible, nor the wine that is fermented in vessels, but the new pouring, the new kneading, are in the sacrament of the Resurrection.

The fresco of the Last Supper in all its variants contains the most complete miracle of the eighth day. Even scenes like the Descent into Hell or the Myrrh-Bearing Women do not depict the Savior's resurrection directly, they remain true to the mystery of mysteries. Only the Last Supper reveals this most sacred, most intimate act, although it does so in the language of symbols. The tablecloth that is shiny white like a mother's milk (Eleshnitsa, fig. 6-1), rolled at the edge like a fish coated in flour (Iliyantsi, fig. 6-2), stretched and starched, with all the details of life – drinking, eating, sentiment – is there. But the details do not dominate the cloth (they do not dominate the earth), because the centre is that cup, precisely. For which, like the Savior, we are chosen, even if we prefer to escape, the blood once spilt by Cain poured back into our bodies. The blood which no longer cries out, which doesn't tempt or entice or accuse, but which we receive voluntarily. The blood that resembles the nebula in the egg of the universe so closely (Boboshevo).

So should we give importance to the devotional bowing of John towards the teacher (Kremikovtsi), to the oratorial postures of the disciples (Eleshnitsa), to the ecstatic stretching across the table (Strupets, fig. 6-3), to the show of hands (Alino, fig. 6-4), like the show of feet ready for washing (Washing the Feet, Alino, fig. 6-5),

16 Paul Evdokimov, *The Art of the Icon*, location 4958.

using the same gesture as that of Adam and Eve when they were caught in sin (Iliyantsi – see the essay 'The Ascension of Jesus')? Well, yes and no.

Nothing is more important than the cup the Savior has accepted and given to us. Needless to say, before that, he resurrected Lazarus, ready to grab his 'reins' before the curious gaze of the crowd (Raising Lazarus, Strupets, fig. 6-6), unwinding his turban (Eleshnitsa, fig. 6-7), attracting his bent body like a snake with a gesture of blessing, the way snake charmers draw serpents out of baskets with their music (Kremikovtsi). Lazarus in his bandages, whose prototype is the infant Jesus.

By his resemblance to Lazarus, Christ prematurely defeats the serpent. As he cursed the tree on which Judas later hanged himself or answered Pilate by washing the disciples' feet. The centre of this process of foreseeing and anticipating events in human terms, of accepting them, which the Savior calls 'fulfillment of the law,' is in fact the manifestation of hope, the seed of which is love. Fulfillment of the law is the opposite of self-reliance. Self-reliance, which is regarded by Church Fathers as a sin.

So truth is to enter Jerusalem backwards, but going first (Entry into Jerusalem, Strupets, fig. 6-8), along the way to curse the empty fig tree in blessing (Cursing the Fig Tree, Seslavtsi – see the essay 'Resurrection'), to wash your disciples' feet, being their *master,* a word that in Bulgarian is a combination of 'God' and 'gift,' *Gospod* and *dar* (Washing the Feet, Seslavtsi, fig. 6-9), to drink the cup of the universe, not just of the world, to pray in the garden when someone nods off (Garden of Gethsemane, Boboshevo) or yawns (St Stephen's, Nesebar, fig. 6-10), to pray while 'dancing' (Alino – see the essay 'The Ascension of Jesus'), to pray while watching over your friends, the way our Father watches over us, and then to let yourself be betrayed, the feathers of soldiers' helmets sticking up above your head instead of angels' wings (Betrayal of Christ, Alino). Betrayed not just with a kiss, but with the same embrace with which the Virgin Mary holds the Infant on her lap, even with a possible wing on the back of his betrayer, had he repented – two opposites shown by the inverted colors of their clothing (Strupets, fig. 6-11). To let yourself be chained, your hands and neck tied like the halo around your head – three nimbuses of the Trinity (Road to Calvary, Boboshevo, fig. 6-12), humiliated and tamed by the prince of this world, reduced to showing mercy, to full kenosis. And, at the end, waiting for your cross to be driven into the ground, to sit on a stone, the way Alonso Cano saw it in his painting *The Christ of Humility* – a cornerstone.

Here is Love, riding a donkey the way a child rides a wooden horse, wrapped in his clothes as in a nappy (Entry into Jerusalem, Bilintsi, fig. 6-13), clean and blissful, stepping into the light with those big feet (Dolni Pasarel, fig. 6-14), with which he might have escaped from death city or sidestepped betrayal, but never did. Before that, he washed the disciples' feet, a scene that forms the antithesis of Pilate's washing of the hands on the next day. Christ has already answered the question, 'What is truth?' before Pilate had a chance to ask it. Let anyone with ears listen! Truth is service, not self-justification. Christ speaks the truth by example.

Fulfilling the law, humiliating fear. Because of masochism or stupid naivety, a non-believer or skeptic would declare. But no, because of what Alexander Schmemann writes in his *Journals*: 'In that Child, there is no need for strength, glory, "rights," self-affirmation, authority, power, and everything else which is requisite only where there is no truth and is therefore not needed by God.'[17]

17 Alexander Schmemann, *The Journals of Father Alexander Schmemann 1973-1983*, tr. Juliana Schmemann (Crestwood, NY: St Vladimir's Seminary Press, 2000), p. 56. The English edition of Schmemann's journals is more succinct than the Bulgarian and doesn't include the second part of the quote: 'and everything else which is requisite only where there is no truth and is therefore not needed by God.'

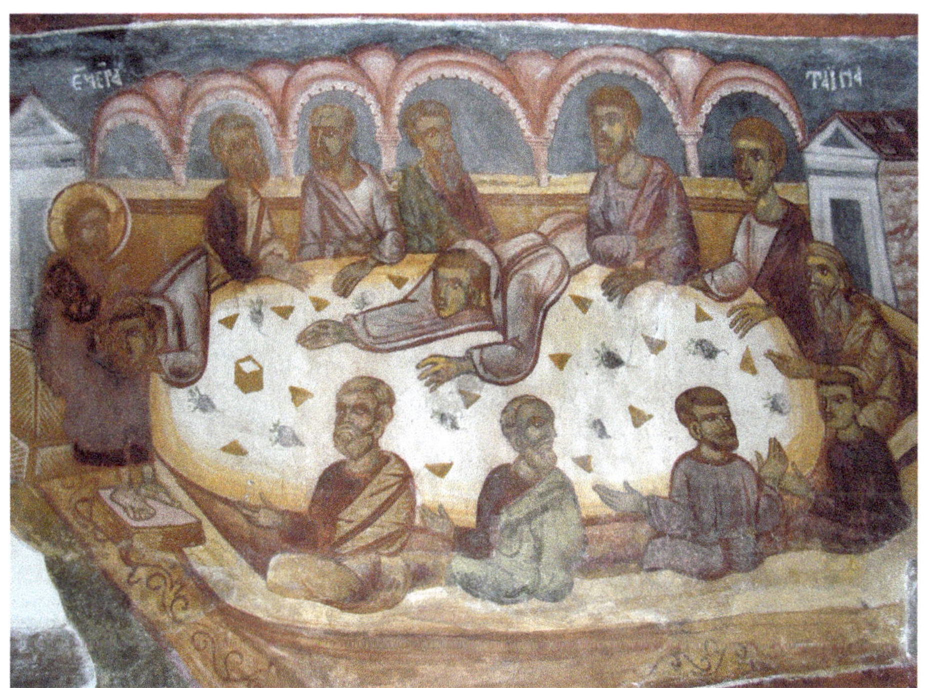

Fig. 6-1

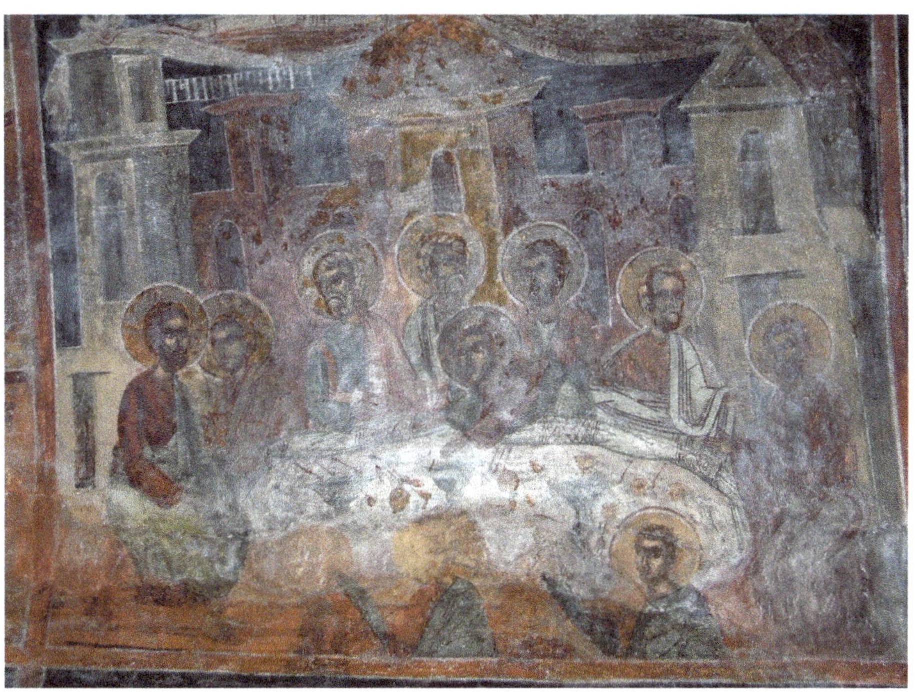

Fig. 6-2

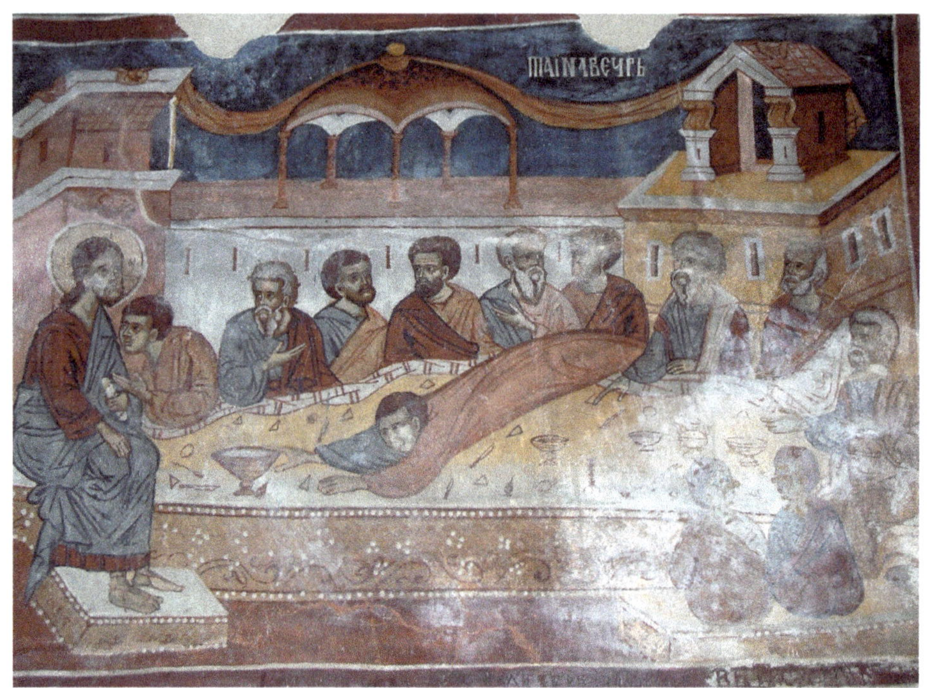

Fig. 6-3

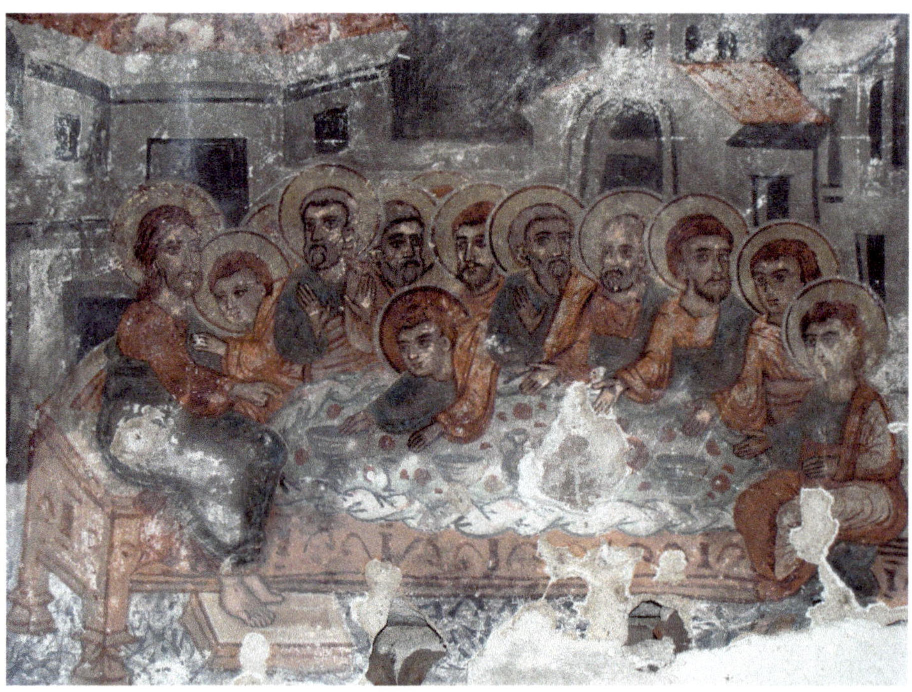

Fig. 6-4

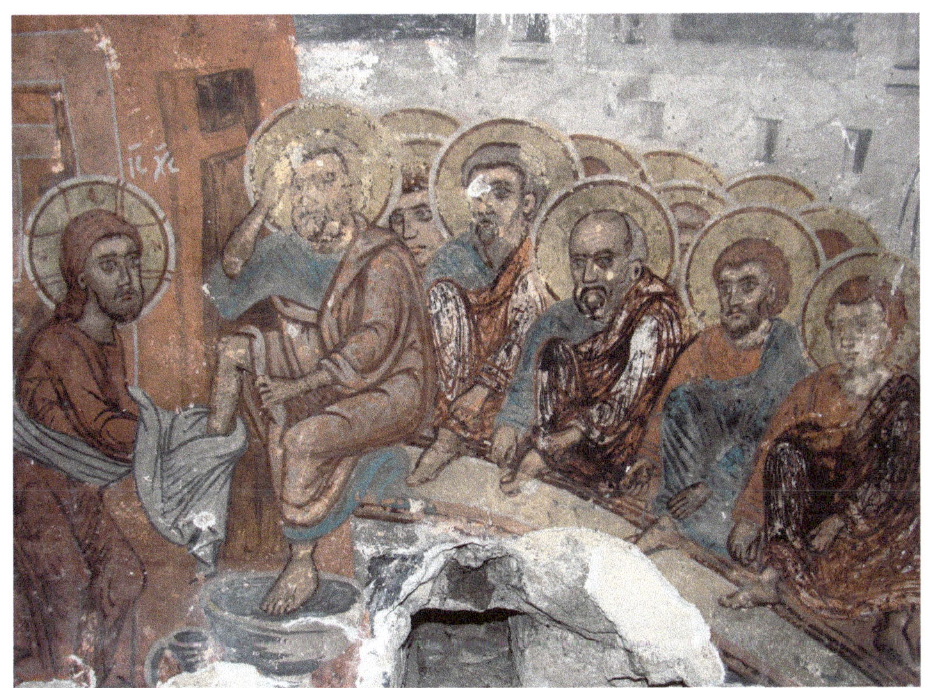

Fig. 6-5

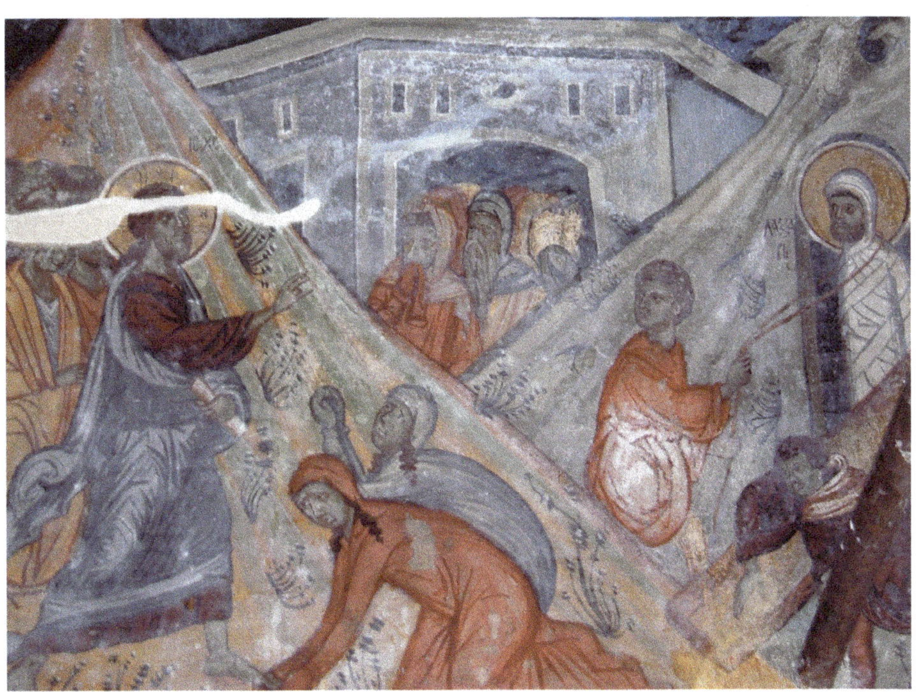

Fig. 6-6

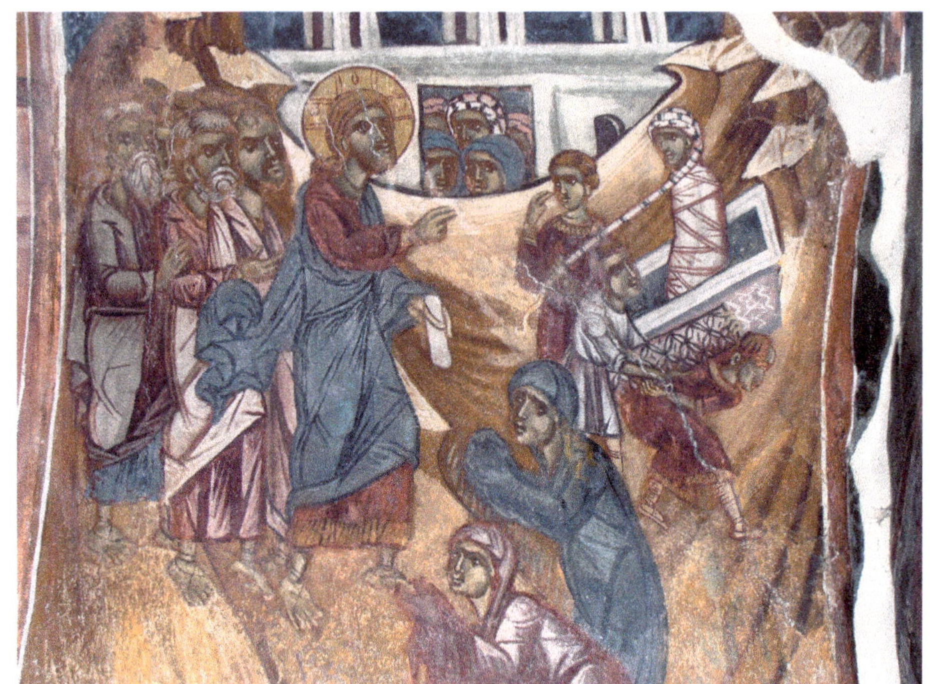

Fig. 6-7

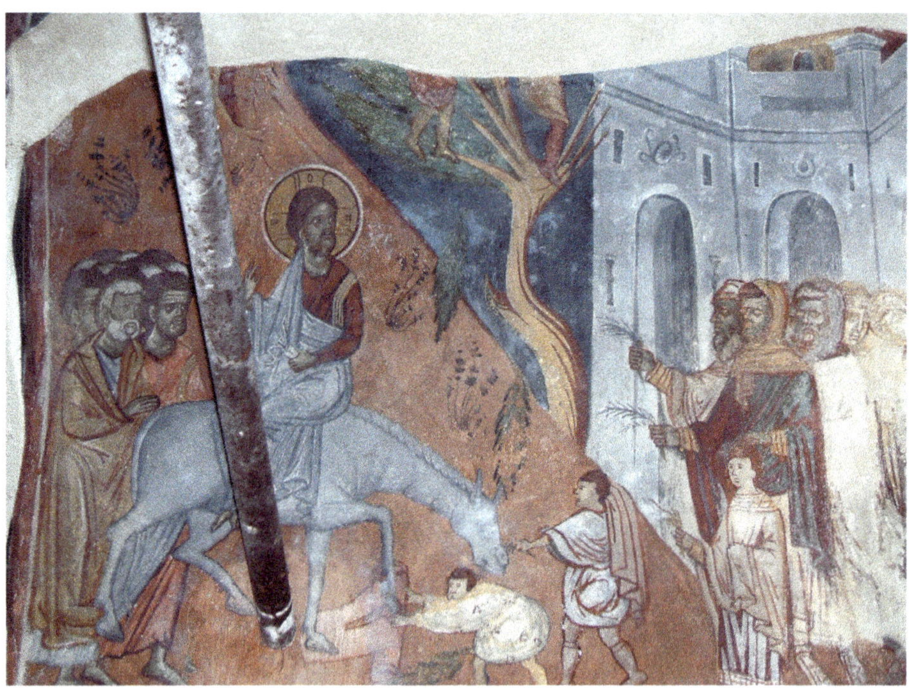

Fig. 6-8

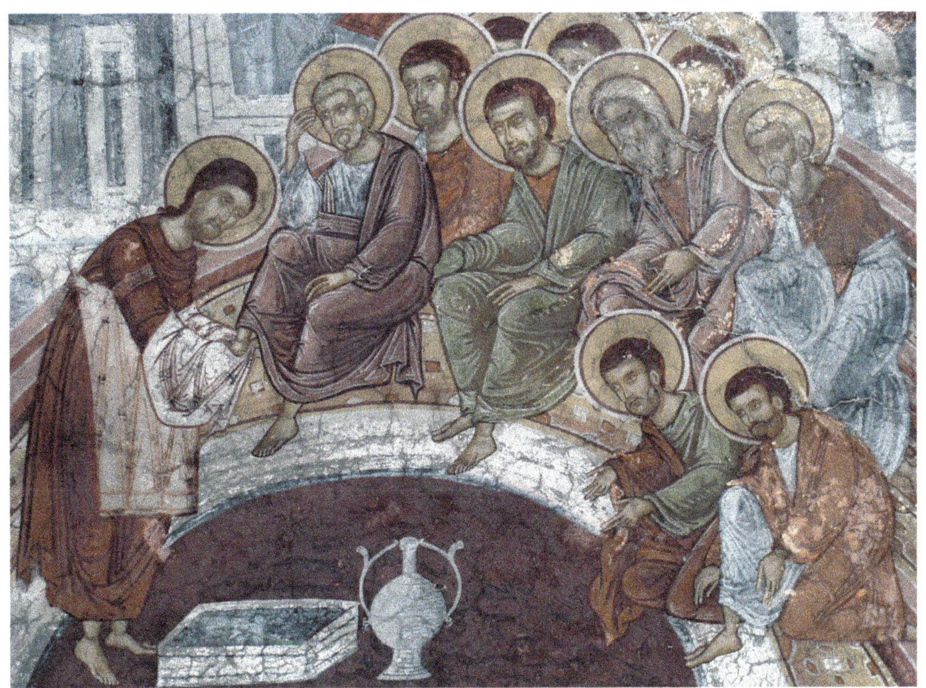

Fig. 6-9

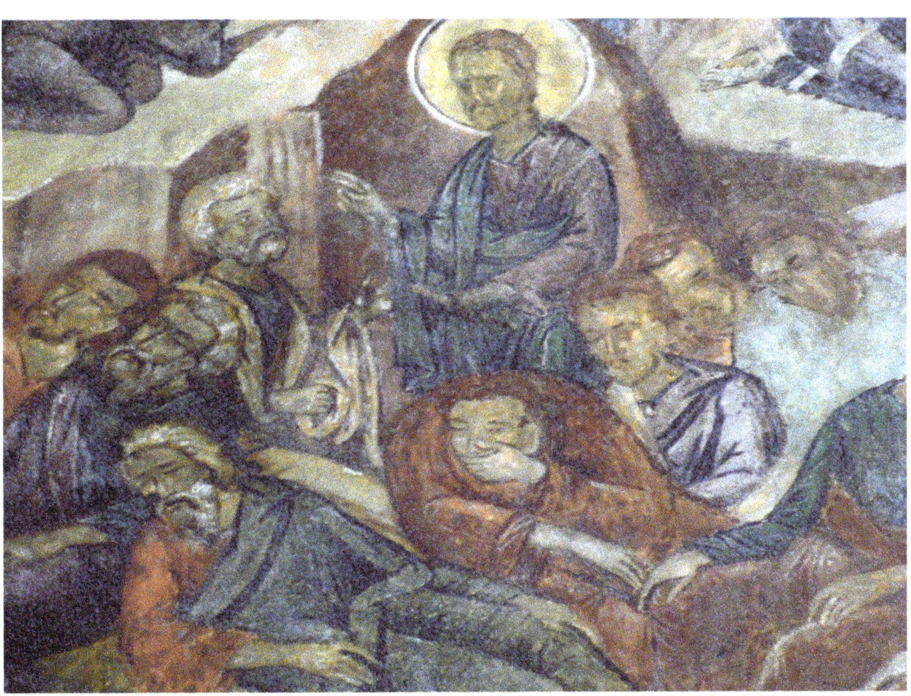

Fig. 6-10

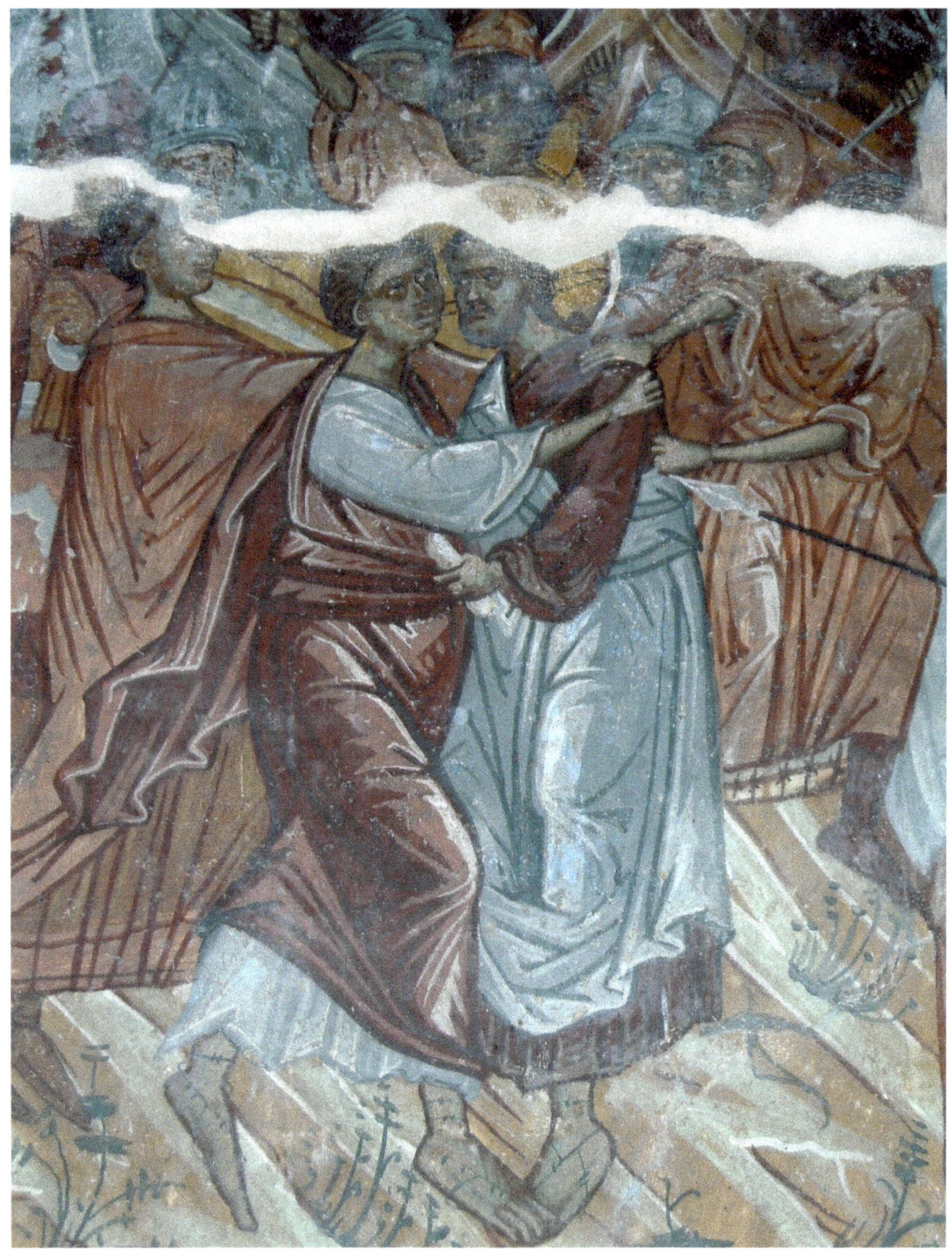

Fig. 6-11

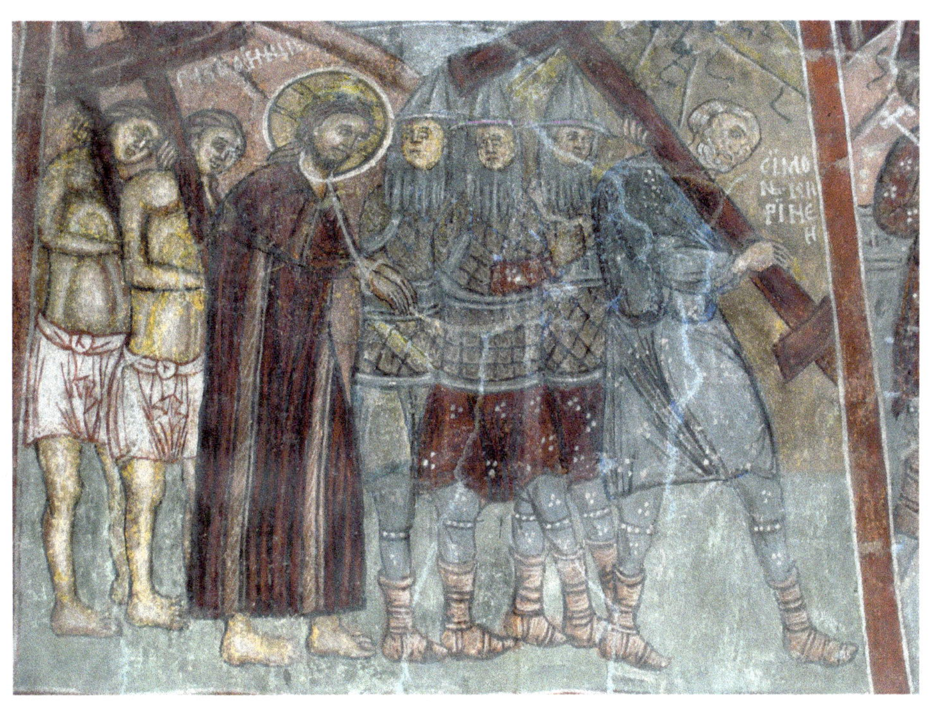

Fig. 6-12

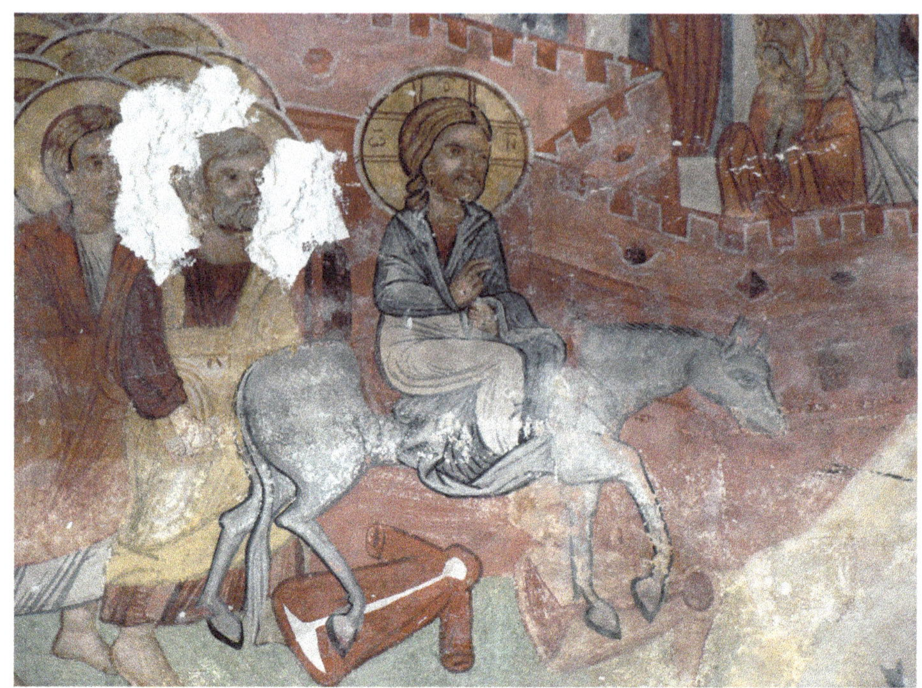

Fig. 6-13

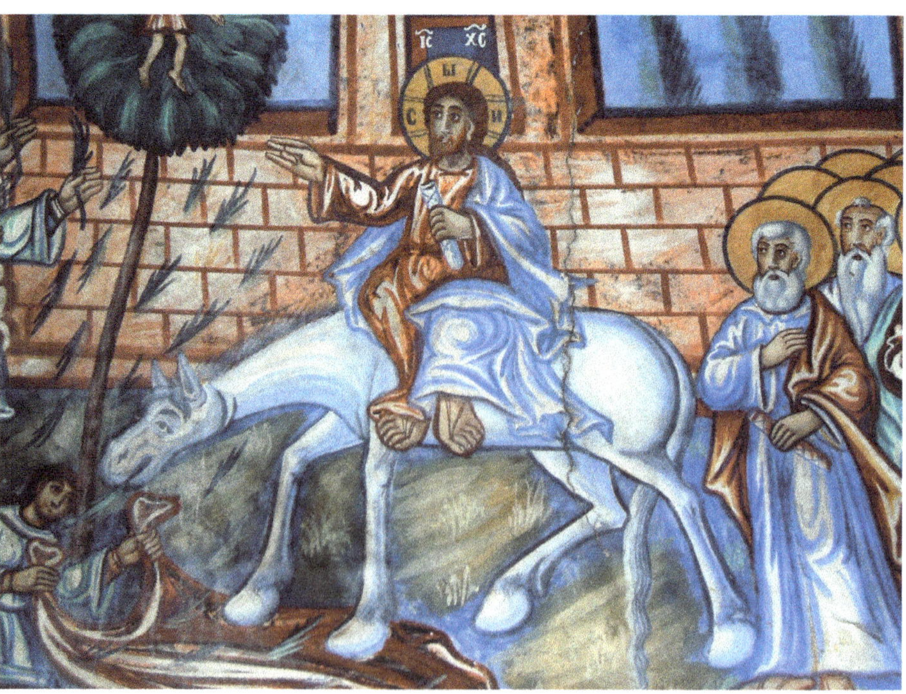

Fig. 6-14

Resurrection

The Fire of Love[18]

18 This essay deals with light in frescoes, through scenes such as Abraham's sacrifice (Genesis 22), healing the sick, cursing the fig tree, washing the feet, the arrest and flagellation of Christ, his crucifixion and being laid in the tomb, and his descent into hell on Holy Saturday.

'The Father is Love which crucifies; the Son is Love crucified; and the Holy Spirit is the invincible power of the Cross,' writes Metropolitan Philaret of Moscow.[19] A statement that provokes the unprepared reader with the cruelty of the Father's mission, of Fatherhood, of fatherhood in general, and relates it in an identical way to one of the most frequently painted scenes from the Old Testament: Abraham's Sacrifice. But while Abraham is tested because of his love and faith towards God, because of whom is God the Father tested, and why does he not stay his own hand if he stayed Abraham's hand and if this is one of the prophecies concerning the coming of Christ, of which he himself says, 'Do not think that I have come to abolish the law or the prophets; I have come not to abolish but to fulfill' (Mt 5:17)? Or else, 'Let it be so now; for it is proper for us in this way to fulfill all righteousness' (Mt 3:15).

These questions, along with others – for example, the conical shape of the sacrificial fire and the angel-cocoon, which comes to announce the replacement of the pillar of fire and the knife with the Rising Light (Abraham's Sacrifice, Strupets, fig. 7-1) – provide the framework for this subject.

The Crucifixion of Christ is its centre – what in fact is the cross, what is Love crucified? Isn't it the shadow of a bird on a hillside, which always runs before it? Or the open arms of a mother before an onrushing child, of the beloved who has been waiting for her lover? Isn't it ultimately, but not in last place, the arm you put around a friend's shoulder, the outstretched arm in bed on which your little son rests his head, falling into a deep sleep?

And if this is Love crucified – the furthest extension of an embrace with which Christ wished to comprehend the whole world, and the Father the whole Christ – then the Crucifixion has less to do with the knife, or cruelty, than with tenderness, agape and life. The cross represents the unending love of Christ the God-man towards his people, of God the Father towards his Son and his people. The Father does not stay his hand, so that the fire of the burning bush can be turned into an Easter candle, love can be humbled, there can be Light to illuminate the whole of creation through a hole in heaven.

Exactly this love was foreseen by the painter of Boboshevo Monastery drawing the Savior's body in a figure of eight with the all-pervasive light of a lamp that shines in the darkness (Crucifixion of Christ, Boboshevo, fig. 7-2). In God, there is no

19 Quoted in Paul Evdokimov, *The Art of the Icon*, location 859.

evil. Even when he curses, he in fact blesses. So in the fresco Cursing the Fig Tree (Seslavtsi, fig. 7-3), light pours from his hand to resurrect the tree's empty womb. Giving off reflections like a sun path on water. Guiding light.

We see Christ-Light in the fresco Healing the Sick (Seslavtsi, fig. 7-4), surrounded by the weak, lame and blind, where he blesses with a right hand that is three-dimensional like the Holy Trinity. From his seated body, his painful grimace, his clothes, we get the feeling of transparency, as if he has already overcome the world's resistance. We see him in the fresco Washing the Feet (Alino, fig. 7-5), his eyes overflowing blue, immersed like the Seven Rila Lakes, like the Charioteer of Delphi, seemingly turned both outwards and inwards. We see him in the fresco Arrest of Christ (Iliyantsi, fig. 7-6), where, pressed by the crowd, he brings dawn to the darkness, like a snowy night or the aurora borealis. We see him in the fresco Flagellation of Christ (Iliyantsi, fig. 7-7), already a pillar of light, streaming, but also passing through him. A prophetic scene before that of the Descent into Hell. The same light we find in the Nativity, the Baptism and the Transfiguration. We see him in the dazzling look of the fresco Nailing of Christ to the Cross (Alino, fig. 7-8), in the infirmity-kenosis that accompanies his gesture and expression (Strupets), because what else is the outer manifestation of inner strength if not descent on light? We see him in the bright whiteness of the fresco Laying of Christ in the Tomb (Berende, fig. 7-9), where his wrapped body resembles a chrysalis like the one in the manger in depictions of the Nativity. And in the fresco Descent into Hell (Seslavtsi, fig. 7-10) we see how the bottom left part of his garment forms a heart – his heart, a gift to us, his children (the clothes resurrect with the body, just as the bleeding woman touches the fringe of his cloak and is healed, or after baptism we put on a new outfit).

In all frescoes of the Descent into Hell, the Savior has taken Adam and Eve, or only Adam, with the gesture of a mother who holds her child, not hand in hand, but, afraid of losing them, with their hand in her grip. In the same way in which the Virgin Mary probably held Christ before he went up to the temple. Christ's fatherhood is linked to the Virgin's motherhood and the Father's fatherhood. 'To the Father's fatherhood without a mother on the divine level corresponds the Theotokos' motherhood without a father on the human level, and this motherhood is a figure of the maternal virginity of the Church,' writes Paul Evdokimov.[20] Just as Christ pulled away in order to enter the temple, so he pulls Adam and Eve

20 Paul Evdokimov, *The Art of the Icon*, location 4106.

away for the kingdom of heaven. Not by chance does the cross in his other hand (in some frescoes, he holds a scroll or shows the wounds in his hands) have more than one transverse beam, like Jacob's ladder to heaven.

The light in murals is most frequently conveyed by the transparency of the image (light white is transparency!) or by white and grey tones (often found in frescoes of the Baptism, the Temptation of Christ and the Dormition of Mary). The light that appears in different scenes of Christ's earthly life shows us the path of salvation. Like the Christmas star, it leads us towards the Savior's manger and towards resurrection. In Bulgarian iconography, the light pours out in scenes of healing, washing the feet, Christ's torments, because 'no one has greater love than this, to lay down one's life for one's friends' (Jn 15:13). This is the light Bulgarian painters have revealed – of taking away pain, of service, of accepting pain. Precisely this transformation from the pain of the multitude to the pain of the One, of the passing of pain from people to the Son of Man, is called service. It is service that illuminates us, through which the frescoes are heaped, one on top of another, in order to draw the form of God's Name.

Christ is the Christmas star. He is born Light; on his earthly path as the God-man, he carries light, he reveals it to us so he can infuse us with it. He is an emanation of the Trinity's light – hypostatic, divine-human, deified – the highest expression of which is his Transfiguration on Mount Tabor. On his human path, Christ repeats the path of the Christmas star. Pre-eternal and life-giving source of Light, he brings it down to earth for us, just as God appeared in the Old Testament as a cloud and a pillar of fire. Christ's light is the guiding star of the New Testament. The pillar of fire and the cloud with all the semiotics of their purpose – for righteousness and the knife – have become the blessed light of Christmas Eve, which completely fulfills the Savior's words, 'I desire mercy, not sacrifice' (Mt 9:13). All-enlightening, holy mercy.

In his *Apology*, Tertullian describes the soul as 'by nature Christian.'[21] The twelfth-century Indian poet-mystic Akka Mahadevi includes in her poems a refrain dedicated to God-Light: 'O lord white as jasmine.'[22] In his animated film *Howl's Moving Castle*, Hayao Miyazaki offers us one of the most beautiful metaphors for

21 Tertullian, *Apology*, tr. S. Thelwall, XVII.6, <https://ccel.org/ccel/tertullian/apology/anf03.iv.iii.xvii.html>.

22 A. K. Ramanujan (tr.), *Speaking of Siva* (Harmondsworth: Penguin Books, 1973), p. 111-42.

light: a young Howl catches a falling star, which he then swallows, only to take it out a few seconds later as a small fire – his heart. The light that is humble, pre-eternal fire and fertilizes our hearts with a soul. The soul that, dedicated to God, is fire, the same fire with which the Savior came to baptize us, of which he says, 'For where your treasure is, there your heart will be also' (Mt 6:21).

The humble, bluish light of a candle gathered around the wick of an old body, over which the burning fire of the Resurrection shines and is passed from hand to hand.

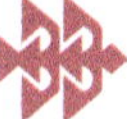

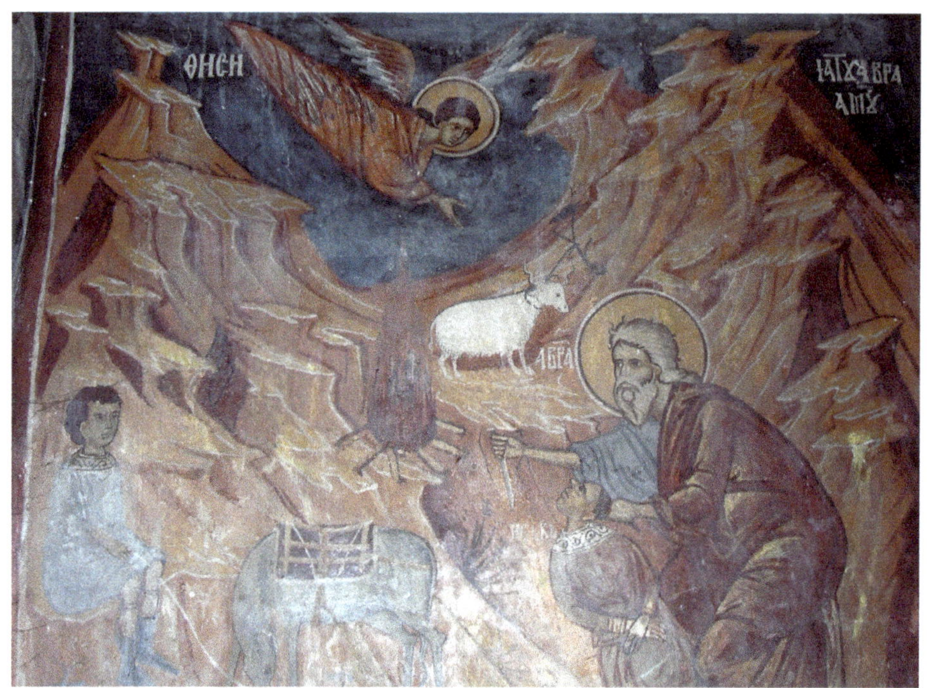

Fig. 7-1

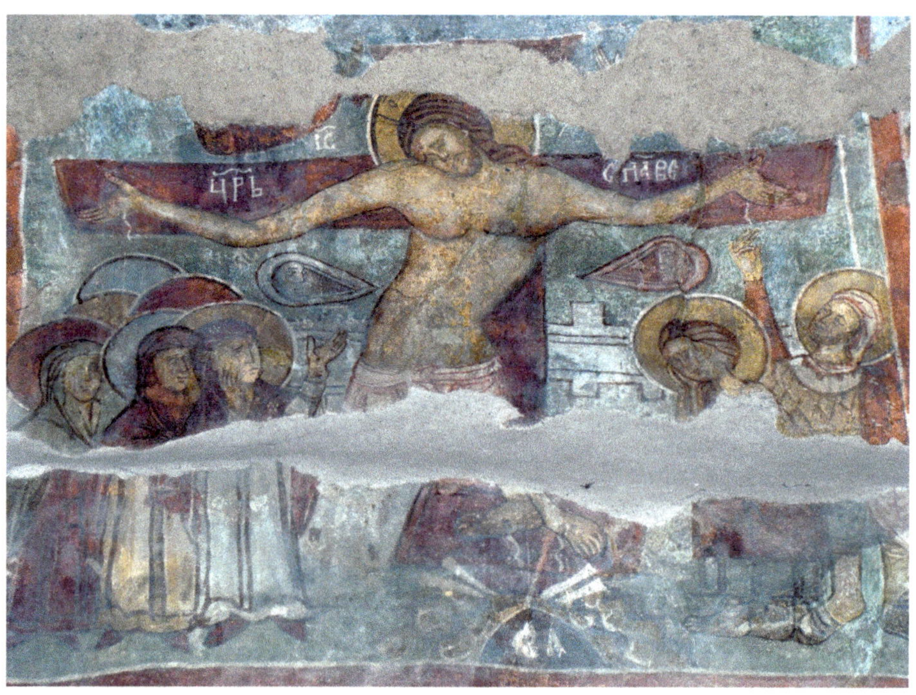

Fig. 7-2

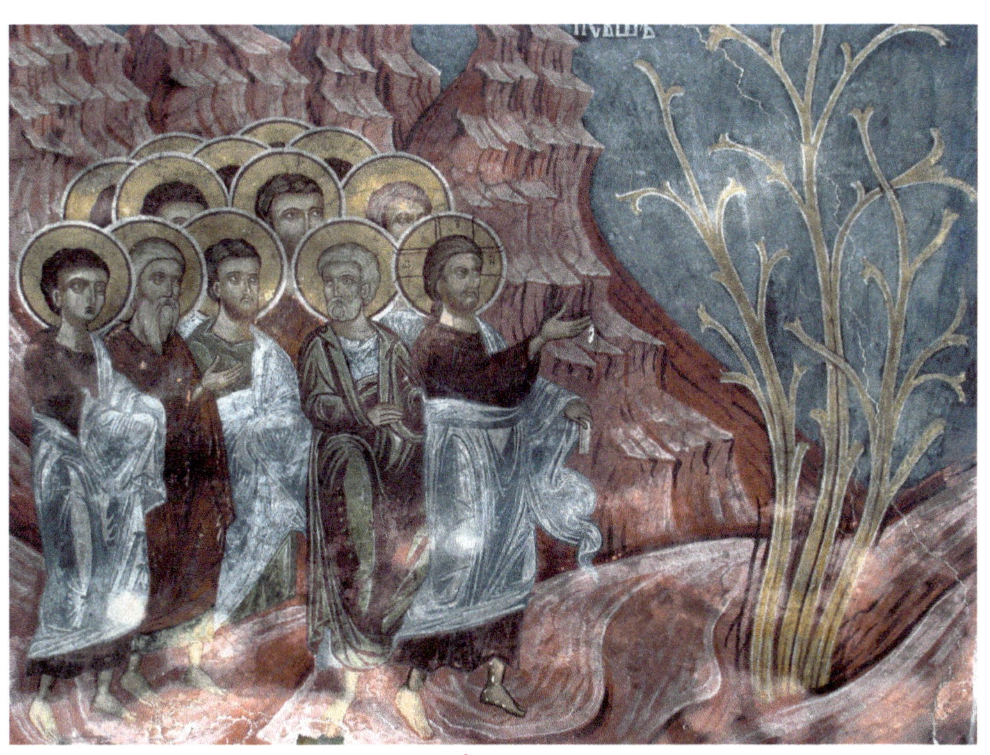

Fig. 7-3

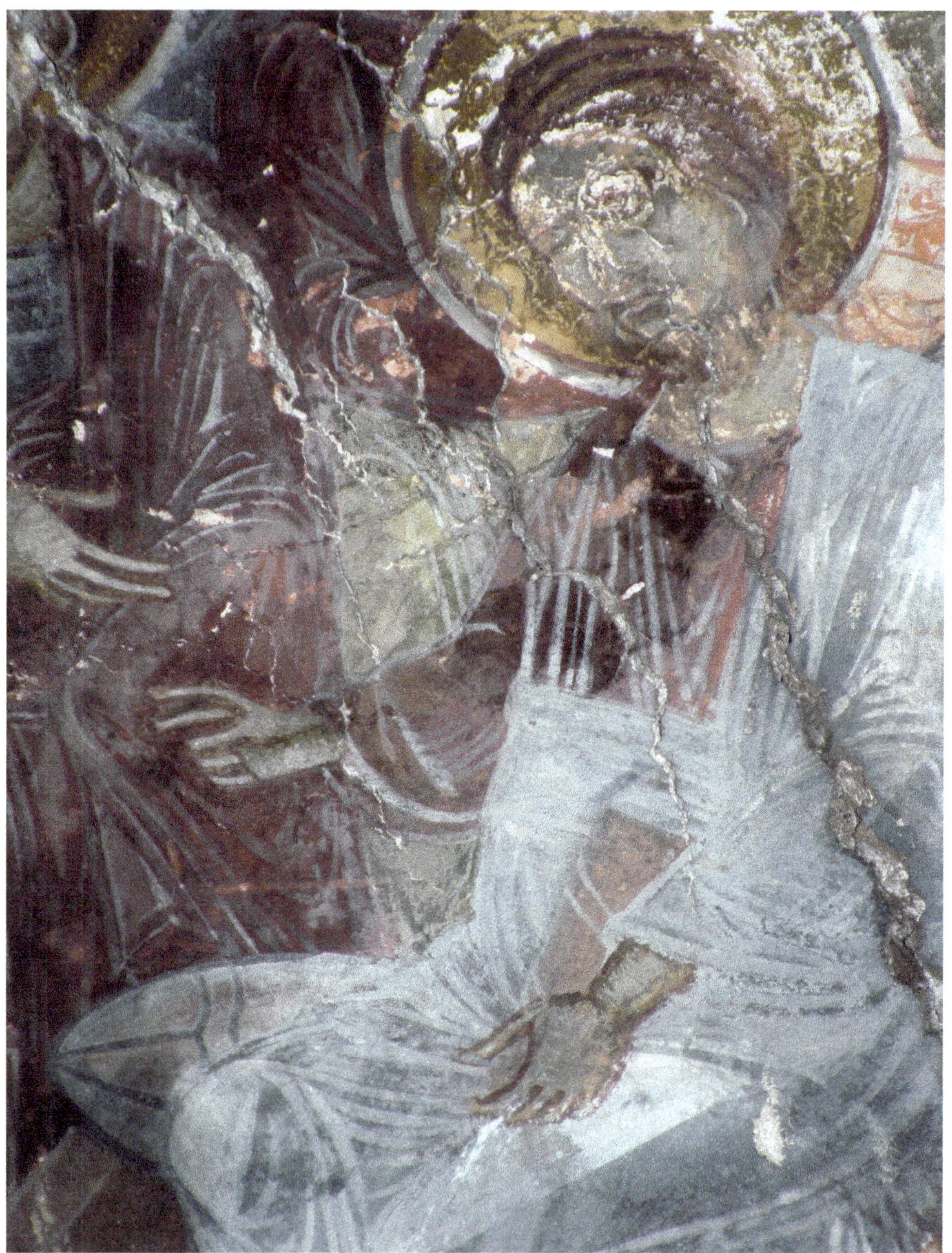

Fig. 7-4

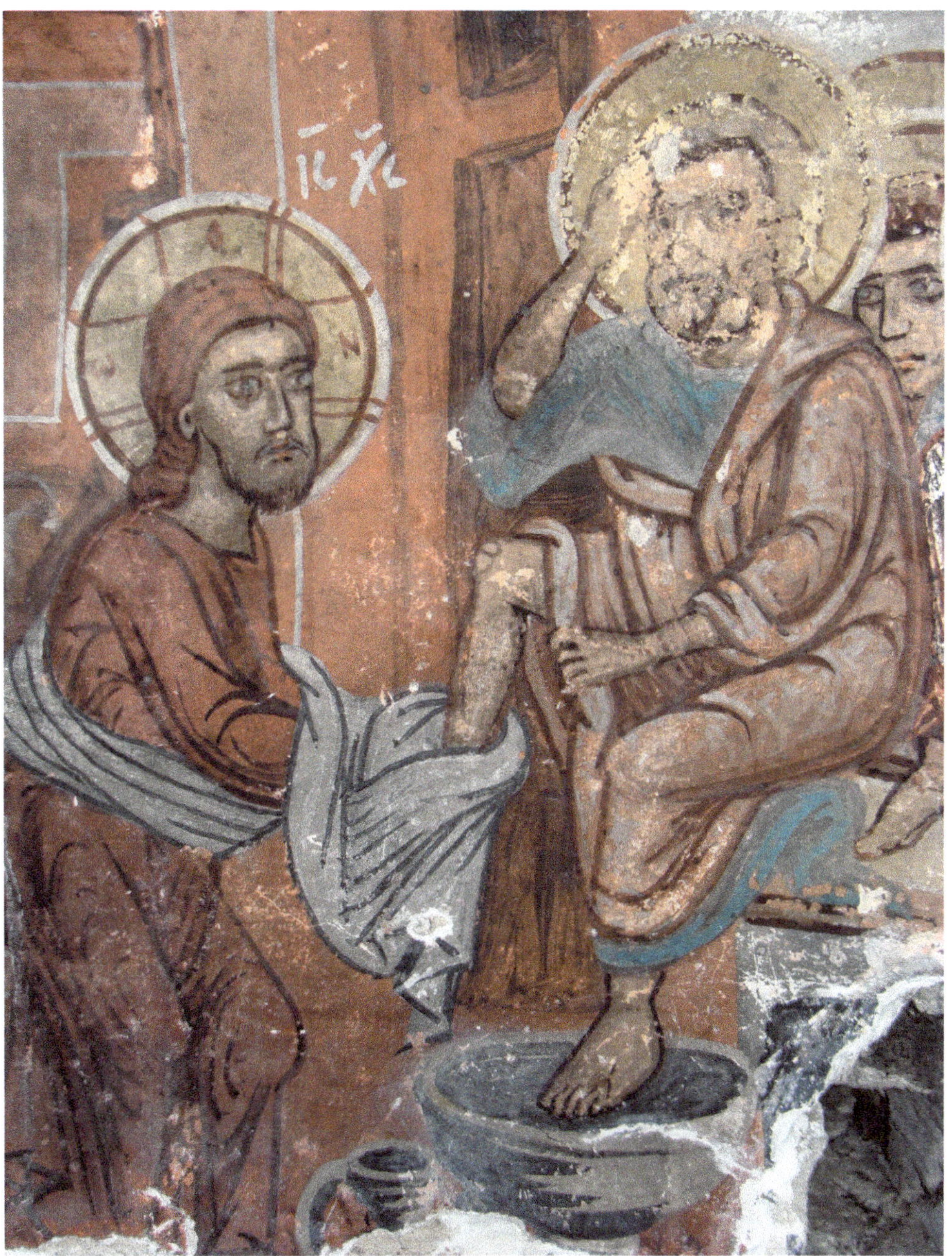

Fig. 7-5

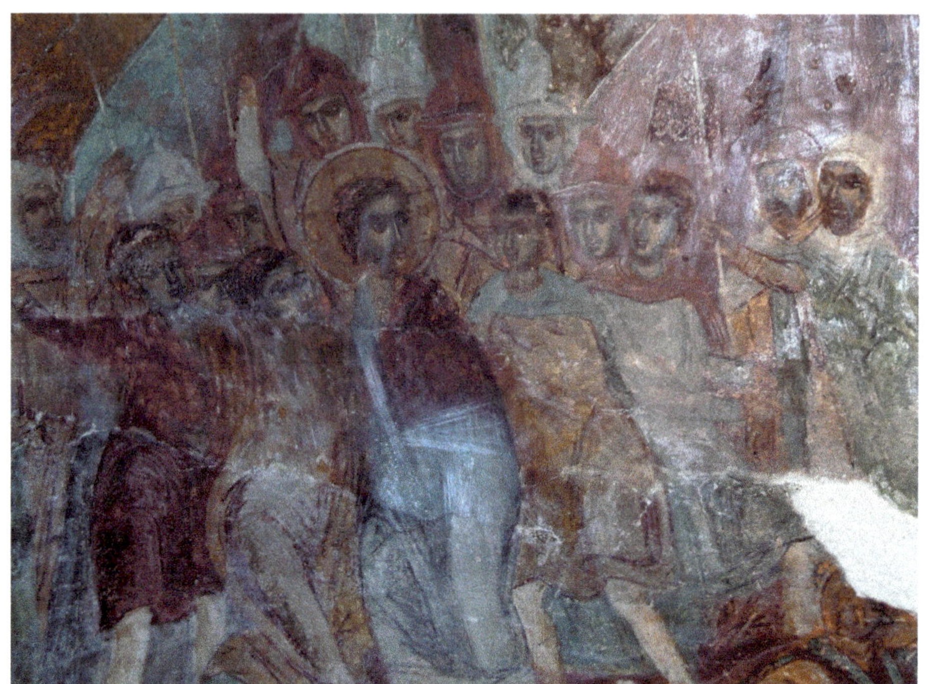

Fig. 7-6

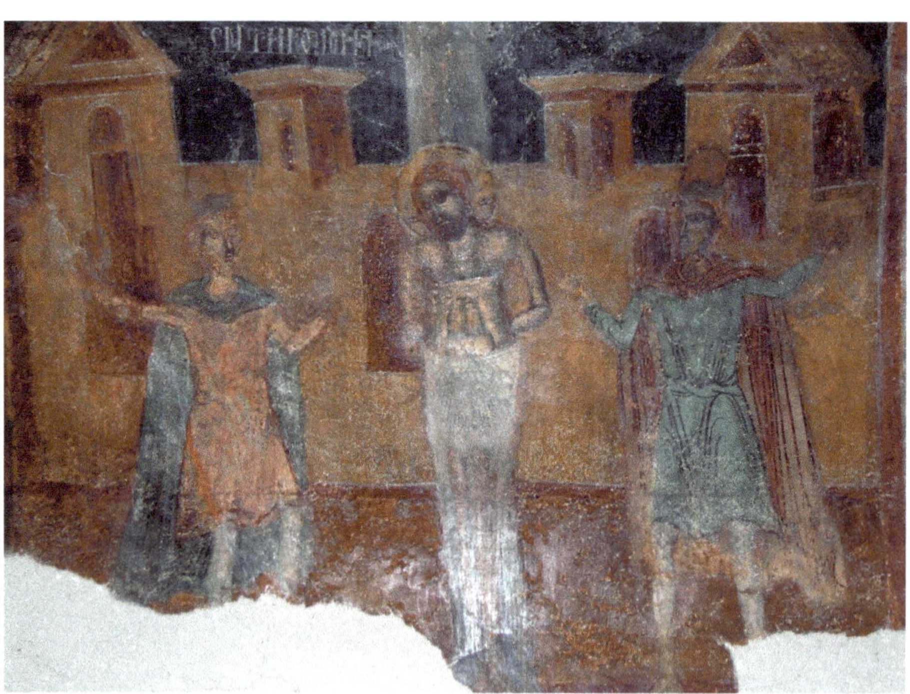

Fig. 7-7

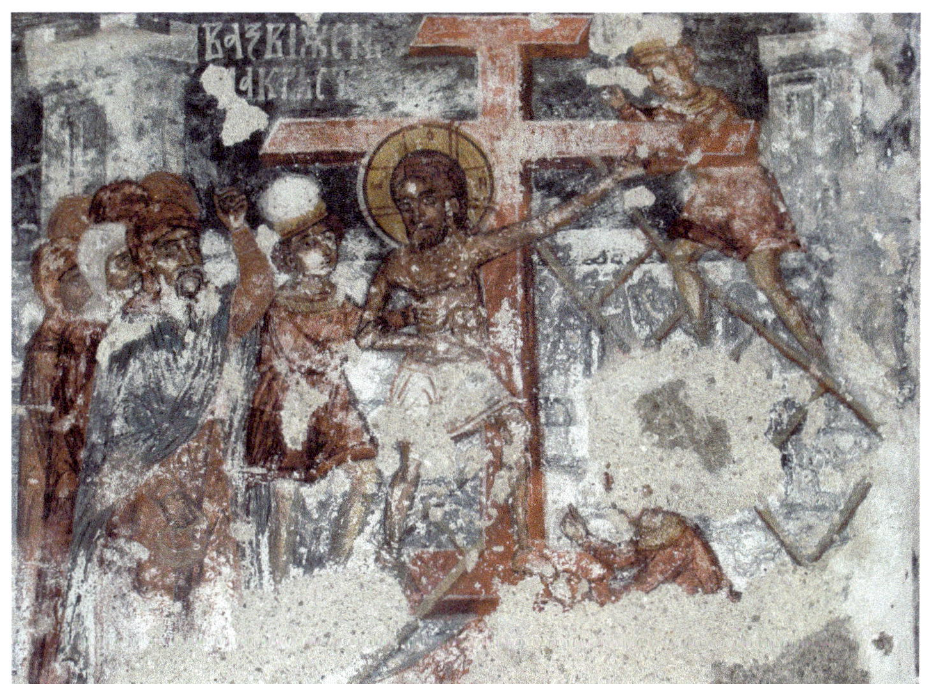

Fig. 7-8

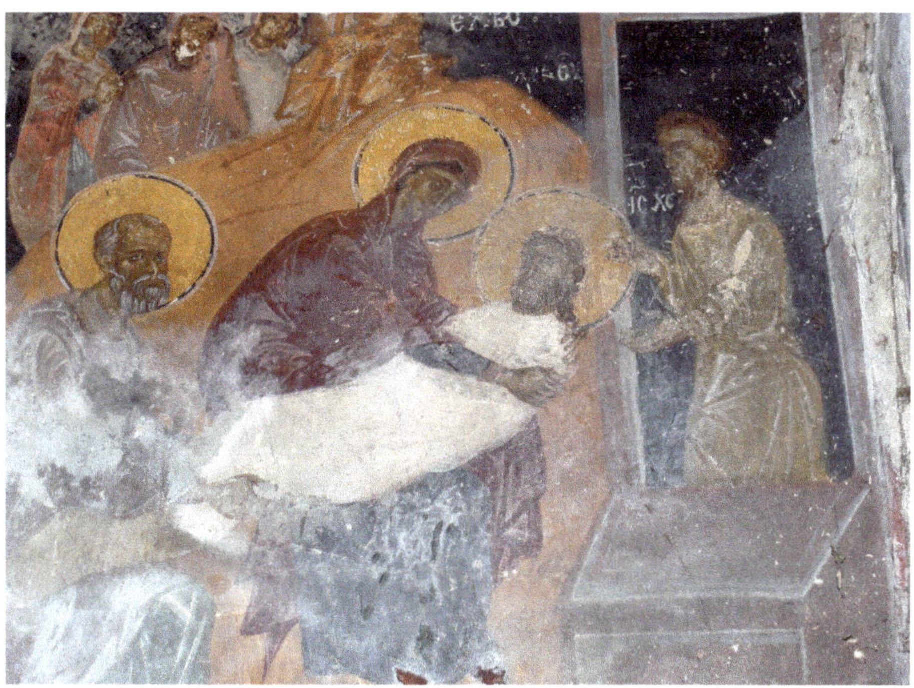

Fig. 7-9

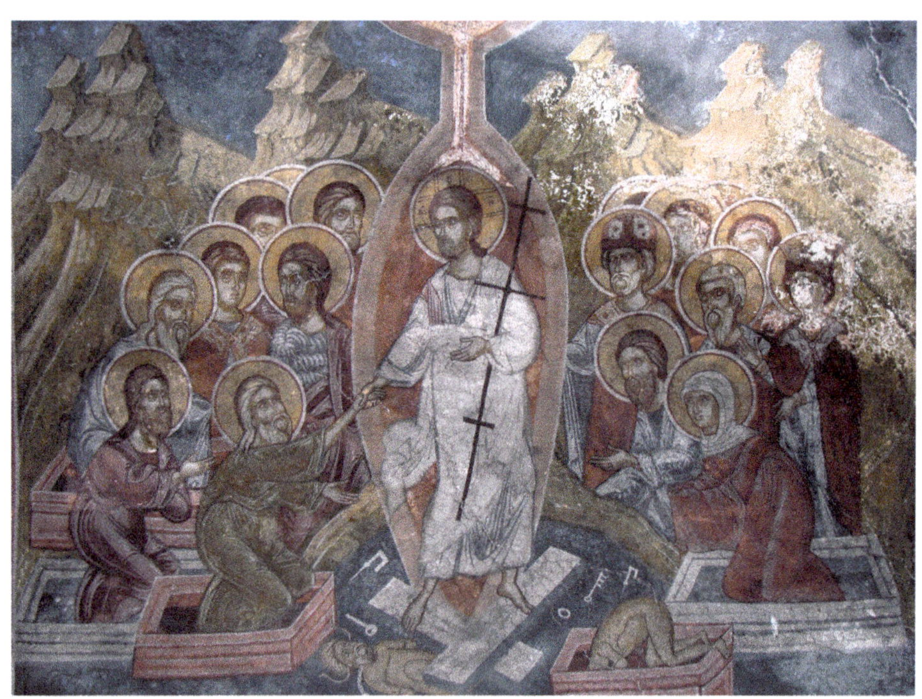

Fig. 7-10

The Ascension of Jesus

The Egg of Faith

For I, the Lord your God, hold your right hand; it is I who say to you, 'Do not fear, I will help you.'

Isaiah 41:13

There is no greater harm in society than the taking away of faith. 'Nature abhors a vacuum' is a saying attributed to Aristotle and so fear fills the empty space. In other words, those forty years walking in the desert with a pillar of cloud and fire as guide are equivalent to Christ's appearance to his disciples after his crucifixion to inspire them with faith – years filled and transformed, revived after the Old Testament, won back by his forty-day temptation in the wilderness.

By his resurrection, Christ does this as well – he reclaims the empty space of fear and temptation for our faith. He refills the empty vessel. Turns water into wine. Multiplies the loaves. Like Easter candles that are lit from each other and spread.

What is fear, then, if not the emptying of content, that feeling of not being accepted by the landscape, where there is nowhere even to lay your head? Turning stones into bread, jumping from a pinnacle, money – everything he had to struggle against before us in order to restore faith.

Faith is the word most often used by Christ. Even more than love, more than the Word. Because faith is a way, if we superimpose the two triads faith-hope-love and way-truth-life from the Bible. Faith in and of itself is love. We have heard it said that love without faith can do nothing, but just as true, even more true, is that faith is love. There is no more heartrending picture than that of eyes staring at you in disbelief. We have seen them on television and in real life – old men in deserted villages, marginalized children, mothers who can't breastfeed their children, all those who are oppressed in one way or another. Bare eyes like snails without a shell. Even if you touch their horns, they have nowhere to go. Except into themselves. Only one thing is left to them – the nakedness called hope. They have been deprived of faith and love. Deprived of that shield of the Holy Spirit, which Christ sends us with his ascension. Perhaps that is why the Ascension is so important, when he, the God-man, the Risen One, returns to the centre of the circle, of the egg, gathers, as it were, in the yolk, and the shell surrounds him – a perfect circle, not just around his head like a halo, around his body like a mandorla, but all the way around (Seslavtsi, fig. 8-1). Christ is the seed of faith.

By his ascension, the Savior repairs the cracked egg, builds the house anew, calcifies the shell around the content. A crack that was caused by the spilling of blood, by the desecrated body of doubt. Not last, his body in the Garden of Gethsemane; first of all, that body permitted in Eden by the snake's penetration of the Tree of Knowledge – a crack in the building which separated God from people for the first time (Fall, Church of the Nativity, Arbanasi, fig. 8-2; Teteven, fig. 8-3). Doubt, which creeps around the cross (Descent from the Cross, Ivanovo, fig. 8-4) and so resembles the snake in the depiction of the Fall, but has been defeated already by Christ, the Wisdom of God, whose type is the serpent of bronze on a pole in Numbers.

Doubt, the taking away of faith, precedes sin – doubt is the reason for sin. After which, the first reaction is fear. Doubt produces fear in creation, in our souls, in the *eschaton*. Doubt is the *eschaton*.

Christ's answer to the Fall in Eden, to every human fall, is the Ascension. After he struggled with temptations in the wilderness for our sakes, he struggled with the greatest of them of all – his own doubt. The Garden of Gethsemane serves as a parallel to the Garden of Eden. In this way, Christ not only redeems us from death with his sufferings, but also from fear with his faith. By accepting a divine and a human nature, he undergoes the Old Testament Genesis for our sakes, just as by accepting the cross we are called to undergo that of the New Testament. To experience him every day of our lives, inserting the experience through will, our own choice, which is the only thing that makes our liberation possible. From death, from fear, from sin. Our willingness perpetually entwined with his. As St Anthony the Great says, 'The virtue that is within us only requires the human will,'[23] for 'the kingdom of heaven is within you' (Lk 17:21).

It turns out that willingness is the necessary minimum that works wonders, turning fear back into faith. That free will given to us by God, without which nothing would be possible. That inner strength, decisiveness, motivation, obstinacy, which must be engaged to get lost faith working. An equation that begins with will and leads to faith. For which Christ himself in the Garden of Gethsemane gives us an answer when, among the sleepy, drooping heads of his disciples, he performs three consecutive acts: he tells them not to sleep, to be awake; standing on a height above them, he prays for this cup to be taken from him; and (on the left of the fresco)

23 Carolinne White (ed. and tr.), *Early Christian Lives* (Harmondsworth: Penguin Books, 1998), p. 22.

he accepts his Father's will. So his call for vigilance, his consciously adopting a protective posture over the heads of his followers, with his Father over his own head, and his humility are three steps in a dance of faith and victory over fear (Alino, fig. 8-5). Already in the Garden of Gethsemane the faith that was desecrated in Eden has been restored. And we, so-called twins, whose faith extends to digging in his wounds, have no other choice but to tread in his footsteps, as in a snowdrift. His mercy towards us and his passion are so strong that he doesn't just sow in us the greatest message of all time – faith – he doesn't just allow wounds on his body, but he allows them to be felt. While with the extended arm of that 'let it be' (Doubting Thomas, Boboshevo, fig. 8-6) he transforms Adam and Eve's apostasy, he turns a gesture of self-justification, of resistance (Adam and Eve, Iliyantsi, fig. 8-7), into a gesture of affirmation, of acceptance. At the Ascension, he is already with both arms wide open, a symbol of ultimate victory.

The similarity between Our Lady of the Sign (Radibosh, fig. 8-8; Strupets, fig. 8-9) and the Ascension of Jesus (Karlukovo, fig. 8-10) is not accidental. Christ goes up to his Father in the same aureole of light with which he touches the womb of the Virgin Mary at the Annunciation, remaining inside her, who is 'more spacious than the heavens,'[24] sown within her, within us. After the Ascension, we are his womb already – and he is our child.

24 A description of the Virgin Mary taken from the hymn 'All Creation Rejoices in Thee,' used after the consecration of the gifts in the Liturgy of St Basil in place of the hymn 'It Is Truly Meet.' The Bulgarian text has 'Ширшая небес.'

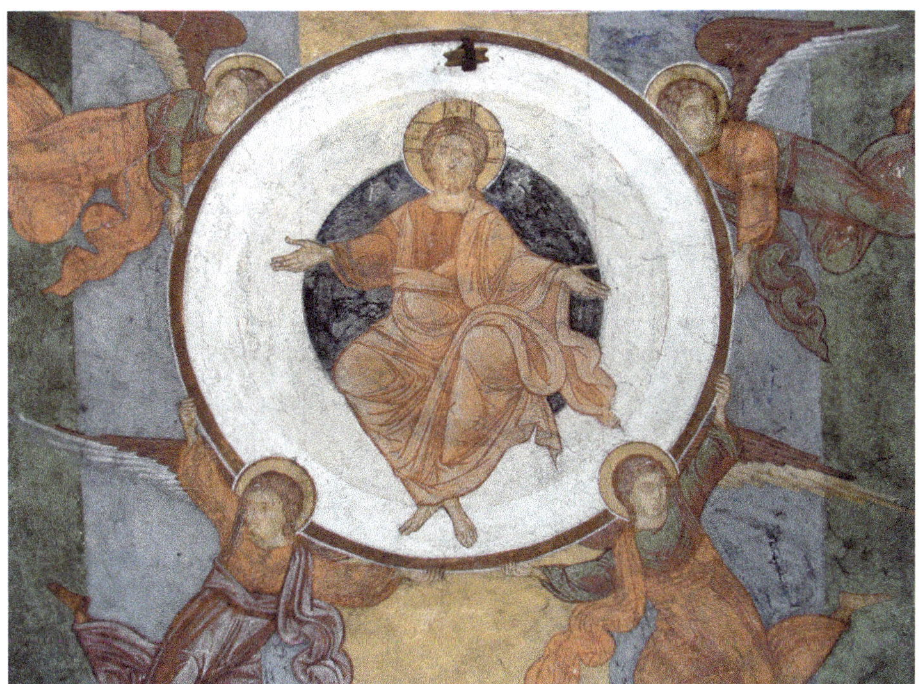

Fig. 8-1

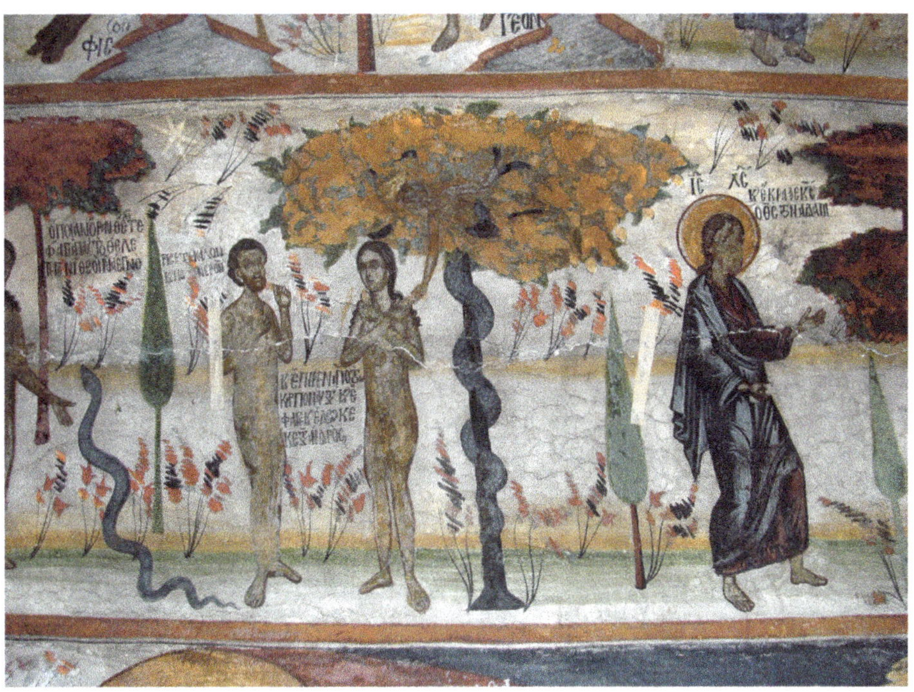

Fig. 8-2

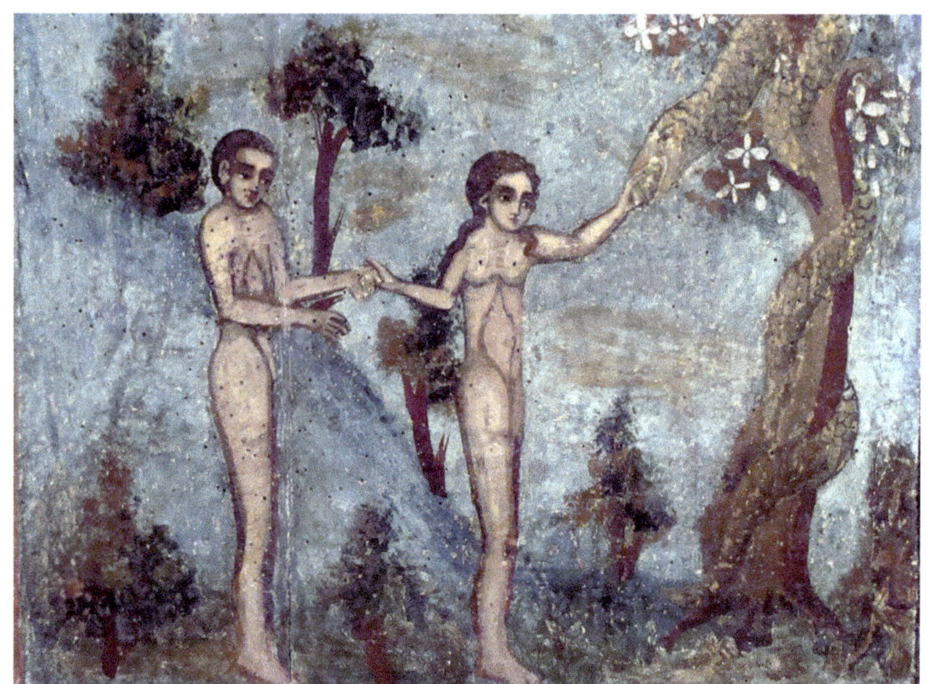

Fig. 8-3

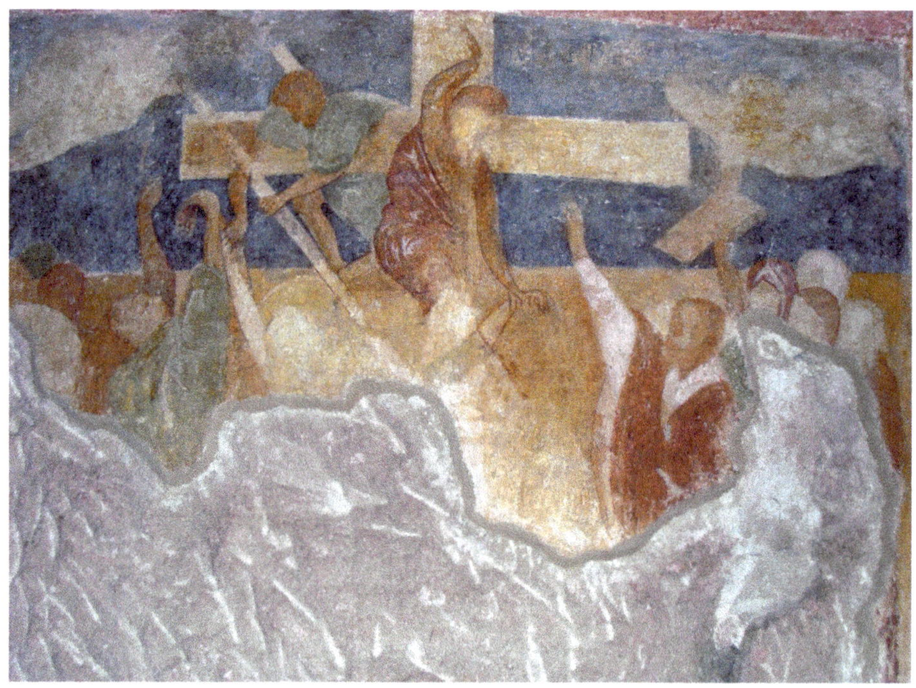

Fig. 8-4

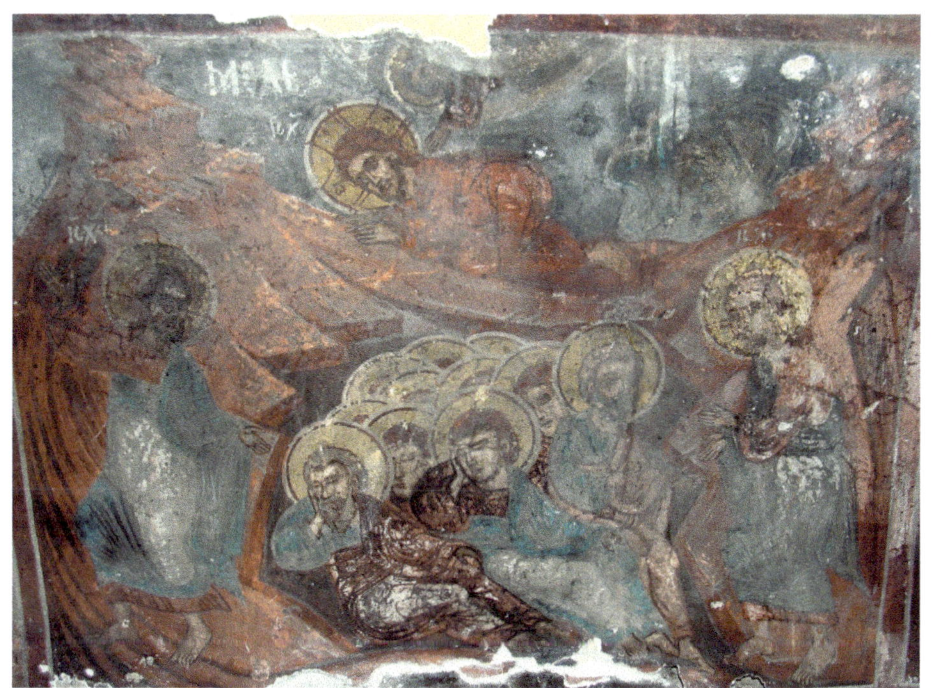

Fig. 8-5

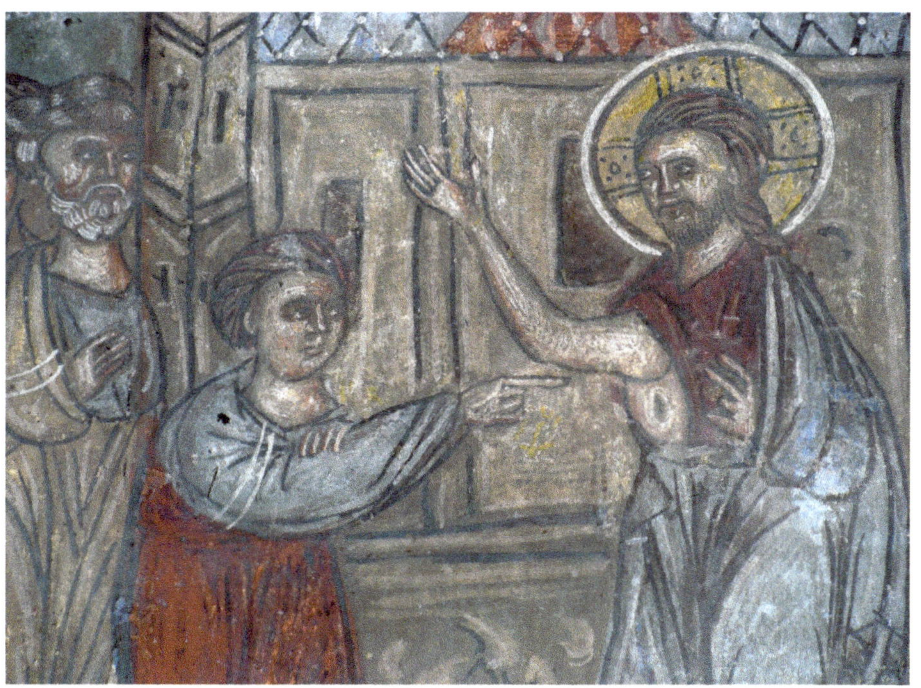

Fig. 8-6

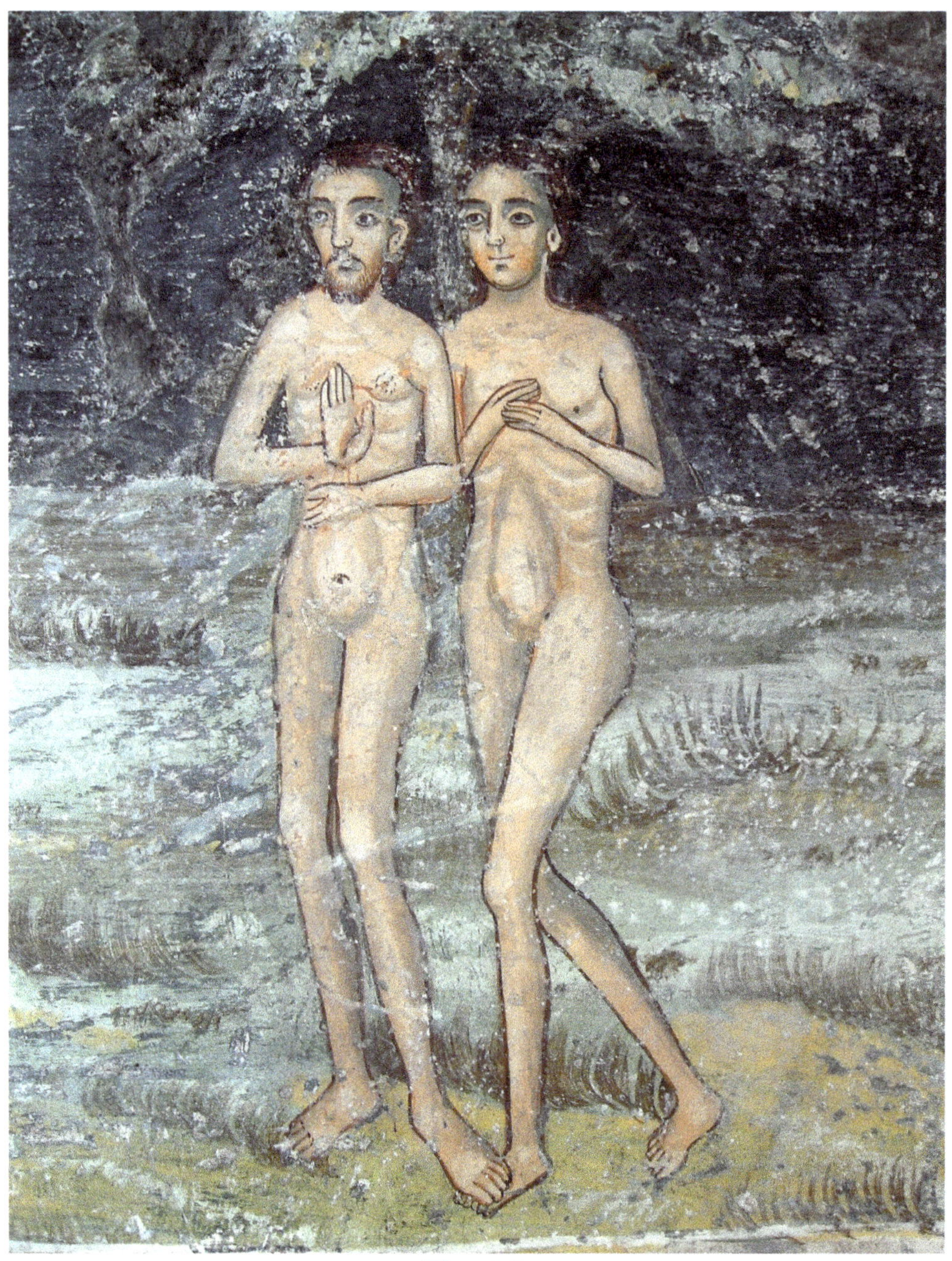

Fig. 8-7

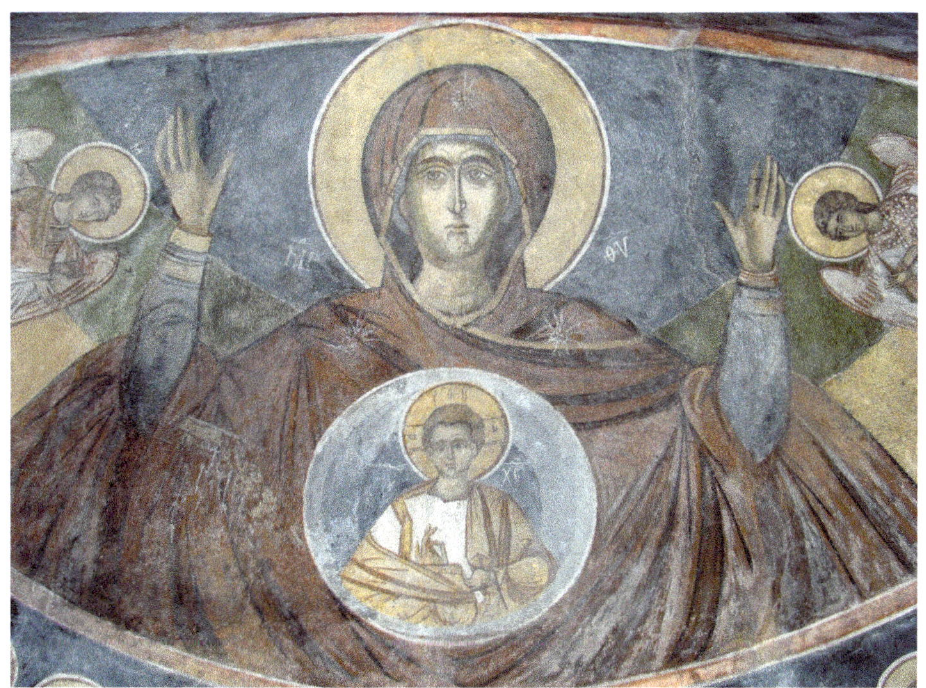

Fig. 8-8

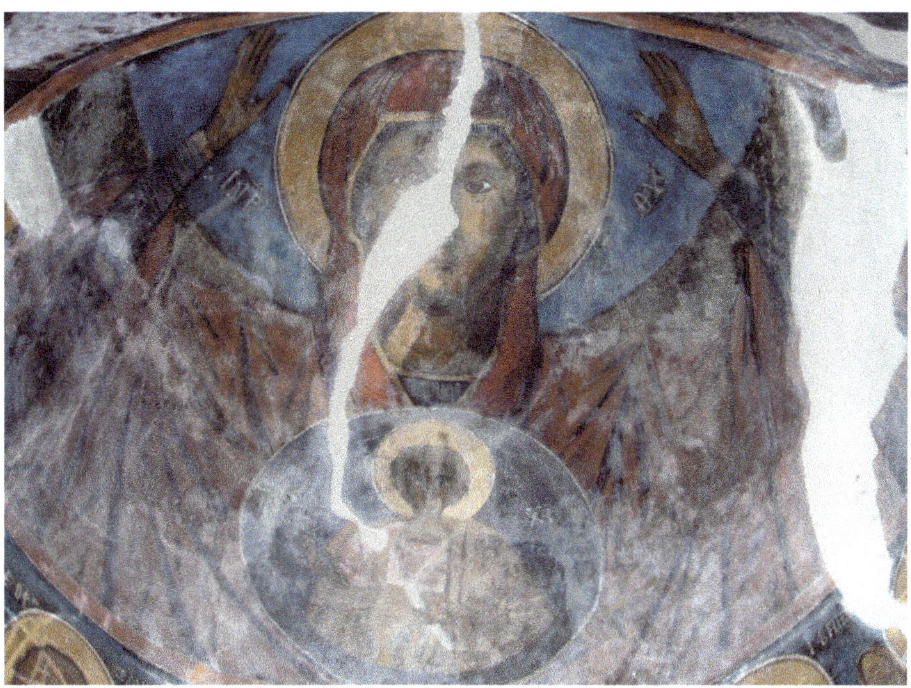

Fig. 8-9

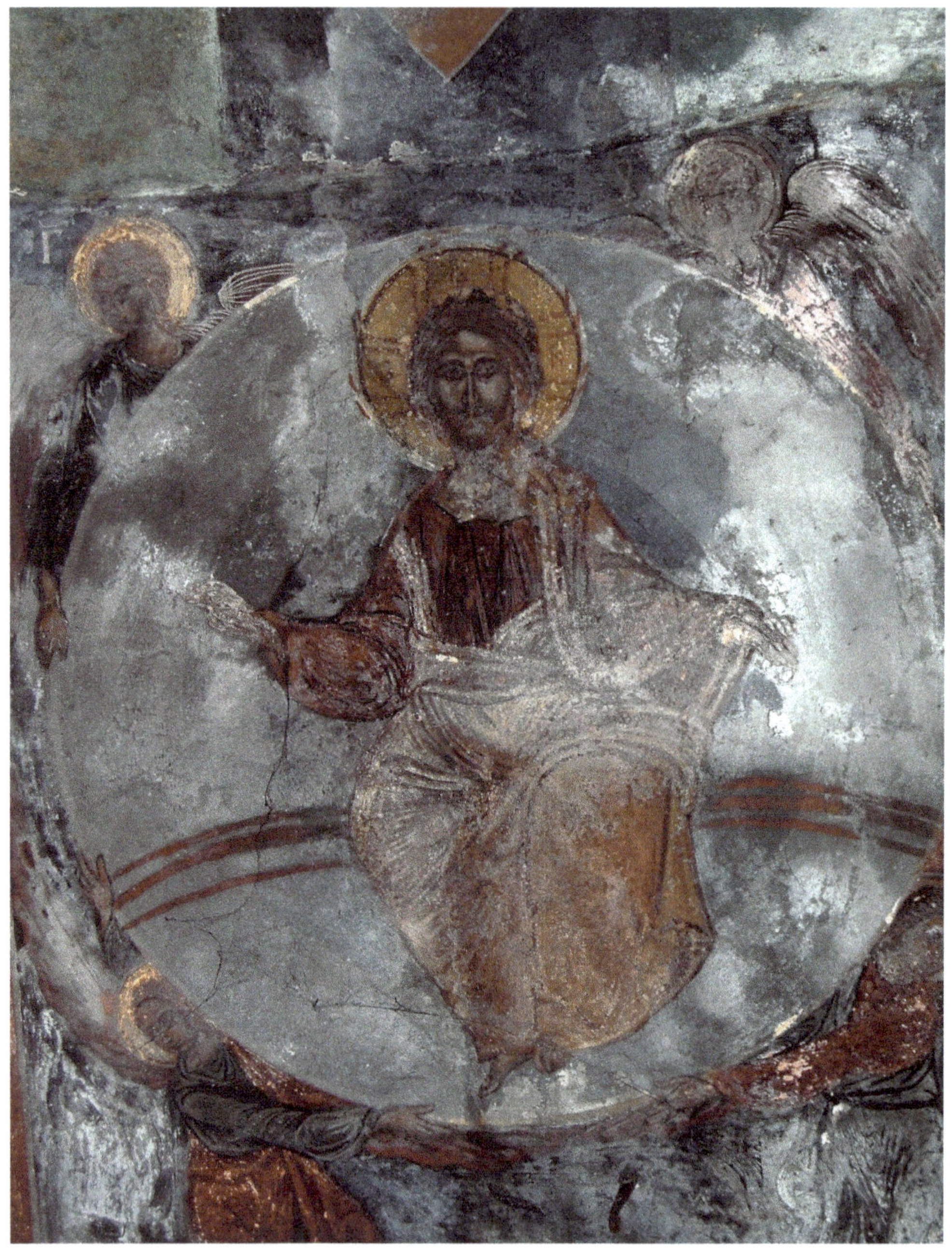

Fig. 8-10

Transfiguration

The Rhombus of Time

There is a direct link between frescoes of the Transfiguration and the Holy Trinity, as there is between time and eternity. It is precisely these two that lie at their base. Jesus Christ is transfigured on Tabor in order to show us time inscribed in eternity and eternity as a continuation of time. He becomes a bridge between time and eternity, between this and the other world, accepting uncreated light before three of his disciples and speaking with Moses and Elijah. That is why the mandorla around his body – unlike that in the Resurrection and the Ascension, which in most cases takes the shape of a perfect circle or an ellipse – is transformed into a light-refracting rhombus, whose rays sometimes resemble wings, emphasizing the linear movement of biological time (Eleshnitsa, fig. 9-1). Time, which in the Holy Trinity from the Church of the Nativity in Arbanasi has already returned to Eternity.

The place of time in eternity, the symbiosis of the two, the importance the Savior gives this 'today,' are the subject of these words of his, 'Give therefore to Caesar the things that are Caesar's, and to God the things that are God's' (Mt 22:21), as they are of his answer to one of the three temptations in the wilderness, 'One does not live by bread alone, but by every word that comes from the mouth of God' (Mt 4:4). In this relative rather than categorical way, using the word 'loaves' instead of 'stones,' the Savior once again underlines the importance of time for eternity only when it is meaningful. It shouldn't go on building with stones or even on what is most necessary, bread (though on that as well), so that we can live in God. Placing bread (this life) and the Word of God on both ends of a see-saw, the Savior is telling us that upwards movement is only possible if we look at time as the face of eternity and at eternity as the padding of time.

Eternity begins here, in this life. As Paul Evdokimov writes in his book *The Art of the Icon*, it isn't some abstract category after time or outside of time, rather 'the temporal reaches its fullness in the eternal "right here and now" […] eternity is not the absence of time but rather its fulfillment.'[25] Eternity is in the multilayered-ness of time. Using three basic figures – the circle, the rectangle and the rhombus (which is just two triangles stuck together) – that is how iconographers have presented it.

In St Stephen's Church in Nesebar, the transfigured Christ is in a rhombus inscribed within a circle; in Alino (fig. 9-2), he already has emerging rays, which in Eleshnitsa have become wings. In the Ivanovo rock monasteries (fig. 9-3), the crucifixion has been inserted between the rhombus and the circle, being a section of both, while the Transfiguration in Strupets (fig. 9-4) is the most expressive of all with its image

25 Paul Evdokimov, *The Art of the Icon*, location 2202.

of the pendulum of a clock, its typical rhombic suspension at the top. Without going against dogma, the icon painter has presented Christ in a very allegorical way – as crucified time in the embrace of eternity. Time raised above the rectangle of the earth and inscribed in heavenly spheres.

These figures are invariably present in every depiction of the Trinity – they are visible in Rublev's archetypal icon (sometimes called the 'Old Testament Trinity'), where the three heads of the angels form a perfect circle above the rectangle of the table (the earth), a cross passing through the centre of the cup. They are included in a particularly striking and original way in the Holy Trinity from Kladnitsa (fig. 9-5), where the circle of the Triune God's face shows three faces in one, the normal oval shape being replaced by a square. Holding the Book of the Gospels, which in this case has blank pages, taking on a more cosmic expression (the infinite, silence, universal language, even fear of the blank page, the unknown). Meanwhile, in the Holy Trinity known as 'Fatherhood' from the Church of the Nativity in Arbanasi (fig. 9-6), inside the rhombus is a circle – God's mantle – with a cross inside it, which the Father has embraced with his crucified Son embedded in the hourglass of his wings. Which is nothing other than an inverted rhombus – the tips of the two triangles point towards each other – the passage of time.

Jesus Christ came to earth and became time. He himself gave birth to time for us – as part of eternity. He revealed not only eternity, but also new time. The only real time. Because, as St Sophrony of Essex writes, 'it is a sin for us to waste the time given to us for knowing God on anything else.'[26]

In the Fatherhood Trinity from Strupets (fig. 9-7), we see the same embedded figures, but here Christ is a fetus in the womb – as in depictions of Our Lady of the Sign, where she is pregnant with him. Here God the Father is pregnant with him. A circle within a square, within a rhombus, within a circle. A circle within a circle. It is impossible to understand what is outside, what is inside (rotating spiral), but does it matter when in their extreme values, in their ecstatic limits, opposite categories become one, seem to blur, the contradiction between them disappears? There is no contradiction between time and eternity.

In all icons of the Trinity – be they Old Testament, New Testament or Fatherhood – the unfolding of the hypostases, their enumeration, goes in a clockwise direction. Father, Son and Holy Spirit are positioned in a movement from left to right, like the three hands of a clock. But there is another image – the Coronation of the Virgin, her 'let it be,' enshrined in the Creed (Dolni Pasarel, fig. 9-8). Here a fourth person

26 St Sophrony of Essex, Духовни беседи, p. 14.

has been included – according to Church Fathers, the number four symbolizes the fullness of the four Gospels, nothing can be added or taken away, the universality of the Word of God. Albeit down below, in recognition of Mary's humility and devotion, the fresco from Dolni Pasarel shows the Trinity in its four dimensions, the triangle has become a rectangle – the earth, fertility. This counting does not omit the Mother of God, as with St Sophia, who embraces her three daughters – Faith, Hope and Love. Father, Son and Holy Spirit. The Way, the Truth and the Life. Or, in human terms, spirit, soul, body (the title of a book by St Luke of Simferopol), something that is impossible without her intercession. Four triads, in relation to which she is already the bride of God, as in frescoes of the Deesis – the praying church, the madness of love, our Mother. The number four.

This fresco – the Mother bowing before her Son with strong, lowered eyes (Kremikovtsi, fig. 9-9), in her maphorion (head-cloth) like fish tails with their rhombuses (Boboshevo, fig. 9-10), the triangle, half a rhombus, in the bridegroom Christ's gesture of blessing (Church of Sts Peter and Paul, Veliko Tarnovo, fig. 9-11) – corresponds directly with the hourglass in the landscape (Dolni Pasarel) or eye (Church of Sts Michael and Gabriel, Arbanasi) of the Nativity (see the essay 'Nativity'). Between frescoes of the Nativity, the Deesis, the Trinity and the Transfiguration, there is an inseparable connection: time-rhombus, time-eternity.

In the Transfiguration, standing between his disciples and the Old Testament figures, Christ sends us a message – so long as we follow him, he will be our link with eternity. As when he turns to Peter and Andrew and says, 'Follow me and I will make you fish for people' (Mk 1:17), or just Peter and says, 'On this rock I will build my church' (Mt 16:18), or casts his net – the waves – towards his disciple (Sea of Tiberias, Seslavtsi, fig. 9-12).

The word 'rhombus' comes from the Greek word *rhombos*, meaning 'spinning top' – like the spinning Mary in depictions of the Annunciation. Symbolically and semantically, frescoes of the Transfiguration are a section and summary of the main scenes in the Savior's life. They are the milestone of church murals.

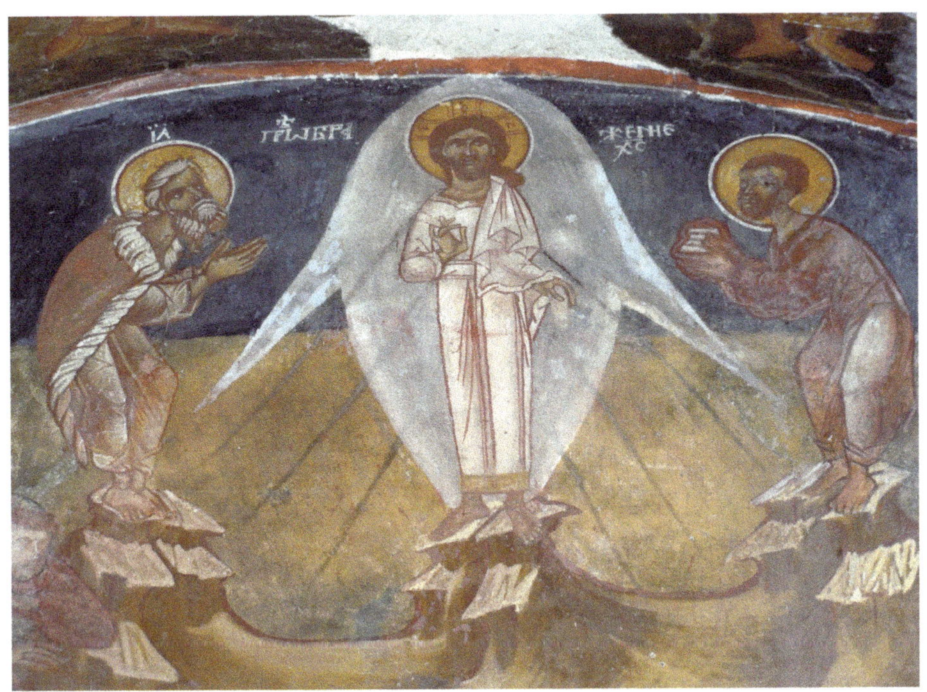

Fig. 9-1

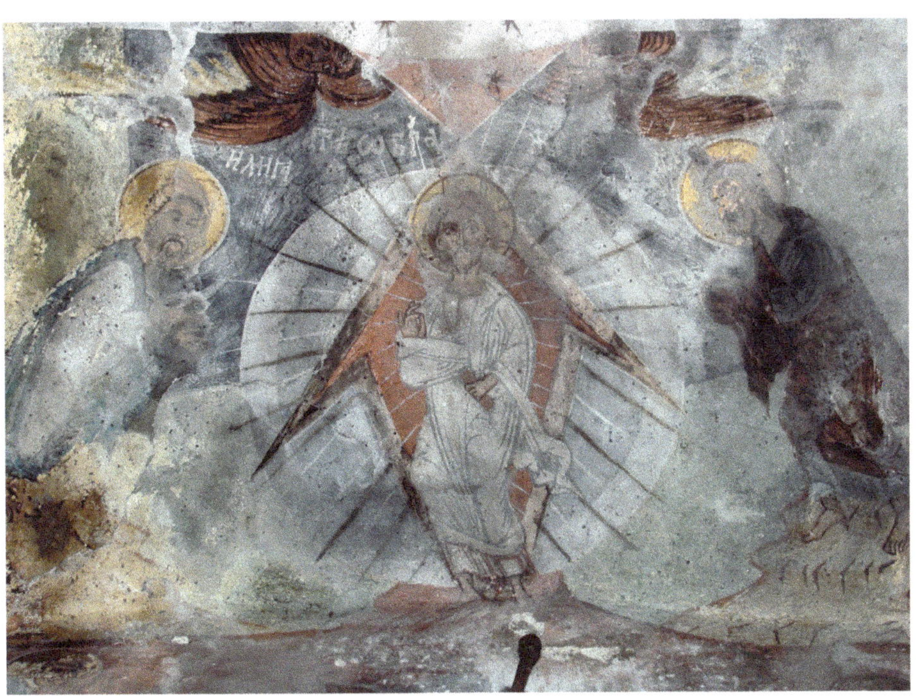

Fig. 9-2

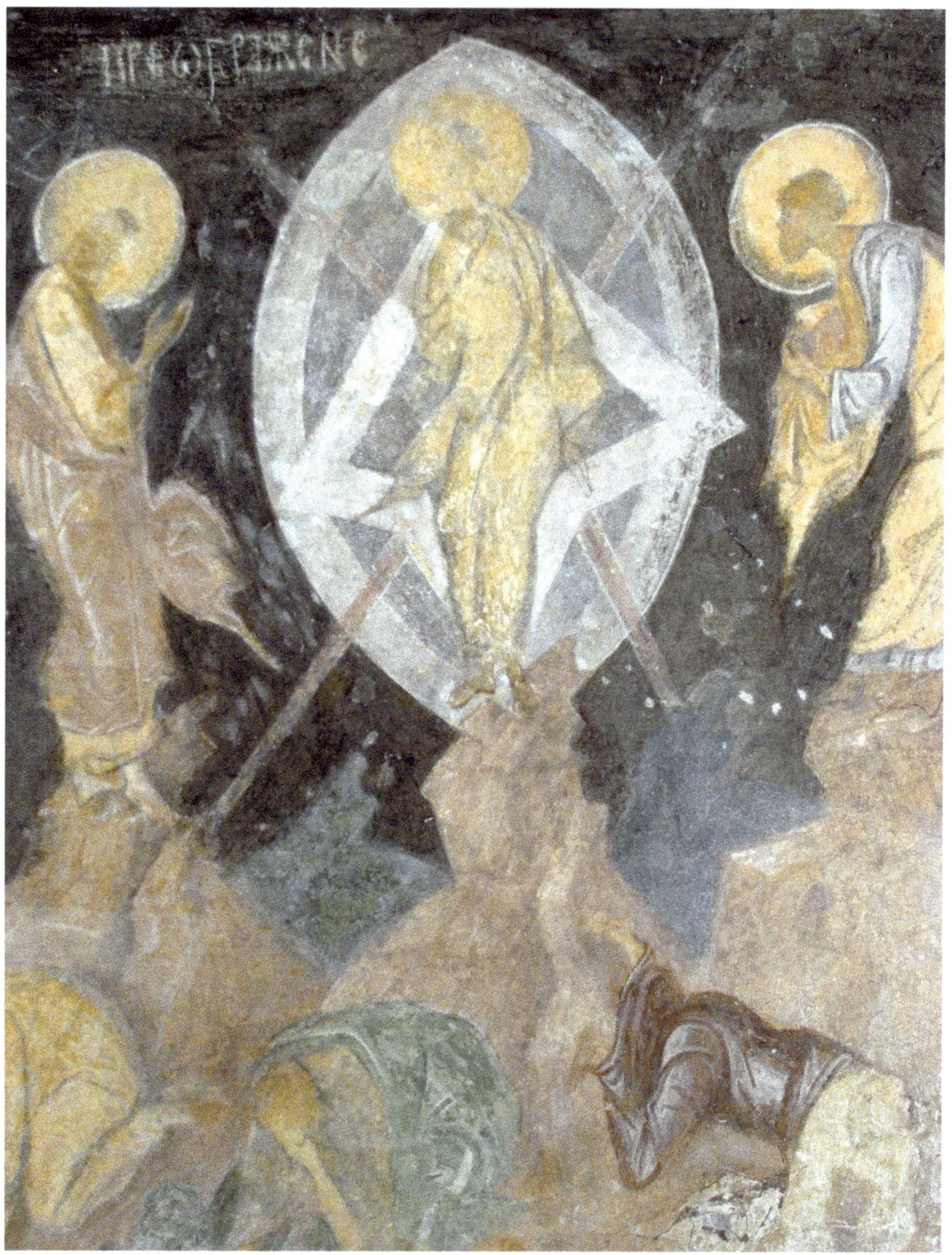

Fig. 9-3

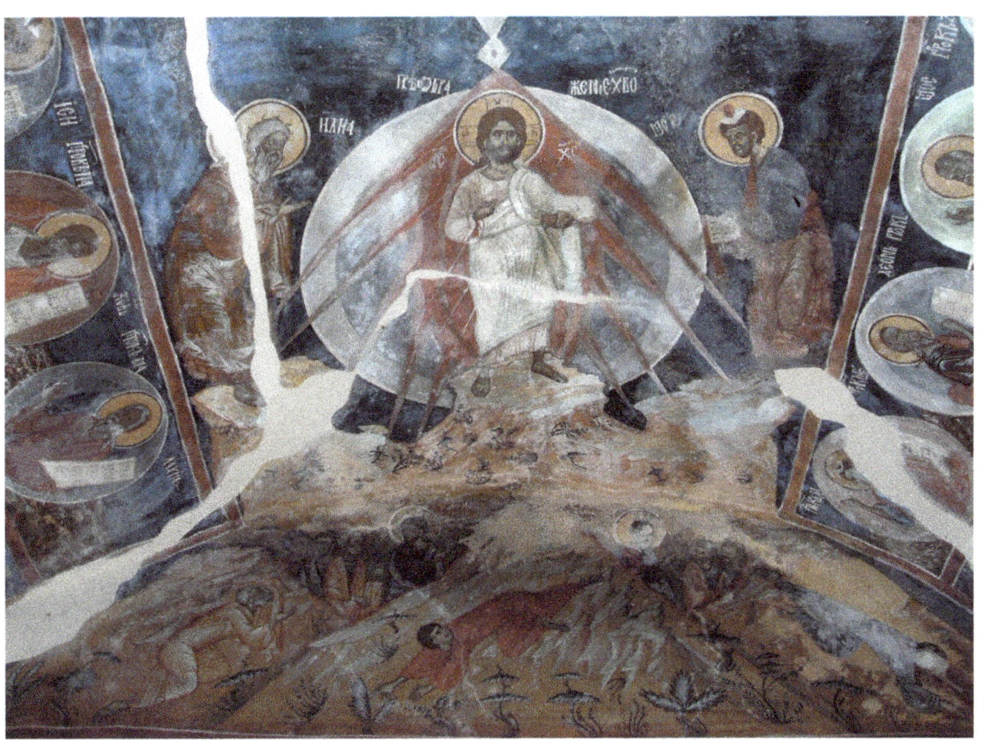

Fig. 9-4

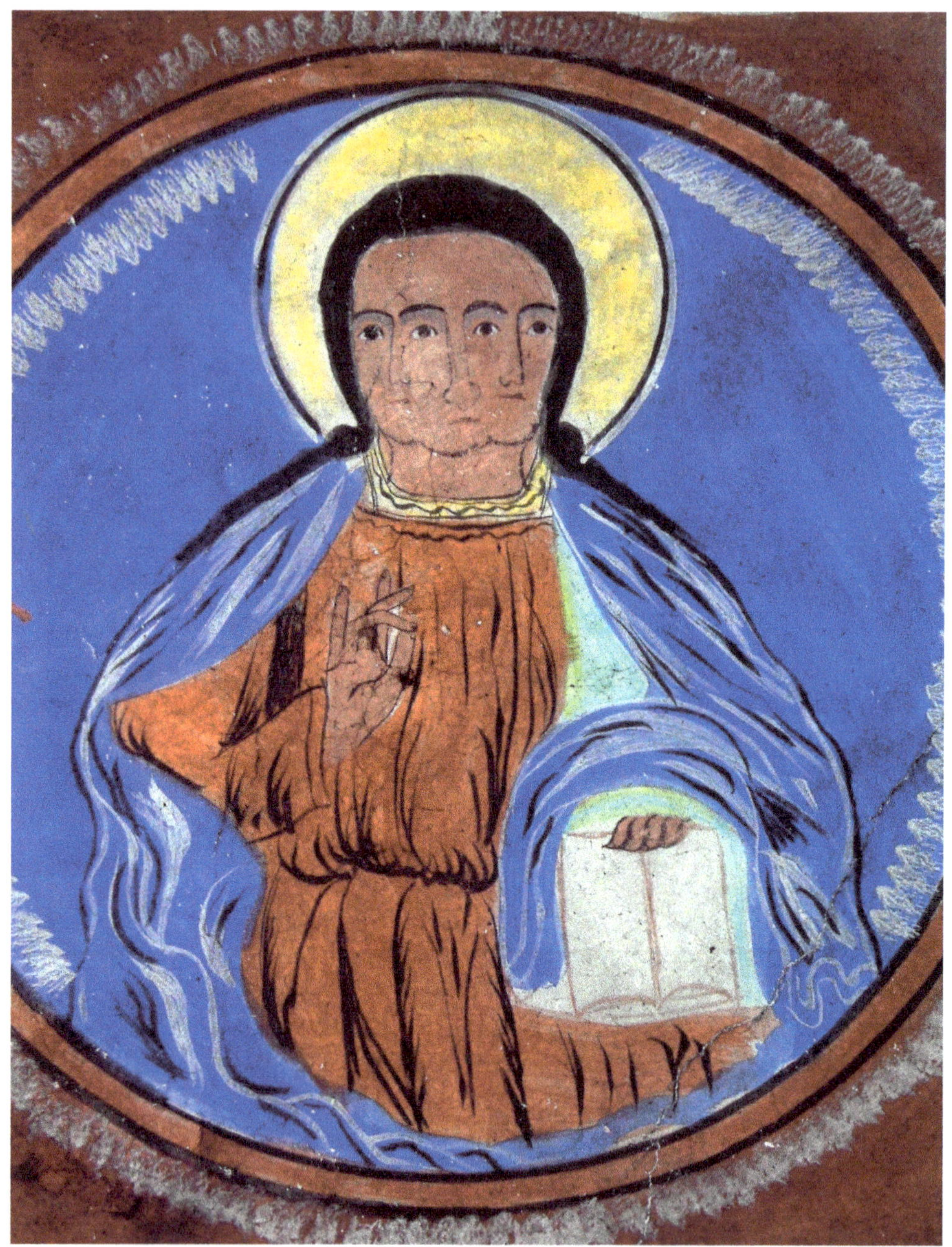

Fig. 9-5

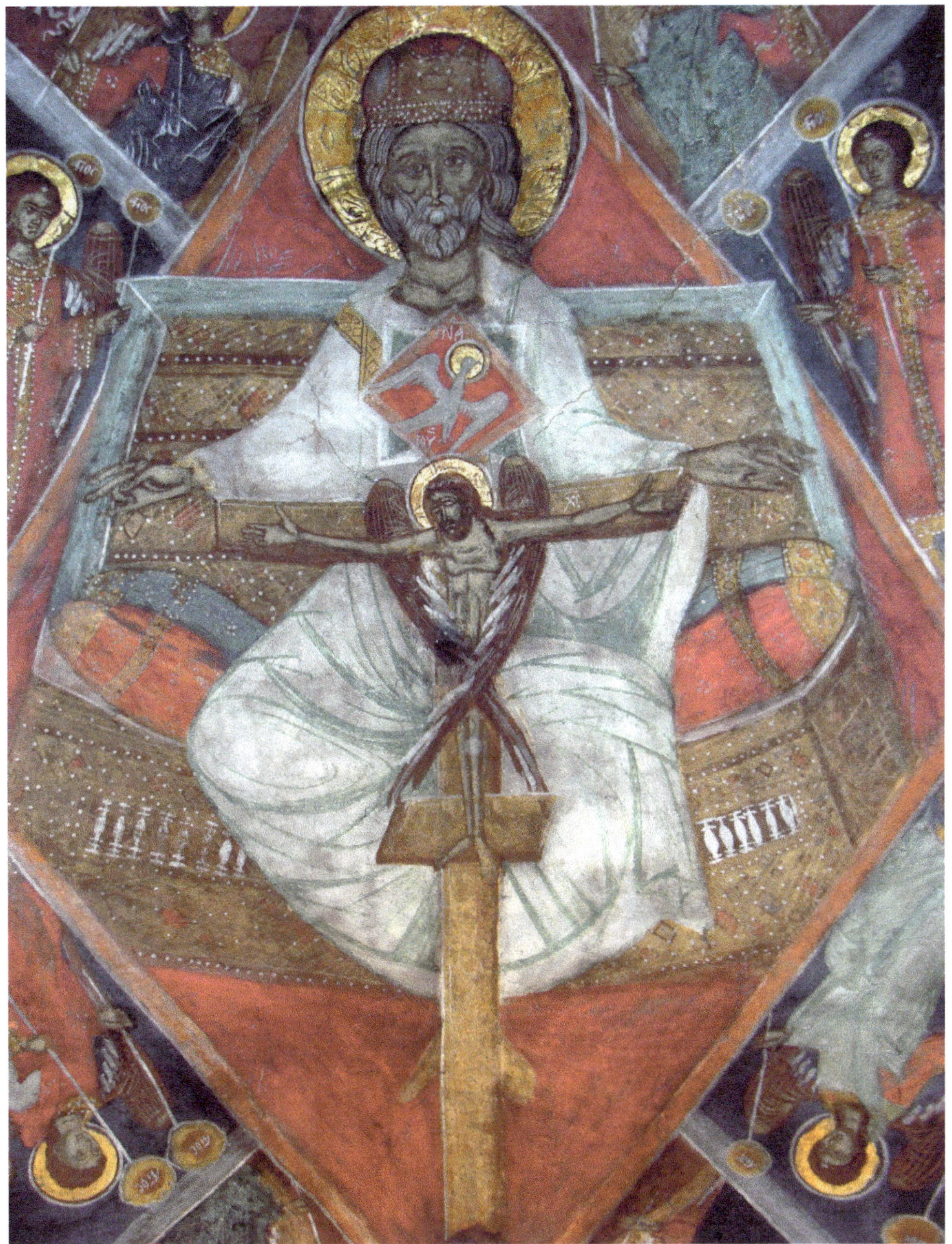

Fig. 9-6

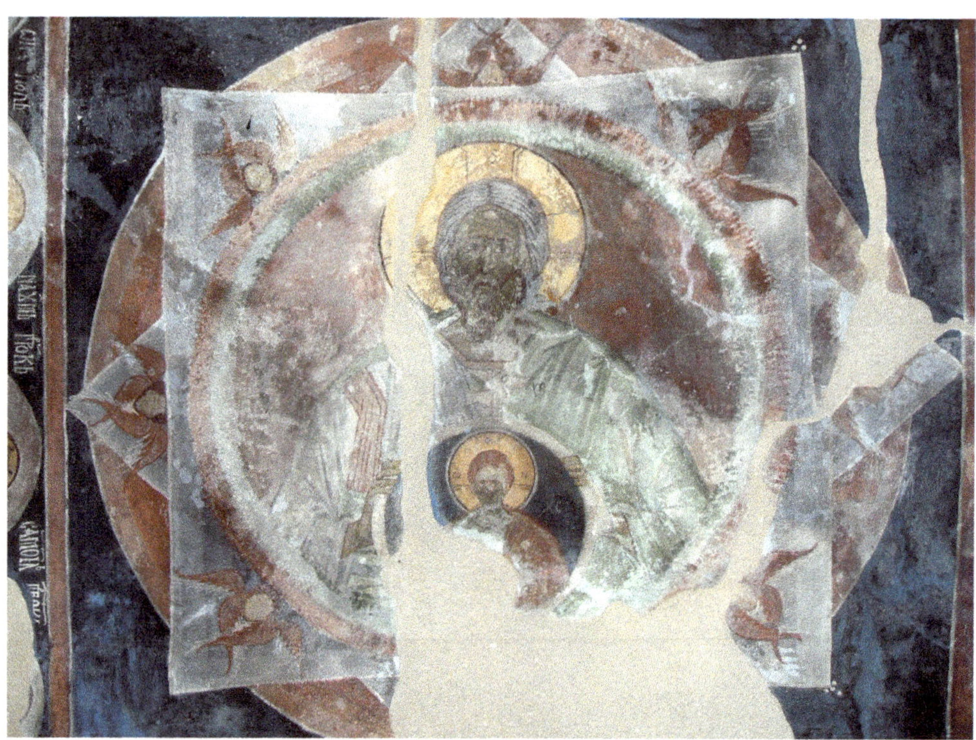

Fig. 9-7

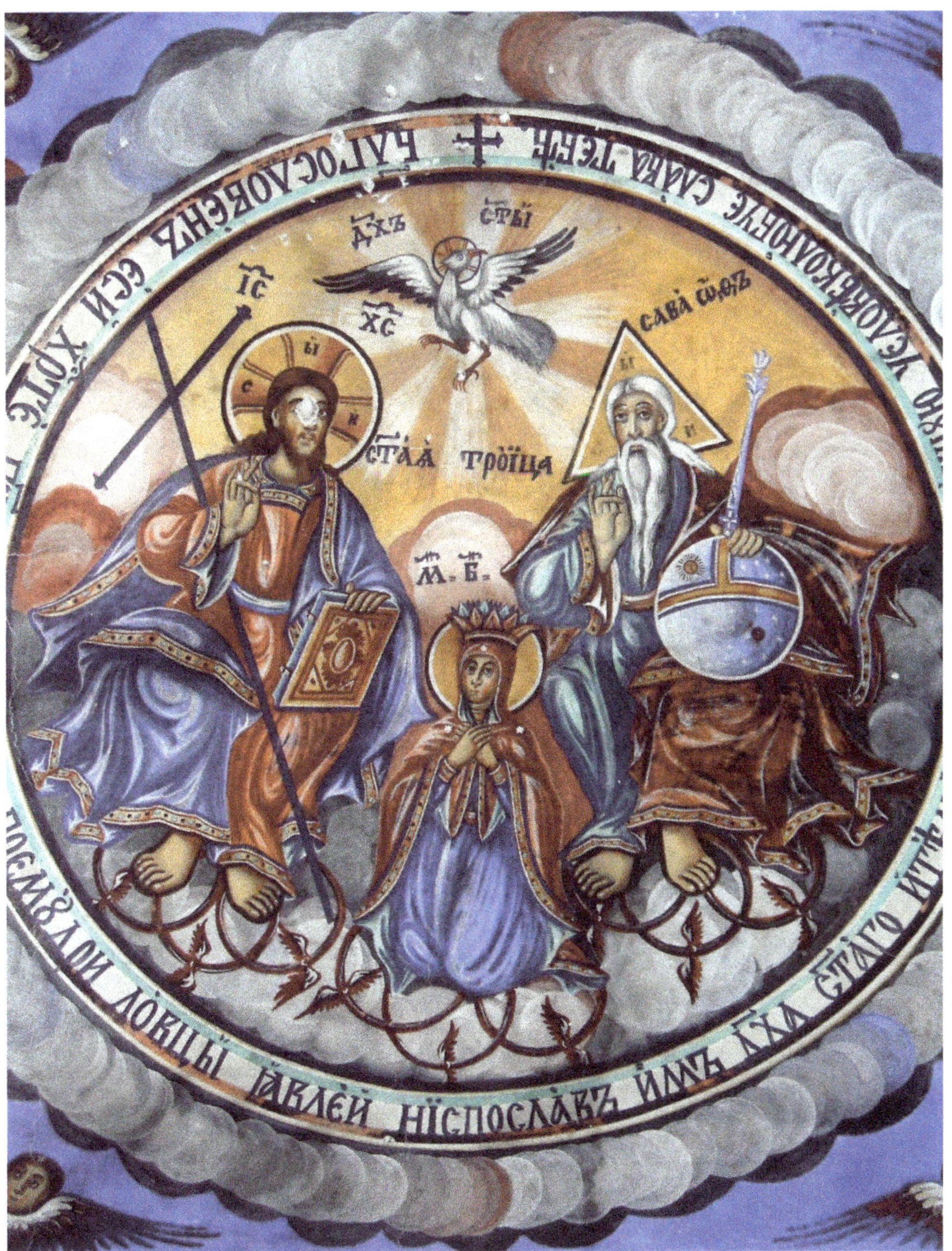

Fig. 9-8

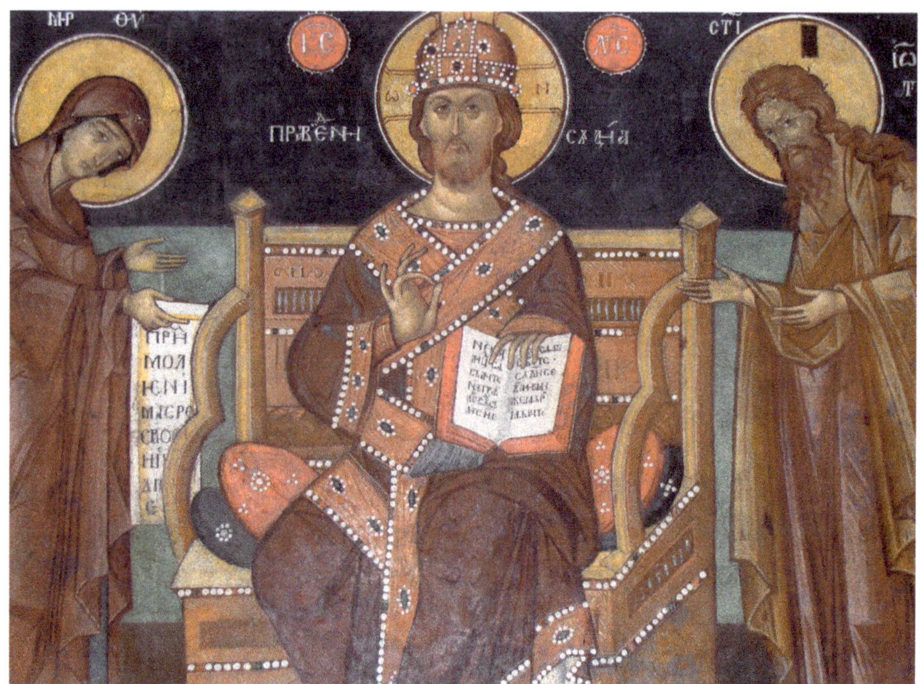

Fig. 9-9

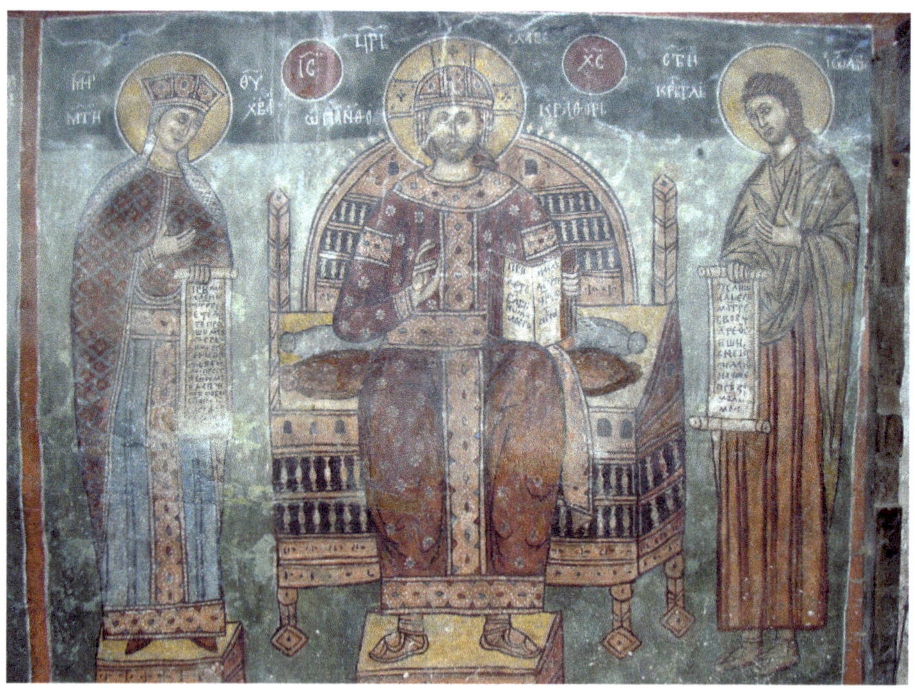

Fig. 9-10

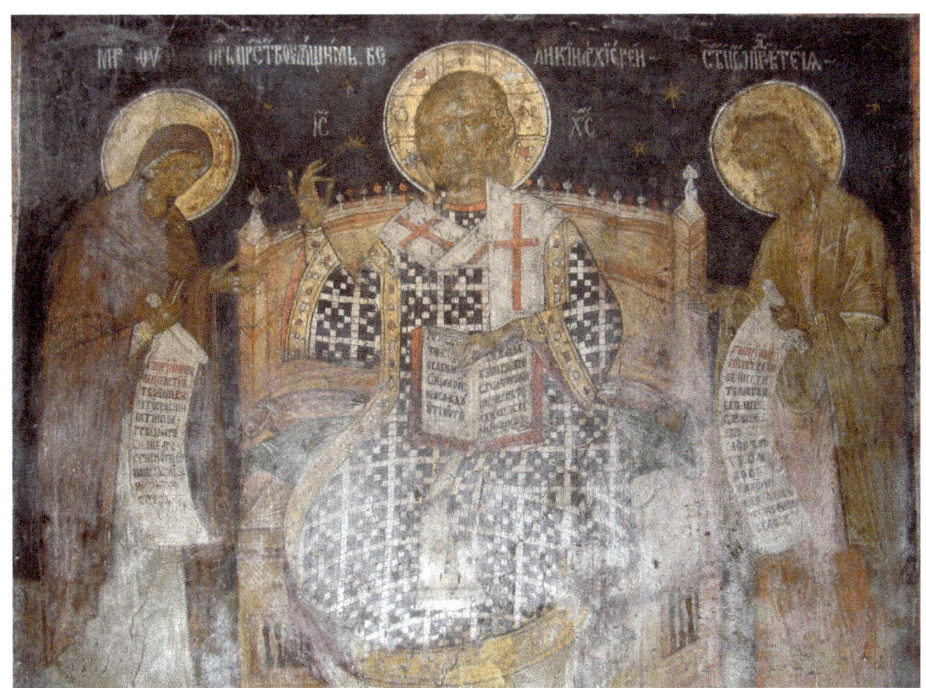

Fig. 9-11

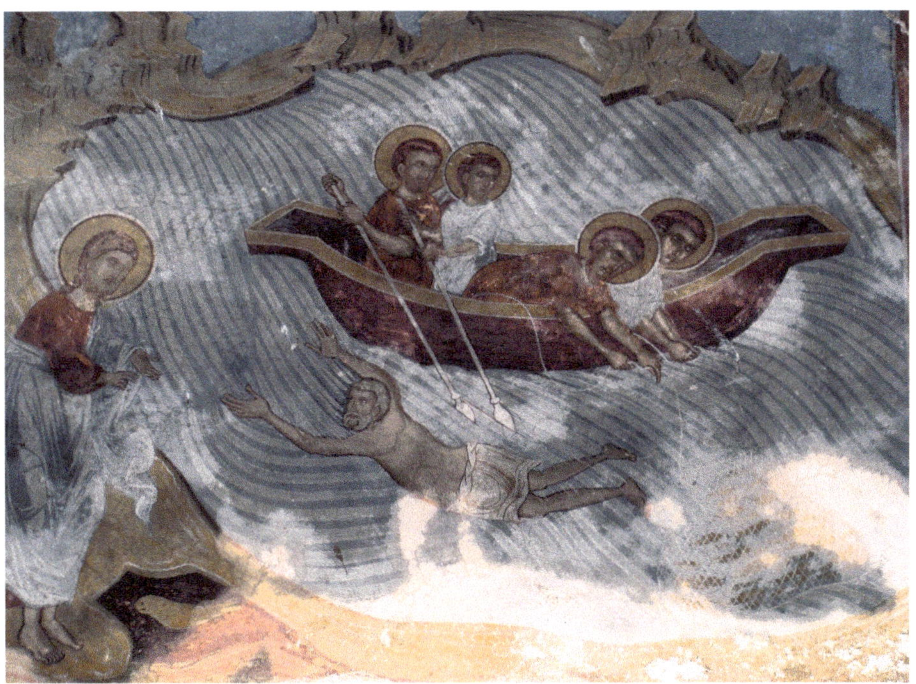

Fig. 9-12

The Dormition of Mary

The New Tree of Knowledge

That sprout, that flower, that apple with its root in the black soil, but speaking with the stars, itself a star, sitting upright between earth and heaven, since she came from the earth, but she is the first human to whom the gates of heaven were opened, our intercessor for eternal life, our Mother, is the Virgin.

Her face in icons with the graceful curve of her neck is a path, an arrow pointing to the Son. Never intrusive, because the power of the Holy Spirit is in that gentle knock at the door. The gesture of her hand, which gathers us as a shepherd gathers their flock, like the eyes of the Child, which never look fixedly, but to the side, from every side, is equally attentive. The Mother's and the Child's hands are big, like the hands of all the saints, and if they come together, they form a whole – the broken fruit in Genesis. Which only the Deesis bridegroom and bride can put back together. From the direction of her heart, Christ blesses us with his right hand, because no one comes to the Father except through the Son and her intercession. The two are one – he, the Child from the Nativity; she, from the Dormition. In an embrace like a cradle, where their haloes meet in the shape of a heart. The Spirit sheltered by Love.

Her soul is sheltered by Love. The ripened fruit from Eden, bigger than its branch, has left its body in the Dormition – not sleeping, death or rest, but dormition, that success in death – and will ascend to the Son, to the leaf of the Tree of Knowledge (Eleshnitsa, iconostasis, fig. 10-1).

So there is an inseparable link between icons of the Mother and Child and frescoes of the Dormition. As the icons are in their relation of the Mother with the Son, so the frescoes are in their relation of the Son with the Mother. In the way he holds her, the way he looks at her. In icons, he is the Child. In the frescoes of the Dormition, the roles are reversed – she is the infant soul. The Child newly received in heaven, our intercessor, because she is our only hope and witness for eternal life. The first human soul to achieve deification. Because if she has succeeded in all her human glory, by God's providence and favor, then so can we by his grace.

The Virgin of the Dormition is also deified time. Eternity, which is not stopped time, but a change in its direction. Her body's position reminds us of a wall clock with the censer as pendulum (Karlukovo, fig. 10-2), a hand-arrow pointing to the Son (Strupets, fig. 10-3). And God's clouds are above her, like those of the Old Testament that accompanied God's people on their way to Canaan, or the noctilucent clouds in the upper atmosphere that are known to science (Eleshnitsa,

fig. 10-4). Rising towards the ether, far above the spiritual forces of evil, above the stench of this world, which couldn't hold her.

The Son looks at her with love. Her soul in his right hand resembles a baby (Berende, fig. 10-5), a doll (Iskrets, fig. 10-6), a bird in its nest (Boboshevo, fig. 10-7), a bird under his wing (Strupets). Even a loaf of bread (Rakovitsa, fig. 10-8).

In the fresco from Rakovitsa, where the upper layer of paint has worn away, the Spirit has remained, since the palimpsest of frescoes is primarily Spirit and then technique. Most of all, a spiritual feat. Something that could also be said of written theology. Or, to quote St Sophrony of Essex, 'ascetics avoid this rational speculation because it not only weakens the intensity of their contemplation of the Light but, indeed, interrupts it, with the result that the soul sinks into darkness, left as she is with a merely abstract rational knowledge devoid of all vitality.'[27]

Yes, the Virgin is apple and bread, the arrow of time and the direction that leans towards the Son. If the Son is the living Word, she is the harvested field, the complete human soul waiting, hoping and succeeding in its resurrection. She is the Mother of us all and the Church of Christ. And the heavenly gates, behind Christ, are always open for her.

A bird swoops down and touches the surface of the windswept water, beside the Chapel of St John the Baptist (Sveti Yoan Letni). The contact creates a circle, but it doesn't break the horizontal symmetry of the waves – it is incorporated. Like a huge apple hanging from a tiny branch. And perhaps the apple from the Tree of Knowledge is bigger than its branch; perhaps the Tree of Knowledge is the only one with fruits bigger than its branches – not the tree in Eden, but that of the New Testament – her tree that cloaks temptation with humility. Climbs the ladder of the ribs to the light. Makes one soul more important than the entire universe, according to Church Fathers – a soul that grows from a fetus into a star, the star of her maphorion.

The landscape seen in the waters of the Pchelina reservoir is the same as the frescoes in the Matthias Church in Budapest or the rock formations of Stakevtsi waterfall. Always with Christ: a small island in the shape of a lamb, a lamb in the pupil of an eye or a crown of thorns to the right of the stone. Above the slightly bowed head, the maphorion undulates with sharp edges – thorns in the outline of her face,

27 St Sophrony of Essex, *Saint Silouan the Athonite*, p. 186.

which will later stick in his forehead. Nothing of the earthly hierarchy penetrates the heavenly, where the fruit is bigger than its branch, the soul is star and bread, the Mother is the Child's bride and the Father is not her earthly bridegroom. Stepping towards this holiness, we must be careful of our hands – unlike the Jewish priest Athonios, whose hands were cut off by an angel and seem to float on the surface (Kladnitsa, fig. 10-9). Very important in depictions of the Virgin are the gestures of her hands. Hers also is the only icon known as 'Three-Handed' (a famous icon in Troyan Monastery, central Bulgaria).

The Virgin Mary is the new Tree of Knowledge, with which everyone records their human success in God: 'Every tree therefore that does not bear good fruit is cut down and thrown into the fire' (Mt 3:10).

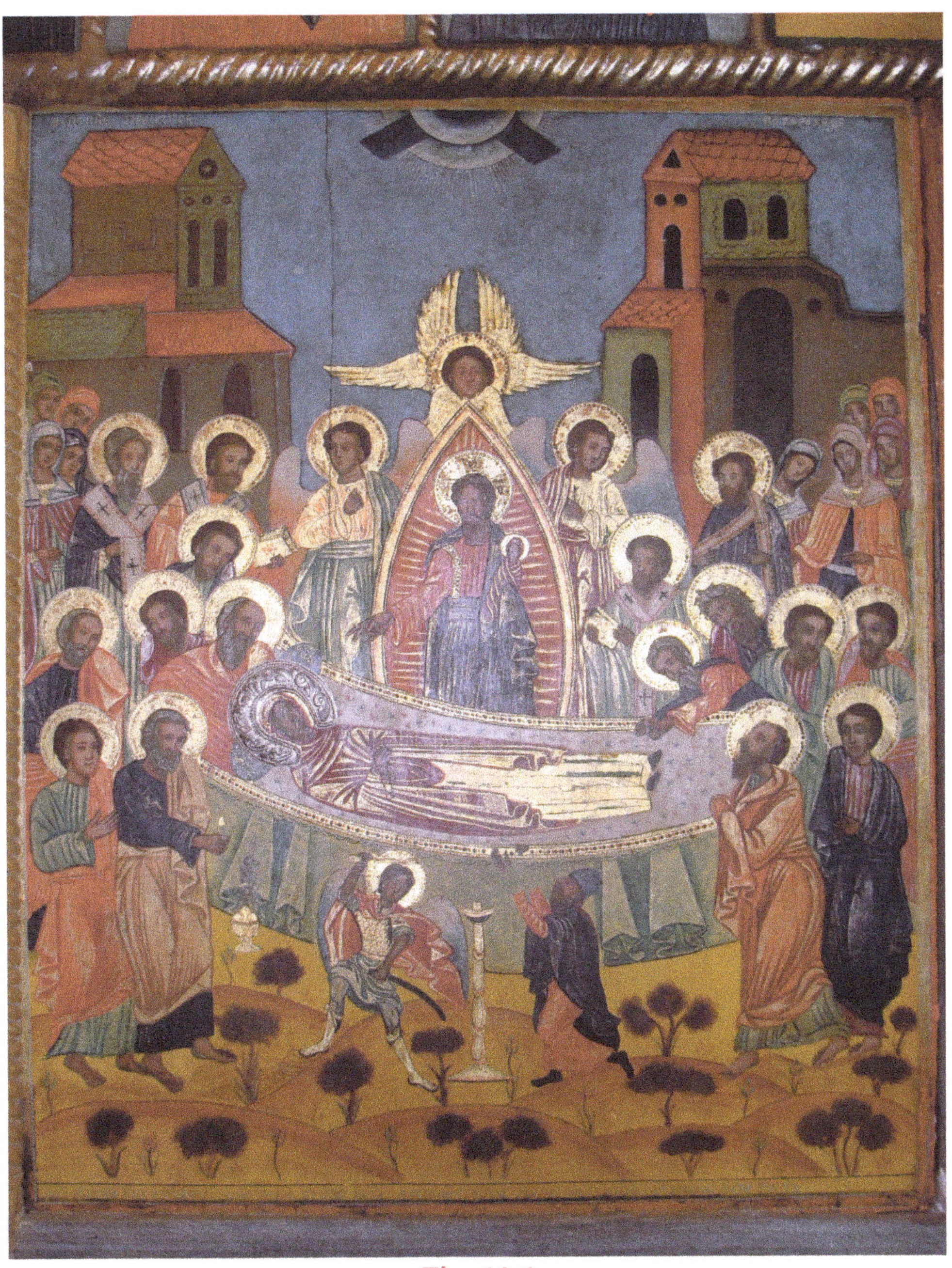

Fig. 10-1

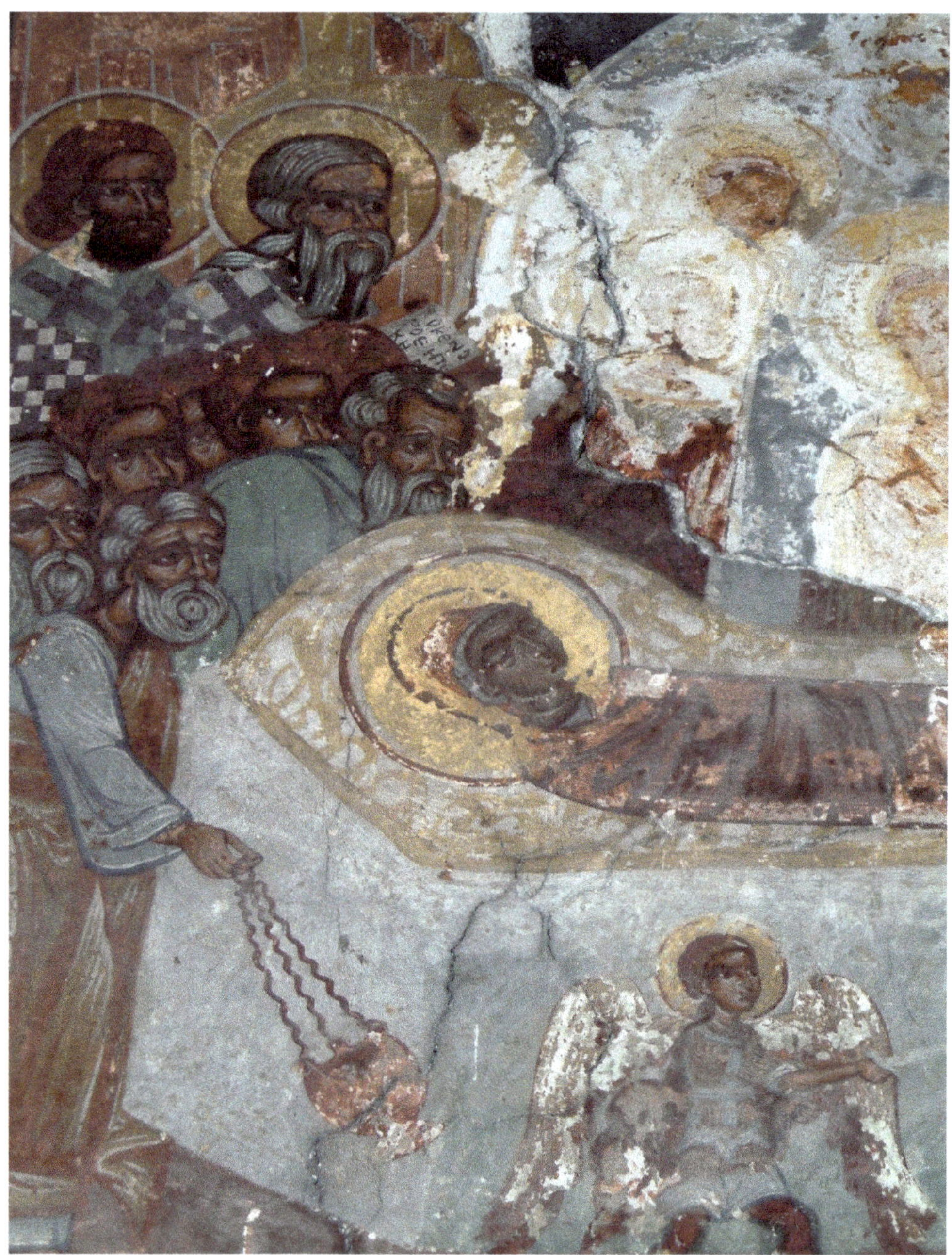

Fig. 10-2

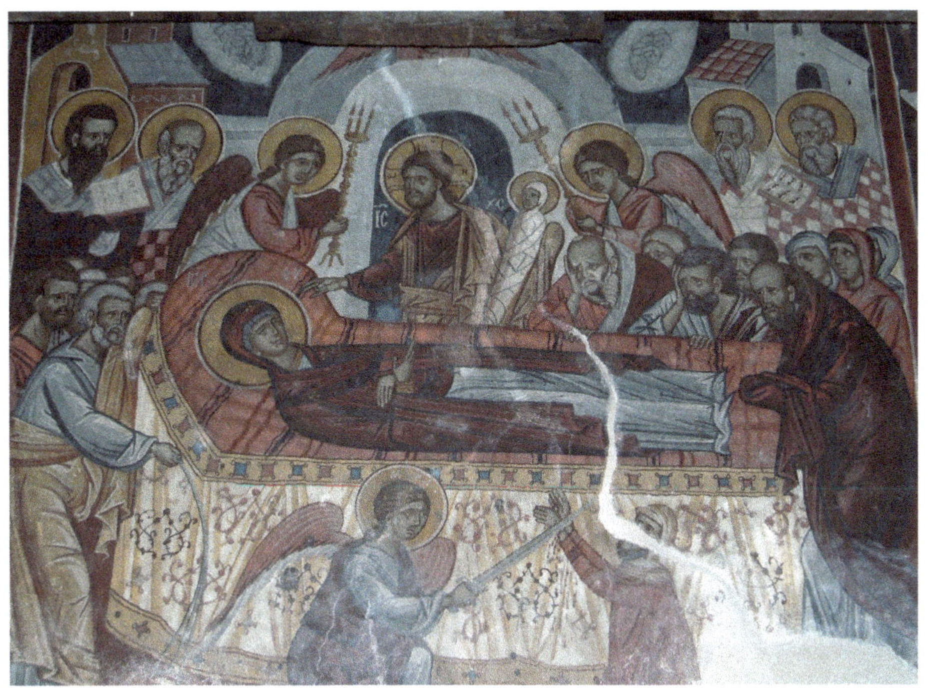

Fig. 10-3

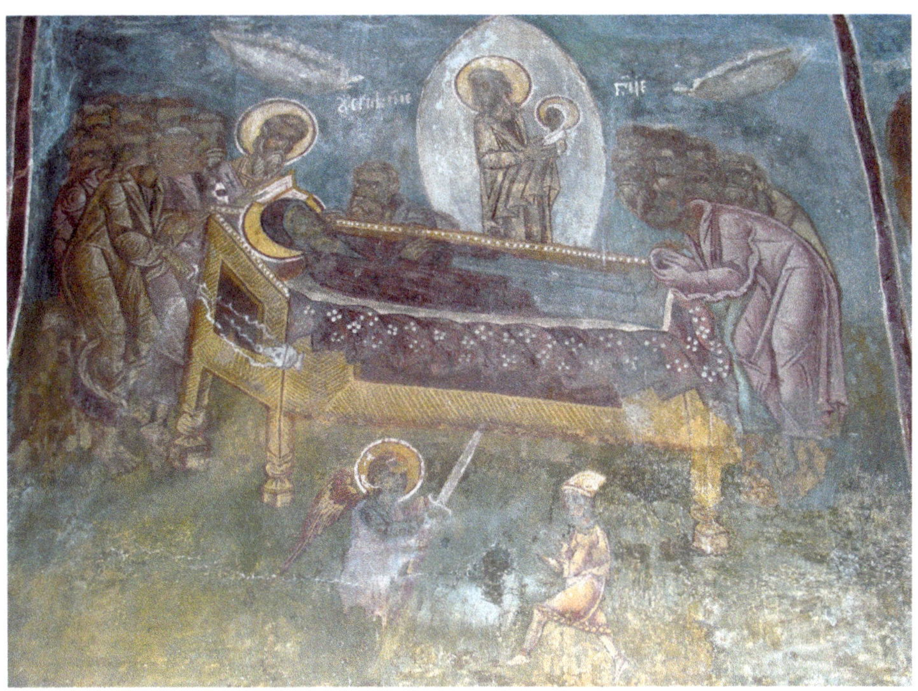

Fig. 10-4

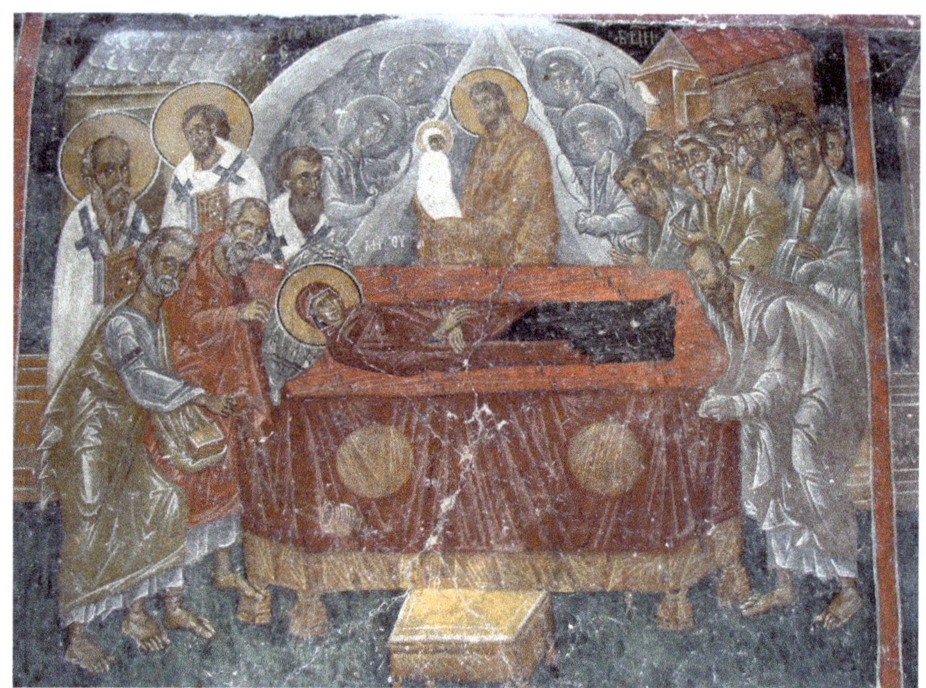

Fig. 10-5

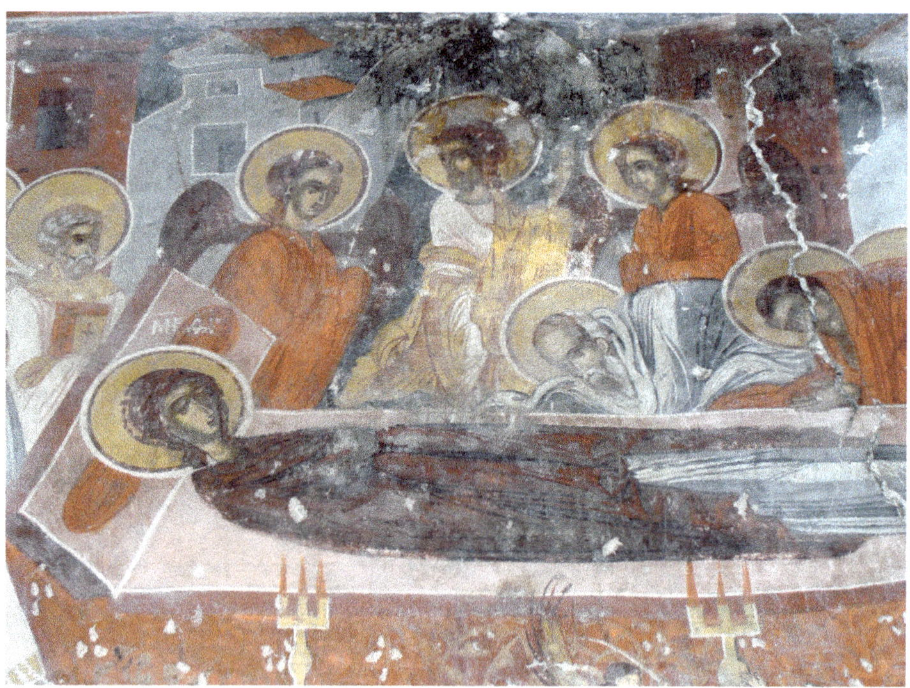

Fig. 10-6

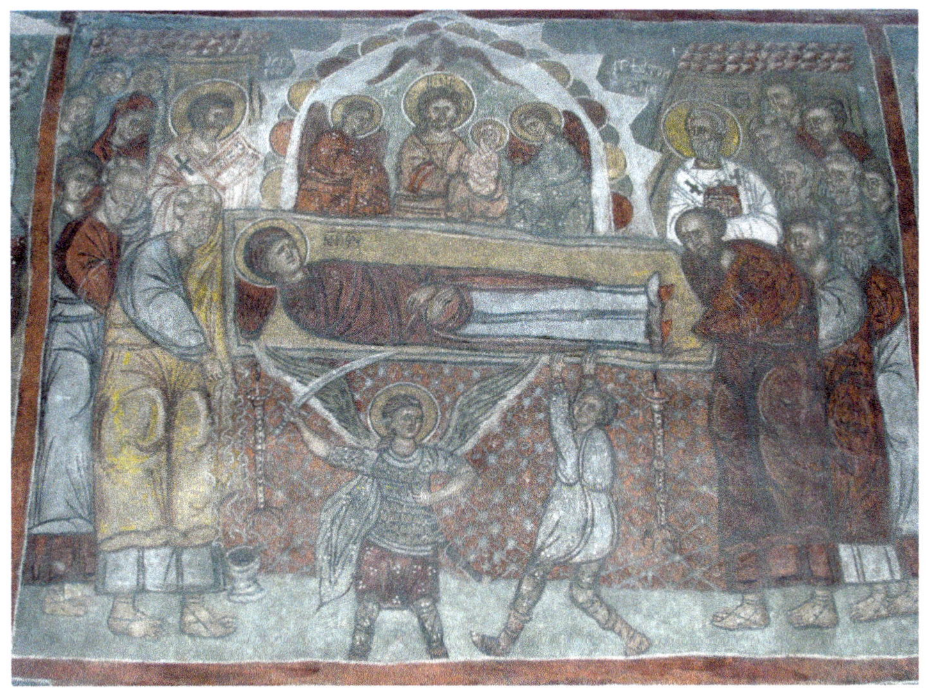

Fig. 10-7

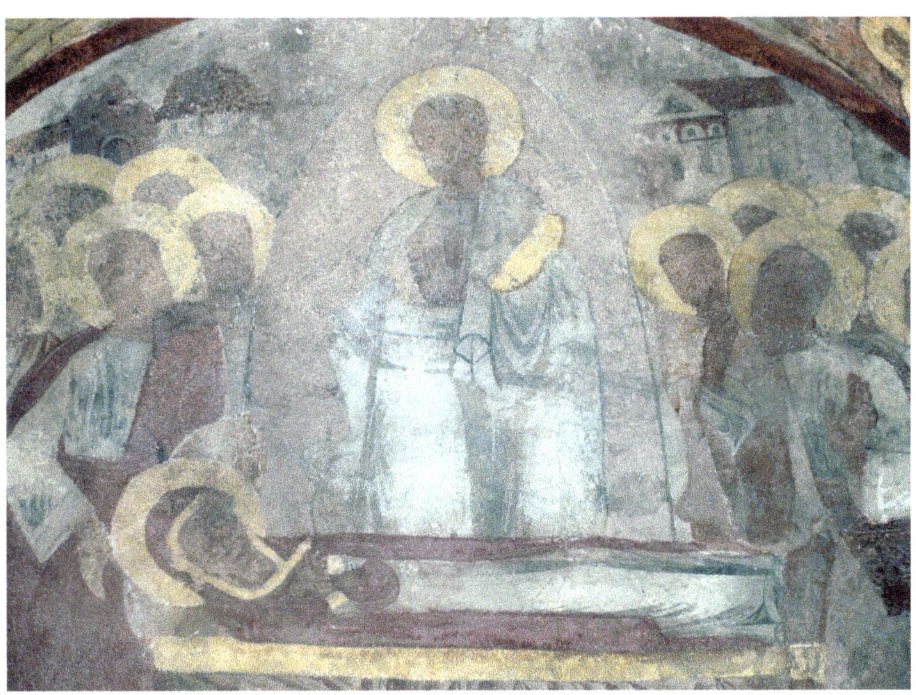

Fig. 10-8

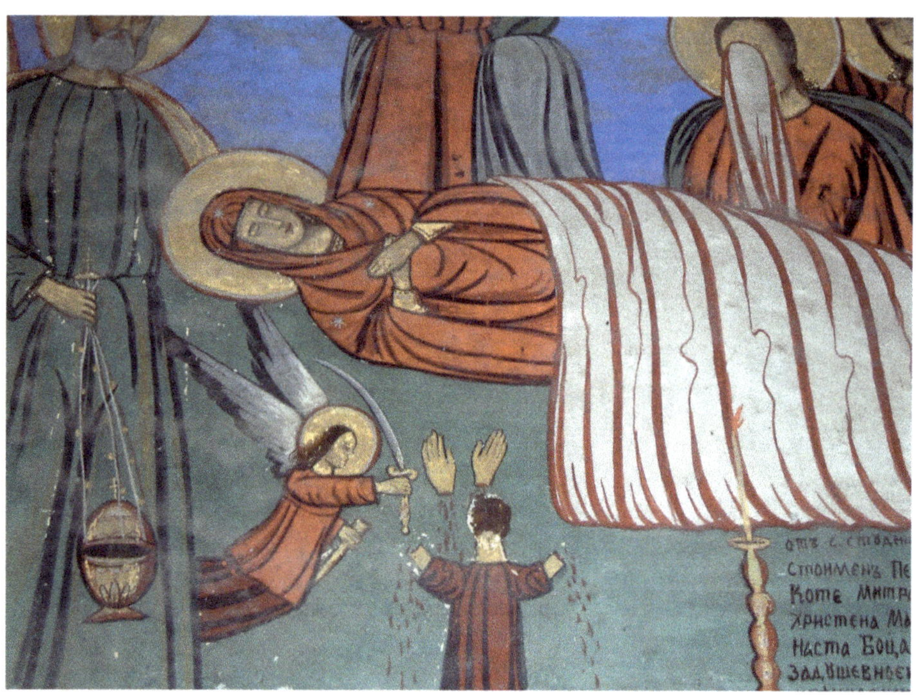

Fig. 10-9

List of Bulgarian Monasteries and Churches Included in this Book

1. Alino Monastery, St Savior (17th century).
2. **Bilintsi Monastery**, St Michael (17th century).
3. Boboshevo Monastery, St Demetrius (15th century).
4. Dolna Beshovitsa Monastery, St Michael (14th century).
5. Dolni Pasarel Monastery, Sts Peter and Paul (19th century).
6. **Eleshnitsa Monastery**, Dormition of Mary (17th century).
7. **Iliyantsi Monastery**, St Elijah (17th century).
8. **Iskrets Monastery**, Dormition of Mary (17th century).
9. Ivanovo Rock Monastery, St Michael (14th century).
10. **Karlukovo Monastery**, Dormition of Mary (17th century).

11. Kladnitsa Monastery, St Nicholas (19th century).

12. **Kremikovtsi Monastery**, St George (17th century).

13. **Kurilovo Monastery**, St John of Rila (16th century).

14. **Malo Malovo Monastery**, St Nicholas (17th century).

15. Nedelishte Monastery, St Athanasius (19th century).

16. **Podgumer Monastery**, St Demetrius (16th century).

17. Preobrazhenie Monastery, Transfiguration (19th century).

18. Rakovitsa Monastery, Holy Trinity (19th century).

19. **Seslavtsi Monastery**, St Nicholas (17th century).

20. **Strupets Monastery**, St Elijah (17th century).

21. Teteven Monastery, St Elijah (19th century).

22. Church of the Nativity, Arbanasi (17th century).

23. Church of Sts Michael and Gabriel, Arbanasi (18th century).

24. Church of Sts Peter and Paul, Berende (14th century).

25. St Stephen's Church, Nesebar (16th century).

26. St Petka's Church, Radibosh (16th century).

27. Church of Sts Peter and Paul, Veliko Tarnovo (16th century).

The eleven monasteries in bold on this list are connected with the name and activity of St Pimen of Zograph (1540-1620), a native of Sofia. According to the life of this saint, at the age of fifty-five, he left Zograph Monastery on Mt Athos after St George appeared to him while he was at prayer and informed him that it was God's will for him to return to his homeland and to become its spiritual shepherd. For a period of twenty-five years, he renovated and painted more than 300 churches and fifteen monasteries from Mt Athos to Sofia's Holy Mountain (the area around the capital, Sofia, which is dotted with monasteries, many of which are mentioned in this book), from the eparchies of Vidin and Dorostol to Lake Prespa.

Tsvetanka Elenkova

Tsvetanka Elenkova was a Bulgarian poet and essayist. Three of her poetry collections have appeared in English: *The Seventh Gesture*, *Crookedness* and *Magnification Forty* (which received a 2022 PEN Translates award). *The Seventh Gesture* also has editions in French (Tertium Éditions), Spanish (Vaso Roto) and Serbian (Povelja), while *Crookedness* has appeared in French (Éditions Corps Puce). Her poems have been translated into more than twenty languages and have appeared in English in the magazines *Absinthe*, *Modern Poetry in Translation*, *New Humanist*, *Orient Express*, *Poem*, *Poetry Review*, *The Massachusetts Review* (her poem 'The Train' was included in this magazine's sixtieth-anniversary anthology, *And There Will Be Singing*) and *Zoland Poetry*. Her poetry and translations into Bulgarian of work by Raymond Carver, Fiona Sampson, Rosalía de Castro and others have been nominated for important prizes in Bulgaria. In 2019 she received the prestigious Pencho's Oak Award for her contribution to literature. She edited the anthology *At the End of the World: Contemporary Poetry from Bulgaria*, which includes the work of seventeen contemporary Bulgarian poets in a bilingual Bulgarian-English edition. She was a doctoral student in theology at Sofia University, where she researched the mystical poetry of St Gregory of Nazianzus. She died in November 2023.

Jonathan Dunne

Jonathan Dunne is a graduate in Classics from Oxford University. He has translated more than eighty books from the Bulgarian, Catalan, Galician and Spanish languages, including work by Tsvetanka Elenkova, Carme Riera, Manuel Rivas and Enrique Vila-Matas. His translations have been nominated for the International Dublin Literary Award, the Independent Foreign Fiction Prize and the Warwick Prize for Writing among others. He has written four books on the spiritual content of language: *The DNA of the English Language* (2007), *The Life of a Translator* (2013), *Stones Of Ithaca* (2019) and *Seven Brief Lessons on Language* (2023). He has recorded a sixteen-part video course on the same theme, 'Theological English,' which is available to watch on YouTube. He directs the publishing house Small Stations Press (www.smallstations.com), the second largest publisher in the United States of books from Spain between 2008 and 2018, according to *Three Percent*. His photographs have appeared in publications in England, the United States and Bulgaria. His work, including the video course 'Theological English' and a series of articles called 'Heart of Language,' can be accessed on his personal website, www.stonesofithaca.com.

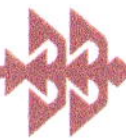

www.ingramcontent.com/pod-product-compliance
Lightning Source LLC
LaVergne TN
LVHW060623110826
845147LV00015B/925

9781960613127